SELECTIONS FROM VINOBA

SELECTIONS FROM VINOBA

Edited and Compiled by:
Vishwanath Tandon

GYAN

ISBN : 978-81-212-0860-4

Published, 2018

Published by

Gyan Publishing House
5, Ansari Road
Daryaganj, New Delhi-110002
Phone: 011-47034999, 9811692060
www.gyanbooks.com
E-mail: books@gyanbooks.com

Printed at: G. Print Process, Delhi.

To
All who have been
kind and affectionate to me

Contents

Publisher's Note

The book titled 'Selections from Vinoba', compiled and edited by Dr. Vishwanath Tandon, was published by Sarva Seva Sangh Prakashan, Varanasi, in 1981. It contains 1,218 extracts (most of these being translated into English from Hindi by Dr. Tandon) arranged under suitable headings and subheadings. The selection covers a wide range of subjects in the fields of philosophy, ethics, economics, politics and sociology.

Vinoba Bhave was not only the closest follower of Mahatma Gandhi during historic days of India's freedom movement, but has left an indelible mark even in post-Independent India with his Bhoodan movement which changed the very basics of how to deal with the conflict between the landlords and the landless in the vast rural India. He followed it up with various other initiatives which, together with Bhoodan movement brought about a sort of nonviolent revolution in the Indian agrarian scene. He showed a rare vision and provided leadership when it was most needed.

It is not generally known that Vinoba Bhave was also a scholar of a high order and could explain the most complex issues in simple and precise terms. He had a mathematical, scientific and at the same time a deeply spiritual mind, which he brought to bear on all matters.

However, most of his writings being in Marathi or Hindi, these have not been easily accessible in English language. Dr. Vishwanath Tandon had done a great public service in compiling, editing and categorizing these 1,218 extracts out of a vast spectrum of Vinoba Bhave's writings.

The book, however, has been out of print for many years. Considering the importance of the book and the need to make it available to the English reading public, Dr. Tandon, even at his present age of 91 years, had kindly come forward to have another look at the contents. Thus has emerged this revised edition, which is being published by National Gandhi Museum, Rajghat, New Delhi in collaboration with Gyan Publishing House, Ansari Road, New Delhi.

On behalf of the National Gandhi Museum, New Delhi, I am grateful to Dr. Vishwanath Tandon, for all that he has done to make this revised edition of his 'Selections from Vinoba' possible and giving us the opportunity to have it published.

Dr. Y.P. Anand
Director
National Gandhi Museum
Rajghat, New Delhi-110 002

Dated: 7 April 2004

Foreword to the First Edition

Almost all who have written earlier or write today about Vinoba Bhave have normally looked upon him as the closest disciple and almost a true copy of Gandhi, and one who has tried successfully to keep up the Gandhian tradition in many respects, if not in all. This estimate may be said to be partially true but not wholly true. It is true as regards the main inspiration and the essence of Vinoba's induction into active life and his participation in the numerous programmes, national and others, even though there too he has expressed prominently his individuality and originality. But, even if it were out of modesty or 'Vinaya of Vinya', Vinobaji himself has said that it was entirely due to Gandhi that he was led into the field of national activities : in the beginning as an Ashramite and then as a leader in his own right of Gandhi-oriented national activities, including Satyagraha campaigns for Swarajya. Both Gandhi and Vinoba looked upon spiritual life as the highest life and God-Realization and/or self-realization in this very life as the greatest achievement. Gandhi plunged into active service of the poorest as the means to that end. Vinobaji renounced life along the path of Shankara, but was initiated into active service of the people by Gandhi before the former had advanced too far in his chosen path. Gandhi took to active life of loveful service, suffering and sacrifice for the people of India and humanity as a spiritual seeker, without even thinking of the alternative way of traditional renunciation. Vinobaji had already left his home and was at Varanasi on his way to the Himalayas to follow the orthodox path of renunciation of worldly life. But Gandhiji's speech in the Hindu University resulted in Vinobaji's adopting the course Gandhi had already made his own.

Vinobaji has acknowledged very frankly his debt to three great persons, to Shankaracharya and Jnaneshwar for his initiation into spirituality and to Gandhi for initiation into selfless service of humanity. Be it said to the credit of both that they acknowledged the particular greatness of each other and respected highly each other's personality.

Vinobaji no doubt acknowledged Gandhi as his Master in many matters but he was never a mere imitator or a blind follower. In addition to being a genuine spiritual *sadhak*, he is a Saint, a *tapasvi*, a profound scholar, and above all an original thinker in his own right. He has rightly warned people not to idolise Gandhi but to look upon him as a man, a votary of Truth and an apostle of Ahimsa. He has spoken of the rich heritage Gandhi has left behind in the form of very great, living and activised ideas. Vinobaji wants us to study Gandhi's ideas in the present context and not to give too much weight to what he could do, as he was labouring under a foreign rule which would have even wished him away ! Vinobaji has published his own view of Gandhi and his differences with him, apart from occasional appreciation, topical comments and observations. Vinoba would like us to look upon Gandhi as an ongoing flow of thought in the interest of human evolution, both individual and social.

It would be a great mistake to write off Vinoba as only a follower of Gandhi. Vinoba has declared clearly almost in the same spirit as Gandhi, that he would not accept blindly even the words of the Veda or Geeta, without a critical look at it and without being satisfied about the truth of it as judged by the tools God has given him. This attitude of his and his active life and thinking for the last thirty-three years after the passing away of Gandhi makes it incumbent on every one who is concerned with India, Indian people, India's destiny to study closely what Vinoba has said and is saying, not only about Gandhi, but about every important aspect of human affairs and activities.

There is no doubt that there are already about a thousand books in English alone on Gandhi. Gandhi's own writings and utterances in three languages, English, Gujarati and Hindi, which are being brought out in English have already run into eighty sumptuous volumes and we are promised ten more. So, one would be inclined to ask, what new light could Vinoba throw on Gandhi's life, thought and action ?

But we should not forget that Vinoba started his active public life of dedicated service with the same basic spiritual inspiration as Gandhi and has averred that his actions are God-guided; though during Gandhi's lifetime, Vinoba busied himself with the activities initiated by Gandhi, he started after his death new activities of Bhoodan, Gramdan and Gramrajya, supplied a full content to the concept of Sarvodaya, added new dimensions to the active principle of Satyagraha, widened the horizon of nationalism by introducing the slogan of Jai Jagat (victory to the world) instead of only Jai Hind, introduced the concepts and appropriate actions about Lok-niti (People's ethos) and Lok Shakti (People's power) as different from governmental policies and power with penal sanctions, gave a new turn to Stree Shakti (feminine power), elaborated the idea of Acharya-Kula (the tribe of teachers), that is a group of people drawn from all social sectors who are above party and power politics, but totally and selflessly concerned with the welfare and progress of the people, gave substance to the Shanti Sena (Peace Army) idea and so on.

It is true that India's spiritual tradition is traced to the Vedas and all who swear of spirituality, point to the Vedas as the original source. But who can deny the enrichment, the ramifications, the varied details and refinements contributed by the Upanishads, the Brahmasutras, the Geeta and the great Acharyas and Saints. So too in the case of Gandhi, with Truth through Nonviolence-Love as his basic teaching. Vinoba who ceaselessly toured India on foot for fourteen years (1951-1965) and has been writing and speaking in limpid Hindi and Marathi all these years in a simple but scholarly style all his own has, no doubt, added to the understanding and interpretation of Gandhi in his own way. Though Vinoba in recent years took to what is called Kshetra Sannyas, restricted movement in a very limited area of his Paunar Ashram, a few miles from Gandhi's Sevagram, it has been a place of universal pilgrimage. A certain calm and equanimity (Shanti and Samya), not shorn of the humane human touch and occasional humour, lights up the personality of the eighty-six year old Acharya Vinoba. He with his beard looks more like a Chinese saint than an Indian Rishi. But Rishi he is, being a Seer (Drishta) of the modern age.

There is a wilderness of Vinoba literature both in Hindi and Marathi. He himself has produced literature on various subjects which interested him. Many, a few of them from abroad, have written about Vinoba and his life and ideas and action. But perhaps people eager to know the essential Vinoba were waiting for a compendium in English which would convey to them his ideas in brief. The author has fulfilled a great want not only in publishing this book in English but in classifying the thoughts subject-wise. There is no doubt that the author has exercised his judgement wisely in categorising the vast gamut of Vinoba's thought. I believe that this publication is a great aid for the understanding not only of Vinoba's ideas, but it has significance as a help for knowing Gandhi's ideas as reflected in the ideas of one who was not only Gandhi's closest associate but a discerning disciple who according to his own God-given light elaborated them, both in thought and action, in the practical world, for more than a quarter of a century after his master's passing away.

Gandhi lived in slave India concentrating on freeing Indians from bondage. After living along with him and working shoulder to shoulder with him in fulfilling that great mission, Vinoba has the privilege of living in free India for re-making it along the dreams of Gandhi. And that is the significance of Vinoba's thought and action. India had only one problem and only one enemy before freedom. Today India faces numerous problems both internal and external. India has to face them as a great ancient cultured nation. In this Foreword, I may not deal in detail with the points of departure and/or difference between Vinoba and Shankara and Vinoba and Gandhi. Nor need I dwell at length with the individuality and originality which Vinobaji has exhibited both in his thought and action. Earlier, I have casually pointed out some such differences, and some traits of originality. After pointing out a few more pointedly, I may conclude the Foreword leaving it to readers to study Vinoba more thoroughly as he represents some of the most important aspects of Indian mind and culture in modern India.

There is no end to the reverence Vinoba has for Shankara-charya of Kalati of the eighth century and he finds no words adequate enough to show his greatness. But his differences— apparent or real—with him, can be discerned by us. Vinoba has substituted his own *'Brahma satyam jagat sphoortih, jeevanam satya-shodhanam'* for Shankara's *'Brahma-satyam jagan-mithya jeevo Brahmaiva NAPARAH'*. It could be said that this is the 20th century interpretation of Shankara's original axiom. Shankara's advocacy of unmixed and fullfledged Advait Vedanta, his denigration of worldly life and of the birth- death cycle, his invocation to take to Sannyas as soon as there are signs of distaste for life *(viraga)*, no doubt influenced Vinoba to leave his home for Varanasi. But though the strong tendency for renunciation and meditation continued throughout Vinoba's life, we entirely miss the other-worldly hankering after escape from Samsar and denigration of life. On the other hand, there is emphasis on a life of service and sacrifice and a continuous deep concern for suffering humanity. It is obvious that this world which is 'a becoming' is a direct projection and manifestation of 'Being' itself according to the Upanishadic seers. In the case of both Gandhi and Vinoba, the quest of 'Being', of God never ceased; in fact it went on intensifying. But the search of 'Being' in 'Becoming itself' and not outside it, proved more rewarding, not only to the two seekers, but to humanity as well ! It may also be pointed out here that there is some obvious difference in the interpretation of the Geeta by Shankara, Gandhi and Vinoba. It may be argued that it is only a difference in emphasis, since all the three were essentially Advait Vedantins. But while Shankara emphasises *'Jnanat eva tu kaivalyam'*, Gandhi emphasises 'Anasakta' action as the Geeta's message. Vinoba stresses what he calls 'Samya Yoga': the Yoga of equanimity of poised consciousness rooted in peace which 'passeth understanding'. This is an example both of difference in emphasis and interpretation as well as the originality of Vinoba.

Now to a few points in connection with the differences in approach and methodology of action between Gandhi and Vinoba. Vinoba has never made any secret about his strong tendency towards what is called Nivritti or quietism or life of contemplation. It is indeed a marvel of Gandhi's influence on Vinoba and Vinoba's own adamantine will, to both of which India stands indebted, for the active life and massive contribution which Vinoba has made to the resurgence of India. In the matter of integrality of vision, in the sweep of universality of interest, in the depth and comprehensiveness of emotional power no one seems to be a match to Gandhi, Gandhi's urge to action also was far ahead of others. So too, his ready response to challenges. Gandhi's originality and inventiveness in finding a new way of life based on the twin principles of Truth and Ahimsa, and in forging a universal weapon of Satyagraha, more civilized and humane than any other, from out of a forgotten kind of resistance offered by a few religious martyrs remains a landmark in human history. Gandhi complimented Vinoba by calling him the First Satya-grahi in the selective Satyagraha campaign in 1940. Vinobaji has done well by cautioning people that Gandhi's was not the last word on Satyagraha and the potency of Satyagraha lies in the future more than in the past. In spite of what Vinoba has tried to add to Satyagraha by saying that it should be gentler and gentlest, one can take him at his word and look forward to its future since violence, both intra-nationally and internationally is fast losing 'its survival value' that is, it is neither able to promise calculated success nor able to save the user of violence from his own destruction! Gandhi believed in organisation and was a strict disciplinarian, though he enforced the latter by his love and moral stature. But for his solicitude to save the Congress organisation, and his timely self-denials on critical occasions, the Congress could not have grown from strength to strength to a pitch of throwing the last challenge in the form of the Quit India Movement in 1942. Vinoba frankly admits that he is temperamentally averse to entangling himself in institutions and organisations. He believes, it seems, in spontaneous organisations which shall find their feet according to situations. Apart from the example of Gandhi who set up and conducted organisations and strengthened them, this weakness of want of organising skill and necessary discipline for it and team work has remained a continuing weakness in our national life. Vinoba, like Gandhi, did not and does not believe in real socio-economic change through mere legislature and to his great credit he initiated movements like Bhoodan-Gramdan. But the steep erosion in the political life of the country could not be stemmed by any of the movements—started either by constructive workers or by Vinoba. The J. P. episode which was not sanctioned by Vinoba proved to be only an episode and the Janta magic rule for a short period instead of providing an alternative to dictatorial rule, exposed once again want of real character in our leaders and the evil of jealous lust for personal power.

However, Vinoba has shown great originality in interpreting Gandhi's ideas and adding some new ideas of his own.

It is expected that this brief but systematic subject-wise exposition of Vinoba's ideas and thoughts by Dr. Tandon would prove useful for real research and study of the legacy Gandhi has left behind him for future generations.

"Sri Arvind Krupa"
Bangalore — R.R. Diwakar
4-7-1981

Preface to the Second Edition (Revised)

Since the book had become out of print and the National Gandhi Museum was prepared to republish it, I thought it better to go through the book and remove its printing errors. While thus examining its citations and comparing them with the originals, it occurred to me that by including some deleted parts, they would better convey the ideas of Vinoba. Thus, in this edition, some of them stand enlarged and one of them has even been substituted by another citation on the same matter. A few footnotes have also been added to help the reader.

The Foreword of Dr R.R. Diwakar had been received so late that I had not been able to express my gratitude to him for it, and now I do it though he is no more with us.

Shri S.K. Bhatnagar, Head of the National Gandhi Museum Library has done the final proof-reading. I could not even help him because of my age. I am thankful to him also.

Lastly, I must express my thanks to Dr Y.P. Anand, Director, National Gandhi Museum, for undertaking the publication of this revised edition. But for his interest in it, it would not have been republished.

Vishwanath Tandon

1159 R. L. Nagar
Kanpur 208 022.
Dated: 20 January 2004

Preface to the First Edition

A *Selections from Vinoba* containing his ideas practically on all important matters needs no explanation. His greatness both as an original thinker and as a practitioner of his ideas was recognized by Gandhi himself. At the Sevagram Constructive Workers' Conference held in March, 1948, K. G. Mashruwala opined that there was none else but Vinoba who could guide them after the death of Gandhi, and Jayaprakash Narayan wrote in 1965 : "Revolutionary and path-finding thinkers in History have usually been followed by mere interpreters, systematisers, analysts. There have been rare exceptions, such as Luxemberg and Lenin in the case of Marx. Vinoba is such an exception in the case of Gandhi."

As the father of the Bhoodan-Gramdan movement, Vinoba acquired an international fame, attracting even many commoners from various climes and regions to be with him for some time and to witness his movement at first hand. Vinoba's thinking, in spite of its moorings in ancient Indian culture and in spite of its being garbed in a language comprehensible to the Indian masses, has an international import. He is a *vishwamanush*, a 'universal man', a 'citizen of the world'.

The inspiration for this compilation came from Nirmal Kumar Bose's *Selections from Gandhi.* Ever since the days of my study of the post-Gandhi Sarvodaya thought, I had been entertaining the idea of doing the same for Vinoba, but it was delayed due to other more pressing preoccupations. This compilation, I think, is the first effort of its kind, and I am sure that others would follow in future, supplementing it and improving upon it.

The task, however, has not been an easy one. First, the full flowering of Vinoba's thinking took place in the context of the Bhoodan-Gramdan movement, and he, for the most part, did not have the time to revise the versions of his speeches before their despatch for publication or after that. This was unlike Gandhi; and one has to depend largely upon such material for the compilation of his ideas.

Secondly, the material is so vast that it is sometimes very difficult to choose out of it. It is all the more so since some have greater attraction for his spiritual ideas, while others are more interested in his social thought. As far as I am concerned, I did not feel myself qualified enough to deal with the former in depth. Hence, I have included them only to the extent I deemed them indispensable for a proper understanding of his social thought.

Thirdly, being a great philologist Vinoba has sometimes been using even common words in their etymological senses, and this further added to the difficulties of translating him into English. Hence, my first preference has been to the passages already available in English. But this material is very small, and I had largely to rely upon the material in Hindi and to translate the relevant passages into English. While doing so, I have tried to avoid editing so as not to intervene between the readers and Vinoba. However, I have been quite often compelled to make slight changes in the available English versions, either to bring them into greater conformity with the original Hindi versions, or to remove what seemed to me slips and printing errors. But in all such cases, English references have been retained. It may also be mentioned that sometimes the passages cited have been culled from longer passages, omitting portions considered unnecessary by me.

In the preparation of the manuscript, I had the assistance of several persons. My colleague, Shri T. N. Atreya, was ever willing, even at odd hours, to help me understand the nuances of some words used by Vinoba and to suggest appropriate English words for them. His deep understanding of Vinoba's ideas and knowledge of the Sanskrit language were of immense help to me. Shri Achyut Deshpande of the Paunar Ashram closely examined the manuscript for Vinoba Vichar Prakashan Samiti and made many valuable suggestions for improvements. He did it twice taking great pains. Shri C. A. Menon, another colleague of mine, was kind enough to go minutely through the typescript to remove its errors and to suggest some improvements in the language. Lastly, my friend Shri B. N. Khanna, a retired Principal of the Uttar Pradesh Educational Service and at one time Lecturer in English, Raza Government College, Rampur, finally went through the manuscript. To all of them I am highly thankful for the trouble they took. However, for all the mistakes still left, the responsibility is mine.

Lastly, my thanks are also due to Shri K. Arunachalam, the Chairman of the Central Gandhi Smarak Nidhi, for encouraging me to undertake the work, to the Vinoba Vichar Prakashan Samiti, which holds the copyright of Vinoba's writings and speeches, for permitting its publication, and to Shri Radhakrishna Bajaj, Chairman of the Sarva Seva Sangh Prakashan, for undertaking it.

Vishwanath Tandon

Gandhi Smarak Nidhi,
Rajghat, New Delhi

ABBREVIATIONS USED

All publications mentioned below, excepting the periodicals, without the name of the authors or publishers, are by Vinoba and the publisher is the Sarva Seva Sangh Prakashan, Varanasi.

AAV—	*Atmajnana Aur Vjnana*. 1959.
AD—	*Ashram-Digdarshan*. April 1963.
AG—	*Abhinava Gramdan*. Feb. 1964.
AK—	*Acharyakul*. 1973.
Ambar—	*Ambar Charkha : Vinoba Ek Vichar*. Ambar Charkha Samiti, Ahmedabad. n. d.
AP—	*Ashram -Prajnopanishad*. Sept. 1963.
B—	*Bhoodan*, an English Weekly. 1956 to 1965.
BAC—	*Bhoodan Aur Congress*. 1955.
BALKOBA—	*Vinoba ke Prairak Patransh*.
BD—	*Bhagwan Ke Darbar Men*. June 1955.
BG—	*Bhoodan Ganga* in 8 volumes. Sept. 1957, July 1957, Feb. 1957, April 1957, May 1957, Sept. 1957, Aug. 1962, and Nov. 1962.
BTG—	*From Bhoodan to Gramdan*. Sarvodava Prachuralaya, Tanjore, Sept. 1957.
BY—	*Bhoodan Yajna*, a Hindi Weekly, 1954-1971.
BYB—	*Bhoodan Yajna Bihar*, a Hindi Weekly, 1953-1954.
CN—	*Crime and Non-Violence* by Vasant Nargolkar, Sulabh Rashtriya Granthamala Trust, Poona, 1974
Diwan—	*Vinoba Ke Jangam Vidyapeeth Men* by Kundar Diwan. Sasta Sahitya Mandal, New Delhi, 1960.
DK—	*Das Saal Ka Kam*. A Conference Report. Hindustani Talimi Sangh, Sevagram, Wardha. Jan 1950.
DV—	*Democratic Values*. Sept. 1962.
G—	*Gramdan*. Jan. 1963.

GG—	*Gramdan for Gram Swaraj* by Vinoba and Jayaprakash Narayan. Feb. 1967.
Gita—	*Talks on the Gita*. Feb. 1959.
Gogras—	*Gogras*, the Monthly of Go Seva Sangh.
H—	*The Harijan*, an English Weekly. 1948-1956.
HS—	*The Harijan Sevak*, a Hindi Weekly. 1948-1956.
JJ—	*Jai Jagat*. April I960.
KD—	*Krant Darshan*. Jan. 1962.
KGM—	Vinoba's Introduction to *Gandhi and Marx* by K. G. Mashruwala. Navajivan Publishing House, Ahmedabad. Sept. 1951.
KG—	*The Khadi Jagat*, a Monthly in Hindi.
KKK—	*Karyakarta Kya Karen*. Dec. 1960.
KKO—	*Kranti Ki Oar* by Kusum Deshpande. May 1956.
KKR—	*Kranti Ki Rah Par* by Nirmala Deshpande. May 1956.
KP—	Karyakarta Patheya. Sept. 1956.
KSP—	*Kuchh Samayik Prashna*. April 1965.
KV—	*Khadi Vichar*. April 1967.
KW—	*The Khadi World*, an English Monthly. 1951-1953.
L—	*Lokniti*. Sept. 1959.
LY—	*Lok-Yatra* by Kanta-Harbilas (Harishchandra). Aug. 1973.
MA—	*Maitri Ashram*. Sept. 1962.
Maitri—	*The Maitri*, a Hindi Monthly. Volumes used from 1970 onwards.
NA—	*Nagar Abhiyan*. Oct. 1961.
Nagari—	*Nagari Lipi : Ek Sangoshthi*, a compilation. Gandhi Smarak Nidhi, New Delhi. Feb. 1974.
PMV—	*Pataliputra Men Vinoba*. Bihar Bhoodan Prapti Samiti, Patna. 1954.
PP—	Prarthana Pravachan in the *Vinoba Pravachan*, published from 1957 to 1959 and 1962 to 1966.
Prerna Pravah—	*Prerna Pravah*. May 1962.
Purnea—	*Vinoba Pravachan (Purnea Zila Ki Yatra Men)*. 1954.
REC—	*Ramanam Ek Chintan*. March 1960.
RKSM—	*Rajghat Ki Sannidhi Men*. Sasta Sahitya Mandal, New Delhi. 1955.

RLO—	*Rajniti Se Lokniti Ki Oar*, a compilation of Sarvodaya Thinkers. Jan.1957.
RR—	*Random Reflections*. March 1971.
RV—	*Rishi Vinoba* by Shriman Narayan. Feb. 1972.
S—	*Sarvodaya*, a Hindi Monthly. 1949-1955.
Samanvaya—	*Samanvaya*, edited by Dwarko Sundarani. Oct. 1965.
Samyasutra—	*Samya-Sutra*. May 1958.
Sansthakul—	Monthly published by Gandhi Smarak Nidhi in English and Hindi.
Sarvodaya Yatra—	*Sarvodaya Yatra*. Bharat Jain Mahamandal, Wardha. 1951.
SAS—	*Sarvodaya Aur Samyavada*. July 1965.
Satsang—	*Satsang* by Suresh Rambhai. May 1965.
SC—	*Sarvodaya and Communism*, Sarvodaya Prachuralaya, Tanjore. 1957.
SE—	*The Sarvodaya*, an English Monthly. 1953 onwards.
SG—	*Sulabh Gramdan*. July 1965.
SH—	*Stri-Shakti* in Hindi. July 1960.
Shraddhanjali—	*Shraddhanjali*. Sasta Sahitya Mandal, New Delhi. 1951.
SHV—	*Shikshan Vichar*. March 1961.
SKA—	*Sarvodaya Ke Adhaar*. Feb. 1956.
SP—	*Sarvodaya Patra*. Oct. 1958.
SS—	*Swaraj Shastra*, translated by Bharatan Kumarappa. Padma Publication Ltd., Bombay. 1945.
SSE—	*Shanti Sena* in English, translated by Marjorie Sykes. June 1961.
SSH—	*Shanti Sena* in Hindi. April 1967.
SV—	*Sarvodaya Vichar*. Sasta Sahitya Mandal, New Delhi. 1950.
SW—	*The Steadfast Wisdom*. April 1966.
SY—	*Shanti Yatra*. Sasta Sahitya Mandal, New Delhi. 1949.
TE—	*Thoughts on Education*. Oct.1959.
TKS—	*Toofan Ka Sanket*. May 1965.

TP— *Third Power*. Sept. 1972.
TTR— *Towards a Total Revolution* by Suresh Ram. March 1968.
Triveni— *Triveni*, compiled and edited by Nirmala Deshpande. May 1957.
VC— *Vinoba Chintan*, published in 60 issues from Feb. 1966 to Jan. 1971.
VKS— *Vinoba Ke Sath* by Nirmala Deshpande. July 1955.
VP— *Vinoba Pravachan*. 1957-1959 and 1962-1966.
VS— *Vinoba Samvad* by Byohar Rajendra Singh. April 1957.
VV— *Vinoba Ke Vichar* in 3 parts. Sasta Sahitya Mandal, New Delhi. 1954, 1946 and 1965.
Vyaparion— *Vyaparion Se*. March 1965.
WP— *Women's Power*. Sept. 1975.
WV— *One Week with Vinoba* by Shriman Narayan. All India Congress Committee, N. Delhi. Dec. 1955.

Besides the above, the published reports of All-India Nai Talim Conferences, Sarvodaya Sammelans and the Arambagh Session of the Sarva Seva Sangh and 1943-1944 unpublished lectures on the Gita by Vinoba, have also been utilised. They have been mentioned in full after the concerned passages.

I
SELF-INTRODUCTION AND ANALYSIS

The Past and the Present

1. I am reminded that on the 25th of March 1916, forty-one years ago, I left my home. I ran away intentionally. I was leading a happy and secure life. But deep within me I felt an anguish. I yearned to see God. I wanted to devote myself heart and soul to self-realisation. I left home for that Search. It continues to this day. It has been a poignant need of my heart. I could think of nothing else...Superficial distractions may have troubled me, but they could never shake my resolve or deflect me. I can say today that my search ever continues. (B, 10.4.1957,4)

Doing God's Work

2. I take up a work only when God beckons me to do it. Here also I have come at His biddings. People enquire whether this work would meet with success or not. But it is not my work; it is God's. I care little whether it succeeds or fails. Personally, my mission will triumph only when truth, love and compassion overflow my heart.......But so far as the work is concerned, the success rests with God. (SE, April-May 1972, 439)

Devotion to Truth

3. My only attachment is to truth. I expect the same of society. It is not proper for me to insist on anything else. Only truth deserves respect. What does not seem to be truth, should be given up, even though it may have been ordained by the Vedas or the Gita or some great soul.

Fearlessly reject an idea of mine which does not stand your test. It will not pain me at all if you do not accept it. On the contrary, I shall be pained if you do something because of me even though it does not meet with your approval. I even do not wish to exercise any moral pressure. No doubt, nonviolence permits moral pressure, but I for one do not like exercising it over anybody. Only accept an idea when it stands the test of reason. (BY, 26.12.1959)

Attitude and Tendency

4. I feel that by nature I am inclined towards meditation. However, no distinction can be made between meditation and action, knowledge and action, service and spiritual practice. Their fundamentals are the same, and they are only different aspects of one and the same. Had it been left to me, I would have lost myself in meditation. But after the departure of Bapu (Gandhiji), I felt that I must take to a wider field of action. While formerly action was going on along with meditation, it was of a special nature and not extensive. Meditation dominated while action only constituted a part of it. But now it is action which dominates. (VP, 29.1.1959)

5. My attitude is spiritual. I left home in 1916 in the quest of the knowledge of the Supreme. That emotion has now calmed down. At present that search is not being made at individual level. The Truth is being sought collectively.
(VP, 1.12.1959)

6. I am not a pessimist because I know that the human soul is all calm and devoid of differences. What look like differences and lack of peace are nothing compared to its exceeding calmness. (SV, 59)

7. My personal tendency has somewhat been against the bonds of institutions......At its back has been a way of thinking. While I believe in the feelings of brotherhood, I don't like those of bondage.
(Hindi Proceedings of 1948 Sevagram Constructive Workers' Conference, 18)

Mission

8. Mine is a mission to bring about a change in the minds of the people. I desire to revolutionise their mental outlook.
(KW, April 1952,219)

9. I am essentially a devotee. I like to read and hear the glory of the Almighty. I have a burning desire to communicate His name and to listen to His stories.... I submit that I have done nothing else for the last seven years of my trek.... I am trying to spread His name while tackling the land problem.

(SE, June 1958, 401)

Influences

10. Gandhiji gave me freely, but I also received from others. Wherever and whatever I got, I made my own. It now forms a part of my capital. I do not have separate accounts as to what part of it was derived from Gandhiji and what from others. Of the ideas I read and heard, whatever appealed to me and were imbibed by me, became my own. Hence, I am a man of my own ideas.

(Proceedings of 1948 Sevagram Constructive Workers' Conference, 113)

11. Some have begun to look upon me as the representative of Gandhiji's ideas.... But there can be no greater mistake than this. It is true that so far my life has been spent in carrying out those programmes of Gandhiji which appealed to me. But this proviso of 'which appealed to me' was always there. I gained from his association and ideas, and accepted whatever seemed correct to me. I left out others. (S, Aug. 1949, 7)

12. I have been nourished on the teachings of Shankaracharya... I owe a deep debt of gratitude to him. He has set an example of desirelessness and non-attachment. He looked upon the temporal world as an illusion and yet he had such compassion in his heart that he trekked throughout the length and breadth of the country three times during the short span of his life of thirty-two years. He fought against the social evils of his times.

(B, 22. 5. 1957,2)

13. I am an humble devotee of Saint Jnaneshwar......I have been nourished on his Commentary on the Gita. Shankar, Jnaneshwar and Gandhi have been the dominant formative influences in my life. I have had the good luck to live with Gandhiji and learn something from him. I am indebted to Shri Shankaracharya for the intellectual grounding and the background of the Vedanta he provided me with. I cannot express in words how much I am beholden to the great saint Jnaneshwar. All I have and all I am is due to him.

(B, 13. 8. 1958,135)

Relationship with Gandhi

14. I rarely mention Bapu's name. Since others do it so frequently, it is but proper for me to desist from it. But my soul is witness to the fact that I am a child of his. I was a mere boy when I went to him in 1916. Since then I have lived under his sole sway and none other's. I have laboured a great deal to assimilate the ideas he has given us, the wealth of thought he has bequethed to us from the beginning to the end. I can claim to have practised thoroughly the ideas he placed before us. (SE, Nov. 1958, 216)

15. I have been endeavouring for these ten years to tread the path he showed us. Wherever he may be, he would be pleased to see the work I am doing.... I have dedicated my life to fulfil the work he had undertaken. The relationship in which I stood to him is beyond expression.

(B, 30. 9. 1959, 176)

Attitude towards Gandhi

16. Gandhiji regarded himself as an ordinary human being. Let us regard him just a man. (H, 23.1. 1949, 392)

17. There is no Gandhism. Gandhiji always protested against any such thing.... Gandhiji was not an individual or a personality. He was a way of living, a manner of looking at things, an attitude and a way of thinking.

(B, 10.12.1958, 268)

18. Gandhiji is not an individual but a thought. If we do not realize it, we do him a great injustice. Considering that he has given us a line of thinking, we have further to proceed independently. We shall be unjust to him if we limit his ideas to his words and actions. (VP, no. 388 of 1957)

19. No matter how pervasive an individual may try to become, he can never reach the stage of identification with an idea. Hence, the moment we speak of it as Gandhi's idea, we make it narrow and it immediately ceases to be so.

(BY, 28. 5. 1965)

20. The world has undergone great changes during the last fifteen years. There has been progress in science. India attained independence and a democratic state was established in it. Independence, democracy and progress in science, these three came to India within the last fifteen years. In their light the outward expression of ideas is undergoing a change, which is so deep that even some ideas get transformed. The present condition is such that if we literally stick to what Gandhiji said or did, we would make no progress. He too has been changing his ideas in his lifetime. Their outward forms went on changing. He did so in accordance with the situations. Yet, he never gave up his basic ideas. We should also do the same. (VC, no. 32-33, 420)

21. He (Gandhi) had the genius to interpret the cultural traditions of this country in terms of nationalism. The Indian nationalism was to him a way of serving humanity. It was not just a political movement. It was essentially a moral and humanitarian concept. (B, 5. 9. 1956,5)

The Philosophy of Life

22. Our three-dimensional right philosophy of life which will bless the world, has a metaphysics conducive to the welfare of all, while its path of action lies in constructive programme and its path of devotion in the observance of non violence and other vows by remembering the name of God and seeking His aid....Hence I should take care that these three go on getting stabilised in my life. (SV, 88)

23. We are universal men. We pride not on any one country, we insist not on any one religion, nor do we enchain ourselves to any one sect or caste. To roam about in the garden of world's best thoughts will be our diligent study, to digest them will be our constant endeavour and to eliminate their contradictions will be our unfailing creed. To develop an attitude of universalism by synthetising the peculiarities will be our endeavour in the realm of thought. (Samanvaya, 3)

II
PHILOSOPHICAL IDEAS

God

24. I positively believe that God exists. As for the lamp in front of us, I cannot guarantee that it does in fact exists. (RR, 233)

25. Some sociologists have arrived at the conclusion that the idea of God is a creation of the unscientific terror-stricken mind of the primitive man. They hold that as the light of science will spread, this darkness present in the form of belief in God will also disappear. Had God really been darkness, His disappearance would both have been necessary and beneficial. The God of those is surely in danger who have conceived Him as different from the soul, as the Creator of the universe and as one who resides in some corner outside the world in the seventh or forty-ninth heaven. But such is not the conception of God taught to us by the Vedanta. The Supreme is the purest form of soul and devotion to God is the acme of self-efforts. (REC, 38-39)

26. **Question :** What do you mean by God ?

Vinoba : If all our earthly body, etc., was taken away, there would still be something left, a consciousness, which is supremely us. There is that something in everyone. And just as our body is a world, so at the same time we are all parts of a greater world and all our consciousnesses are parts of a mighty whole. That is God. (H, 2.1.1954, 350)

Forms of God

27. **Question :** Then is God abstract ?

Vinoba : Oh yes, God is abstract. (ibid).

28. People always ask me to define God, whose name I take so often. God means truth and love. Where these two exist together, God manifests Himself. (B, 16.5.1958, 5)

29. Truth, love and compassion, these have been regarded to be the forms of God. This is the quintessence of all religions. (PP, 13.7.1957)

Proofs of God

30. Mystics are able to see God with their eyes. Men of God all over the world testify to this fact. (B, 16.1.1957, 6)

31. **Question :** What is the irrefutable proof of the existence of God ? Similarly, what proof is there of the existence of soul? If it be presumed that an animate being is the product of a combination of inanimate elements, then it follows that with the destruction of the body life too disappears. It has no existence after it. What arguments can there be against it ?

Vinoba : Some of your questions pertain to the intellect, and some to the heart. Even though the intellectual questions be secondary, their satisfactory answers are needed for the satisfaction of the intellect, specially of those who have received modern education. There are innumerable people in India in whose minds such questions do not arise at all. They accept things out of traditional habit and faith. But such questions do arise these days in the minds of the educated persons, all the more so due to science. It can be said that science has exposed some areas (to such questioning), while in others it is not so. The most important thing is that science is humble. It always adds 'in the present state of our knowledge'. Not that, there is nothing more to know. There is much, but we have not been able to know it so far. Hence, with respect to those areas we can neither definitely say 'yes' nor 'no'. Take the case of God. While an atheist will say that He does not exist, science will not say so. It will say that it is an open question. A decision on it must await research. At present we cannot say anything.

But the intellect has to be satisfied. There are persons who say, "We don't accept those things which are not acceptable to reason" Just like faith, there is also blind 'lack of faith'. Of course, if reason says that there is something beyond it, then it must be accepted. The existence of God is felt (and not proved rationally). If the existence of soul is disproved, the existence of God would stand refuted. His existence depends upon the existence of soul. Hence we must find out about its existence.

To the question if soul exists, the answer is that it exists and it is different from the physical body. If the body suffers from some disease, we go to a doctor. If there is a defect in our spinning wheel, we go to a carpenter. The spinning wheel does not itself go to the carpenter. Hence, just as we are different from the spinning wheel, we are different from the physical body. Not only so, we go further in that we are different from mind *(mana)* and intellect *(buddhi).* People sometimes complain, "The intellect is not working well these days. It gets greatly tired. It does not work as much as it did during the youth." Now what is that which utters all this. Evidently, it must be something different from the mind.

Thus soul is a consciousness different from the physical body. Had it not been there, man would not have talked like that... This faculty of identifying oneself is 'consciousness'. So much so that a man even gives instructions as to what is to be done after his death. No machine would do it.

Another thing is also to be realized. If there is something in the body, a similar thing is also in the universe. If there is blood in the body, there is water outside. If there is breath in the body, there is air outside. Since there is the sun outside, there are eyes inside. There is consciousness outside and so there is also consciousness inside.

God is an axiom ; soul is an axiom. It is different from the body, mind *(mana)* and intellect *(buddhi).*

(Culled from VC. no. 7, 5-9)

Utility of Faith in God

32. Universal brotherhood will not be established in the world unless the paternal authority of God is accepted.

(RR, 115)

Beginning of Belief in God

33. If anyone believes in the goodness of man, I shall be satisfied. Belief in human goodness is the beginning of belief in God. Therefore if one believes in the essential goodness of man, he will be on the right path. This will naturally deepen his experience and he may reach the stage of realizing God.

(B, 23.5.1956, 7)

Theists and Atheists

34. We call theists those who do not get disappointed. The definition of a theist is that he has faith in the inner light.

(BG, VI, 139)

35. According to me, an atheist is he who does not believe that good actions produce good results and bad actions bad results. To me a theist is one who believes in the theory of Karma, even though he has no faith in God. (BY, 22.3.1956)

36. I prefer honest atheists hundreds of thousand times to those theists who take the name of God but exploit men.

None becomes religious by invoking the name of religion, and nor does he become a devotee by taking the name of God. One who lacks integrity in life, non violence in conduct, religiousness in dealings, cannot be a theist. A sincere atheist is nearer to God than a nominal theist. (VP, 2.6.1959)

Responsibility for Atheism

37. I have not the least doubt that the progenitors of atheists are (the so-called) theists. They gave birth to them. Had we really been theists, our life would have shed light all around and there would not have been any atheist. It is a consequence of the institutionalization of religion. (BG, VI, 36)

38. More atheism has been spread by conflicts among theists than by atheists themselves. (VP, 9.6.1959)

Why Atheism ?

39. Teachings of prophets may have some significance in personal life, but we never make an effort to relate them to our everyday social life. Religion hardly touches our business life and politics. I am not surprised that many of our young men have begun to lose faith in God. This is the natural result of our hypocritical faith and double standard of life.

(SE, Oct. 1956, 116)

No Greater Atheism Today

40. Atheism is no new phenomenon. It is as old as faith in God.... There is no reason to hold that atheism is more prevalent these days. (PP, 5.2.1957)

Disrespect to God

41. Exploitation of our fellow-men means disrespect to God. If we harbour pride and consider ourselves in some way superior to others, that too implies disrespect to God. In the same way, if we say 'this is mine, I am the owner of wealth, I will not let others make use of it', then too we disrespect the Lord. For He alone is the owner and all must equally share all wealth which is His gift. (H, 1.5.1954,69)

Who is a Devotee ?

42. What is devotion ? Is it the worship of an idol in the temple and the offerings of flowers and the burning of incense before the temple gods ? That is only an elementary lesson. If it is not developed further and applied to all walks of life, temple worship will become a ceremonial and will have no deeper meaning. Devotion must express itself in our day to day life. Compassion, love and sympathy are the outer expressions of devotion. A person who has real devotion will see the image of God that resides in every human heart.

(B,9.1.1957, 3)

43. The highest way of devotion is surely shedding all narrow personal self-interest. The one characteristic of the devotee is that he reduces himself to zero and believes that whatever exists around him is the manifestation of God who is perfect. The devotee shall always bear in mind that all men and women who live around him are so many forms of his Master and he is their servant. This is true service, true surrender as the servant to the Master, and indeed this is true devotion.

I must, however, warn you that if one who has devoted himself to the service of all around him begins to feel that he was doing something big, something particularly meritorious, and so begins to cultivate pride within himself that he is superior to his fellows on that account, then surely his service of his fellow-men will not be devotion. (H. 9.4.1955, 41)

Worship of God

44. The form of the worship of God has changed. Those who would not realize it, would be doing wrong things in the name of devotion. (PP, 3.2.1957)

45. God is truth, all good, fearless and devoid of animosity. If we worship God but do not develop His qualities, we should consider our worship to have been in vain. (VP, 6.6.1959)

46. We continue to worship with flowers and fruits but without genuine devotion... God is to be sought in our hearts. He can be worshipped only with flowers of real devotion and the fruits of an incessant quest of true knowledge. (B, 9.5.1956, 5)

Idol Worship

47. Many people have opposed image worship. Foreigners, and even thinkers of our own country, have found fault with it. But the more I think of it, the more I realize its beauty. What is the meaning of it ? It is the art of experiencing the whole universe in a little object....This is not mere imagination, it is a matter of direct experience. (Gita, 151)

48. The service of the people is our idol worship. A cluster of five to twenty-five villages, our area of service, is the abode of God. (KD, 3)

Why Various Forms of Worship ?

49. God has innumerable attributes. A devotee worships Him as One endowed with the particular quality he finds himself lacking in....This has led to variations in the forms of worship. (HS, 15.8.1948,207)

50. Different religions differ from each other since they have developed in different regions. However, they all aim at worshipping God. He has innumerable forms, and may even be said to be formless. Of these innumerable forms, some prefer one and some others.

This variety in worship removes the monotony of life. Just as several melodies go to make music complete, similarly the various forms of worship make the devotion complete. (PP, 17.2.1957)

The Functions of Prayer

51. In spite of the fact that the various religions, all built up by the services and sacrifices of many great men, have some major or minor differences in their doctrines and observations, there is no difference of opinion in any religion on this matter that prayer performed collectively or individually, by repetitious of His name or in some other way, is indispensable both for the individual as well as society, for his or its life, moral uplift, purification of mind, search for truth and maintenance of mental equilibrium in the sorrows and attachments of life. (H, 16.10.1949, 277)

52. Prayer is the last act of our daily routine. During working hours we do many acts of commissions and omissions. At the end of the day, we stand before Him and say : Merciful and Omniscient Lord ! Thou knowest everything, even without our expressing them in so many words. But we feel a consolation in speaking about Thee in our language. So we pray, let us not take credit and feel proud of whatever good acts we have performed. Save us from pride and give us the wisdom to do acts without egotism. We might also have committed wrongs, some knowingly and others unknowingly. Forgive us all these failings. By forgiveness we do not mean that we should escape from the punishments for such acts. Do punish us, for thy punishment itself is forgiveness. But have favour on us and guard us against committing such sins.

If we open our hearts before Him in this way, we would experience as if a wondrous beam of light entered our heart and illuminated and strengthened our being. There is no source of energy in the world which, if we draw from it, does not decrease, except the one emanating from God, who is within us. (ibid, 278)

53. I always compare prayer to a bath, food and sleep. It has the virtues of all the three. Sleep gives rest and replenishes energy. Prayer also provides rest and imparts spiritual strength to man. While food nourishes the physical body, prayer does the same to the mind and heart. A bath cleanses this body, while the prayer purifies the mind and heart. Thus, what all these three do together for the physical body, prayer does for the mind and heart. (KP, 28)

54. Through doing his duty, man tries to clean his mind and heart. But as he does this, a point is reached when he gets tired. Then the soul begins to pray, "Oh Lord ! I have come to the end of my efforts. Give me more strength, more power." Until a man realizes that he cannot achieve success by his own efforts, however hard, he cannot understand the secret of prayer. (Gita, 190)

55. Prayer is an effort of a living being to remember God gratefully. (A D, 22)

Genuine Prayer

56. Prayer is no mechanical activity. It is not simply performed by words of mouth.....It involves the practice of passing the whole day in the light of the spirit of the words of the prayer, impressing one's heart with it. (S, Aug. 1950, 141)

The Value of Silent Prayer

57. All of us describe God reverently in our own ways but it has not been said that a particular description is His best or complete description. God is still satisfied with it just as a father is satisfied with the inarticulate expressions of his tiny child. Even so, silent prayer is accepted as one of the best forms of prayer. If children and parents sit together in silent prayer, it is a good practice and elevates society. The habit of silence will be conducive to peace and non-violence.

(SE, Sep. 1959, 56)

58. Silence expresses the feeling for God more than words ever can. Everyone can contemplate on the God of his conception when he is silent. It is only in silence that one can experience God in the recesses of one's heart. In silence, one's intellect is submerged in the feeling for God.

(B, 4.7.1956, 3)

What Name to Remember ?

59. **Question :** Of all the different names of God, which one should we take ?

Vinoba : If it is the quality of kindness which is lacking, remember Him as kind and merciful. If truth is lacking, remember Him as the personification of Truth... He should be remembered by the name which corresponds to the quality that is to be adored. (S, July 1952, Appendix I)

Prayer, Individual or Collective

60. **Question :** Which prayer is better, individual or collective ?

Vinoba : Both have utility in their respective fields. Collective prayer is necessary for social consciousness. Unison of voice strengthens the feeling of unity. At the same time, individual prayer should not be given up. (VS, 49)

World, Happy or Unhappy ?

61. I have often said that the world is essentially full of happiness; it is we who have made it full of sorrow and suffering. People ask me, "Why then have saints spoken of it as a place full of unhappiness ? Which is the correct view ?" My reply to them is that both views are correct. When saints speak of it as a place full of sorrow and suffering, they have in their mind the world contaminated by evil thoughts and evil desires—the world where there is envy, lust and anger. ... .When I speak of it as a place full of happiness, I have in my mind the ideal world, the divine world, the world where there is equality, love and compassion. Look at the sun. It shines equally on all. Look at the Ganga which offers clean and cold water to everyone who goes to her. God's work is full of happiness and beauty. But the world which man has created is full of sorrow, because he acts on the principle of division, namely, that he must work only for serving his interests. He creates walls to exclude others from what he considers his own. But there are no walls in God's creation.

(H, 21. 8. 1954, 199)

62. As a whole the world is good. Evil is accessory to it, a shadow which brings out and emphasises the good. (SW, 112).

Diversity in the World

63. This diversity is the source of all the joy that is in life. Had He fashioned the world on a pattern of uniformity, life would have lost all charm.

Every man has his own capacities which are different from others. If we are able to synthetise them and utilise them to good advantage, it will be a source of ever-new zest in life. But in the absence of wisdom to utilise these diverse capacities they will collide against one another and in consequence produce clash and conflict and unrest in society.

(H, 28. 8. 1954, 205)

Order in the World

64. There is an order in the world. Due to it, whatever we all do is not necessarily because of our planning. There is another plan and things happen in accordance with it. (AP, 56)

God's Will in the World

65. This world is God's and it runs according to His will. We all dance to His will. We all move at His will.

(H, 20.11.1954, 306)

Individual Soul and God

66. **Question :** What relationship is there between the individual soul and God ?

Vinoba : Both are essentially one. They only differ in power and capacity. Pure individual soul is itself God. (VS, 11)

Difference between Man and Animal

67. Man is not simply an animal. The predominating quality of an animal is vitality, *prana*. It is not so with man. The word *manusya,* man, stands for one who contemplates, who thinks.

In the case of animals their capacity is limited. But it is not so with man. (VP, 13.10.1959)

68. Man can take to a new action. He can embark on a new adventure. He can rise higher or go down....There is an alternative before man, not so with the animal. The question of morality pertains only to those who have an alternative. Man can perform both virtuous deeds and sins. An animal is tied up with his physical body, while the man is not so enslaved. He can attain liberation of the soul.(BG, VIII, 158)

69. Man differs from an animal in that he is not satisfied merely with meeting the demands of the body. There is the urge in him to get rid of social bonds and to identify himself with the whole world. This is the thirst of the soul. In case the two are satisfied together, there would be peace and amity in society. (H, 27.11.1954, 315)

God's Gifts to Man

70. God has bestowed three gifts on man—speech, organs of actions and a sympathetic heart. (VP, 23.7.1957)

The Test of a Man's Development

71. A man can measure his development by the extent he has been able to control his mind and heart and his mind has calmed down. The original state of the soul is that of calmness. Hence, real progress will be presumed to lie in the attainment of the utmost tranquility. (KKR, 101)

None is Perfect

72. My intellect is not prepared to accept any man as perfect. (KKO, 28)

Incarnations

73. Every age has its particular aspiration and there are individuals who inspire people to collective action for it by giving it a form. After his death, such a person is treated as an incarnation. In the absence of the people having favourable aspirations, great men remain seekers, *sadhaka.* They do not appear as incarnations. (VP, 28.3.1959)

Mahatma

74. It is pure imagination to think that someone is a *Mahatma*, a great soul and another is an *Alpatma*, a small soul. There is only soul, which is neither great nor small. It is termed Mahatma when its qualities find greater manifestation and Alpatma when they are manifested to a less extent. Manifestation is one thing while qualities are another, (Prerna Pravah, 107)

Man, the Moulder of His Age

75. I am animate, the age is inanimate. Hence, I shall mould my age. (KD, 132)

Human Nature

76. A man has both good and evil desires, but, on the whole, it is the good desires that prove more powerful and it is they which bring him satisfaction. (Purnea, 52)

77. A man's heart, we must understand, is always good at the core. It may get rusted outside due to various external factors; its internal goodness remains always the same, whatever the outward appearance. It is, as I often say, like a cabbage whose outer layers may go bad but the inside layers retain their freshness. (H, 19.12.1953, 334)

78. By nature, man is noble. That is why he pays respect to righteous persons and not to thieves and dacoits.

Man is forced to act wrongly by the force of circumstances. He is carried away by the currents. But the moment he would realize it, he would change at once on one plea or another.

One good point about those who are really wicked is that they have great faith in God. They are quite near to those who are really virtuous, like the two ends of a circle. That makes their conversion quite easy. (Triveni, 30)

79. It is true that faults are to be found in man. But these belong to the beast in man, not to the human in him. Humanity is good, and makes its way forward progressively towards the good. The heart of humanity is constituted of goodness. (SW, 112)

80. People might have become devoid of morality, but they have not acquired love for immorality. They love truth and morality. (S, May 1952,1547)

81. The present lust for money is due to the existing economic structure being based on it. If the social order be such that people get work and their needs are satisfied, selfish people will be turned into good people. (Satsang, 62)

82. To believe that man's nature is wicked is an affront to the whole of mankind and an acme of pessimism. If by nature he is so, there can be no hope of educating him. (VV, II, 16)

Good Qualities, Our Entrance

83. Even if a mansion has thousands of doors, none can enter it through the walls. Similarly, it shall not be possible to enter the heart of a man of great qualities through his defects. On. the contrary, if someone wants to enter into the heart of a very bad man, he can do so through the few good qualities he has. (Triveni, 25)

How to Reform a Person

84. Even if a really bad person appears before you, think that he is Lord Himself. Even a villain will become a saint. (Gita, 121)

85. Let us only think and talk about the good qualities a person has. A mother only speaks of the good qualities of her child, not of the defects. She has faith that the defects are sure to disappear. An intelligent mother attempts to develop good qualities in the child by removing the defects without exposing them. (VP, 23.5.1959)

The Supreme Aim of Life

86. The barrier set between Brahma, the Eternal Reality and myself is the illusory obsession that I am the body. The shattering of this illusion is the removal of the final veil. The expression, *brahmanirvan,* implies that human life finds its final fulfilment in merging with the Brahma. (SW, 132)

87. The attainment of happiness is not the purpose of life, for it is a quality of the soul itself. None can survive without joy, no matter whether there is less or more of it. The real purpose is self-realization. (VS, 18)

88. The supreme ideal of a man's life is Mukti, liberation. (Triveni, 20)

The Meaning of Mukti or Moksha

89. India has always upheld the ideal of Mukti, liberation. But what is liberation ? Liberation consists in ridding oneself of the narrow personal ego and in merging oneself in the larger self of the society. (H, 5.12.1953, 314)

90. 'Moksha' is liberation from attachment, anger, lust, illusion, ignorance, etc. If these perversions have been got rid of, Moksha has been attained. (S, Aug. 1951, 885)

The Fulfilment of Man

91. The fulfilment of being born as a human being does not lie in the enjoyment of physical pleasures, but in making others happy, no matter how little it be. (Sarvodaya Yatra, 18)

92. A life full of service is 'life'. The rest of it is only a form of death. But if the service is not selfless, it does not remain service. (S, Sep. 1954, 72)

The Problem of Evil

93. Sarvodaya does recognize the power of evil. But it also recognizes the power of good, which is greater than the power of evil. We must face the evil boldly. We must understand that it is, in reality, a reaction and has no existence of its own. (B, 17.4.1957, 3)

What is Happiness ?

94. Happiness does not mean the pleasure of the heart or mind. Pleasure has little to do with happiness. Happiness is abiding, pleasure is transient....Many people today are suffering mentally and emotionally for the sake of their country. They find happiness in such suffering. This is because suffering is sometimes salutary, as it is when accompanied by a sense of benignant service. What is sweet or bitter to the tongue is not necessarily sweet or bitter to the person....Health means physical equilibrium. Health is one thing and excessive physical exuberance another....In the same way, the pleasure which excites or thrills is not really happiness. True happiness is something else. It is to be found in peace, not in a disturbed or agitated consciousness. Its source is tranquillity of spirit. (SW, 80)

95. When a man ceases to think of his person and dedicates himself to the good of society, he will be happy. It is out of the identification of oneself with the body or of self-aggrandisement that misery and unhappiness are born. (B, 6.3.1957, 5)

96. We feel happy only when we are overpowered by the feeling of oneness. (B, 23.4.1958, 5)

Ananda, Joy

97. We should avoid the extremes of both elation and depression. A really joyful man is he who maintains his mood even in unhappiness and regards his soul to be unaffected both by delight and misery. Only then he can experience real joy. (VS, 1)

Why Unhappiness ?

98. Life has become unhappy these days for two reasons. We have accorded greater importance to things which have increasingly less importance to things which have greater. The second reason is that one hand (one part of society) works against the other. If both join together, the whole life would be happy. (PP, 12.1.1957)

Happiness and Misery

99. Some consider unhappiness to be a great calamity and happiness to be a great blessing. I do not think so. I am of the view that both misery and happiness are calamities. We can only be safe if we are able to maintain equanimity of mind, which differs from both. (PP, 30.1.1957)

100. Do not think that we should have only happiness. A man should have a little of happiness and a little of misery. Only then his mind will be calm and awake, and it will think of God. (VP, 20.1.1963)

101. There has been an enormous increase in what are called the amenities of life ; heaps on heaps of articles of comfort and convenience have been manufactured. But look at it a little more closely and you will understand that this enormous increase in comforts, indeed is the mother of all the appalling misery. Happiness and pain are oftentimes spoken of as opposites ; but they are parents to each other. Happiness begets pain, and pain begets happiness. (KGM, 3)

Man's Enemies

102. Desire, anger and greed are the three great enemies of an aspirant. Greed is the most universal and subtle among them. (B, 5.9.1956,7)

103. In reality, the enemy is not outside but inside. Our indolence, desire for indulgence, mutual quarrels, ego preventing unity between us, ignorance, these are the enemies, and they appear externally assuming the form of outsiders. Hence our first task is to destroy the inner enemies, and then the external ones would disappear without efforts. (VP, 20,1.1963)

Death

104. Constantly thinking of death is a means of avoiding sins. If death is always staring him in the face, with what strength can man commit sin ? (Gita, 99)

105. In this chapter (the 8th) it is stated that the thought that is uppermost at the moment of death prevails in the succeeding birth. The soul sets out for the journey ahead, with the provision for the way. Taking today's earnings with us, after a night's sleep, we begin tomorrow. In the same way, with the accumulations of this life, after the heavy sleep of death, we resume the journey in the next birth. (ibid, 90)

106. A very difficult problem before an aspirant is that in spite of continuous efforts to cultivate good Sanskaras, ideas and habits, an undesirable word heard forty years earlier, recurs to the memory. To obliterate these memories, God has planned death so that no old memories recur in the next birth.

(Prerna Pravah, 132)

107. A righteous man does not die. As long as he is alive, he is confined to only one physical body. But when he dies, he does not remain imprisoned in one body. If a godly man leaves the body and he has no desire left, he lives in the world through many bodies, and it is what is termed liberation.

(VP, 15.12.1959)

108. **Vinoba :** We should remember that not only is there joy in life but joy in death as well. If we are ill and suffering and our body is ailing and nobody can help or relieve us, death becomes a joy, and a healthy man should always look to death with joy.

Herald Elwin : You said you would look forward to death with joy. Can you say more on this ? It seems to me that even if the hereafter be beautiful, death nevertheless is a parting from good friends and the last glimpse of a lovely world. Also, however strong the faith may be, surely what happens after death must remain a question-mark.

Vinoba : We cannot have all sweet, there is sweet and sour. There is sadness at death, but we are also released from a useless body which has become of no value to us, an encumberance. We ourselves go on. We take on all which is of worth with us.

What is the present ? There is past, present and future. The past is infinity, the future is infinity, the present is but a second or less. That is life. Before us was infinity; after us is infinity; these sixty years or so are less than a second in the ocean of time.

Yes what happens after-death remains a question-mark. But science has shown us that nothing is destructible. Everything that is, always is, only it breaks up sometimes and goes to different forms. Our body cracks up but what is us remains.

We know there was an infinity of time before us. We can know that there will be an infinity of time after us..... What is of value to us we will take on. Ask anyone what happened to him in his first four years of life, he will know little. And of any other four years he will remember some, not all. But what is of value to him he brings on with him and so after death what is of intrinsic value to us we will take on.

Herald Elwin : So you think that some of what you are now is something you have brought with you from another time?

Vinoba : Yes, certainly, We continue to add to ourselves until we have no longer need of an earthly body to help us. Then we have achieved ourselves. This is the Hindu philosophy.

(H, 2.1.1954, 349 and 350)

Heaven and Hell

109. Happiness hereafter is an illusion. You should be concerned about happiness here. Ask yourself, if your mind is full of greed, hatred and lust. If it is, you can never be happy........ If you have a mind which is calm and undisturbed, you will never bother about what will happen hereafter. If you don't have it, you will never have happiness hereafter, do what you will.

Heaven and hell, happiness and sorrow, are created by our own actions. (B, 17.10. 1956, 7)

Rebirth

110. For me, past and future births are as much established as this one. I am of the definite view on this that no matter wherever we look at the creation, we cannot point out its beginning and end..... If we hold that neither we existed earlier nor we would survive death, several questions crop up. But they all find answers if we know that this innate form is without any beginning or end.

Moreover, if we hold that it has a beginning and an end, the law of Karma becomes meaningless....It is demolished. This is the second proof of rebirth.

The third proof relates to direct experience....Some persons have been observed telling the events of their previous births. Purer and clearer the mind, the more it is able to recollect its past birth. It is, of course, not a detailed recollection but a hazy one. Special events of the past birth can be recollected. It is said that Jnanadeva had written that he was a ruler in his previous birth. Dr. Mrs. Annie Besant too had related some happenings of her past birth and such stories have also been told about Gautam Buddha.

I was with my mother at Poona, then a child of three or four years. She was to take me to some place. I gave the description of the house she was taking me to. I told that it had such a courtyard, such a wall and so on. And the house turned out to be exactly like that. It is quite possible that it was all accidental. Though this incident is no positive proof of previous birth, my mother could have said that I had remembered those things because of my some connection with it in my previous birth.

Secondly, I have a feeling that in my previous birth I was a Bengali. The ground for it is that travel-minded as I am, I reached Bengal during my wanderings and found that I could pick up Bengali much more easily than other languages. This, however, is only a conjecture of mine.

Thirdly, there were several attractions at Baroda, but they did not allure me. Once a friend insisted on taking me to a picture. I went there with a mat and fell into sleep. This gives rise to a feeling in me that I must have had some experience of these undesirable things in my previous births and that is why I am not attracted by them. However, I had a fondness for chess and used to play it. Once I dreamed of it and then I felt that it was overpowering me. Therefore I stopped playing it from the next day. I can call it to be an acquisition of this life. All this creates a belief in rebirth. Thus, on the basis of conjecture, experience and the passages of the Shastras, it is definite that there is rebirth, though there may be differences, regarding details. (VC no. 7, 10-14)

111. An important idea in Hinduism is that of rebirth.. According to it, if a person is not able to complete the work he is doing in any particular birth, he tries to complete it in the next. Thus he goes on evolving. (HS, 11.4.1948, 62)

112. After once being born as a human being, one would, later on, either get human birth or some higher one. However, if some desire of his is so strong that it could only be satisfied as an animal, he would get that birth and would even relish it. (VS, 45)

113. It is a mistake to think that one is born rich or poor in accordance with his deeds in the previous birth being good or bad. Good deeds of the past birth result in good thoughts and freedom from egotism, while evil actions give rise to evil desires and to proclivity for wrong deeds. (Triveni, 34)

114. An individual soul has its own regular chain of Sanskaras, tendencies, and one is born of particular parents accordingly. His own regular chain constitutes one line and a second one is constituted of family tendencies. The individual soul is born at the point of their intersection. (KKR, 129)

The Law of Karma

115. We shall certainly reap in the next birth the consequences of the actions of the present one. But some good and bad deeds are so intense that their fruits are experienced in this very life. (ibid, 73)

116. The Indian people have some wrong conceptions. They think that pleasures and pains experienced by us are the fruits of actions of the previous births. Hence everyone must put up with one's fate. This is a mistaken idea. No doubt, everyone has his own destiny. Yet, some part of it is common. We are born in the same village because of it. Similarly, we are born as human beings because of it. Thus what comes to be destined does not pertain to an individual alone.

The very idea of an exclusive individual's destiny is incorrect. It goes against experience .. .A person smoked a Bidi and threw it on a house. That house caught fire and by and by the whole village was on fire. Thus, all the villagers came to suffer. (VC no. 7, 19-20)

117. The law of Karma is not to penalise you. The award of punishment is an indication of God's love. He wishes to reform you. ...There is something over and above justice, and it is Mercy. We must reap the consequences of our evil deeds, but if God takes mercy on us, we can be exempted from them. No matter how wicked one is, if he is repentant he becomes a good man. (ibid, 20)

Freedom of Man

118. Man can be worse than a beast and, if he likes, even better than a god. (H, 3.4.1954, 35)

119. Man has enough freedom to carve out his future. He has been given a free hand to decide what he would like to become in his next birth. God will not impose His will on us in this matter..... If you want to continue whirling in the cycle of life and death, He will ordain it. Or if you want to move closer to God with the hope of merging in Him one day, it is also possible. (SE, Aug. 1973, 52)

120. A cultivator fixes a stake on the ground and ties the bullock to it. The bullock grazes all around according to the length of the rope. Similarly, we have also been fastened to a stake by God. The length of the rope differs from individual to individual. Whatever it is, it constitutes the limit which cannot be crossed. However, he is free to roam in any direction within it.

Now it is for an individual to find out the length of his rope. Everyone desiring to become a Gama or the President of India, cannot do so. But everyone can become a man of steadfast wisdom, a *stithprajna,* and, if he wishes, can even attain liberation by realising God. We cannot go beyond the length of the rope, but we certainly can free ourselves from it. (KKR, 72)

121. We get the physical body in accordance with (the actions in) the previous birth, but as soon as we have been born, the effects of our previous life are over. After that it depends on ourselves how we would act. This would determine our next birth.

What is termed as 'fate' are the efforts of yesterday and the efforts of today would determine the fate of tomorrow. (KKR, 72 and 73)

The Meaning of Dharma

122. The word *dharma* is comprehensive. The ethics which sustains our life is called *dharma.*

Dharma deals with several matters—Soul, God, worldly life, the life hereafter and the rules of conduct in this world. All these form its subject matter. (BYB, 24. 7.1953)

The Components of a Religion

123. A religion deals with several matters. One is 'worship' involving direct relationship with God, the second is 'ethics' concerned with truth, nonviolence, etc. The third includes 'customs' and 'practices' which pertain to various rites performed at death, birth, etc. The fourth is mythology, stories, etc. Thus a religion has several components. (S, June 1951, 769)

The Common Elements in Various Religions

124. The more we concentrate on the fundamental oneness of humanity, the more do the different religions appear as enriching and strengthening one another. I regard the different religions as merely different forms of worship. Each form has its distinctive merit. When the different ways meet together all. these merits gather together and make a rich and full pattern. (H, 17. 6. 1950, 139)

125. All religions lead to God. They are like different roads ; one seems to go to the east, another to the west, but still everyone leading to and terminating in God.

(D. D. in H, 27. 6. 1948, 150)

126. The ethical principles are the same in all religions.

(S, June 1951, 769)

True Religious Attitude

127. We would be greatly harming ourselves if we make our religion something like a prison house. With changing times the external form of a religion too must change. The vitality of Hinduism lies in its broad-mindedness. Hence, possibly none else has done so much harm to this ancient religion than its narrow-minded followers.

We should ponder over the correct religious attitude. It was natural if in the beginning some fixed rules were prescribed for the preservation of the religion. But now when the way of devotion has developed and become comprehensive in India, to restrain anybody from entering places of worship is to harm the religion itself. The methods of worship vary, and hence our attitude should be that of synthesis. (KKO, 124, 125)

An Organized Religion

128. I do not like at all the idea of organizing religion. As a matter of fact, organisation and religion are contradiction in terms. Due to organisation, religion has not become that force it would otherwise have become. Surely, the progress would have been slow, yet the condition would have been far better than what it is today. (H, 11.12.1954, 331)

The Condition of Religions

129. There are many who pride in the name of religion, there are many who start trouble in the name of religion, but there are few who practise the essence of religion. (PP, 28.5.1957)

130. Religion and love must flow freely within a society. We like to keep our God in a distant heaven. We are afraid to bring Him down to the earth. We invent a Vaikuntha or Kailash for Him. We are doing everything in our power to segregate Him from everyday life. Instead of religion entering the market place, the market has entered the temple and fouled religion. It has become hypocritical and soulless. (B, 12.9.1956,7)

131. Christianity is prevalent in Europe and America. Perhaps no other religion puts so much emphasis on nonviolence as Christianity does. It has laid great stress on Love in very unmistakable terms. There would be very few people who have not read the Bible. They teach the Bible in schools also. They eulogize Christ but at the same time they go on increasing their armaments.

Similar is the case with the Hindus. They would talk of oneness and One All-Pervading Spirit. But in practice they would indulge in the worst of caste distinctions and even untouchability. So is the case with the Muslims and the Buddhists. Everybody thinks that the teachings of their religion are not useful for the transitional period, that is, the present.

They are only meant for the time when society will have reached perfection. (B, 14.1.1959, 308-309)

True Religion

132. What is called Dharma today is not really Dharma. It is 'faith'. That is the appropriate term for the prevailing religions. ... What we call *dharma* is yet to come into existence. (VP no. 422 of 1957)

133. Times have changed. New problems face us. Our religion must also express itself in a new way. Old, outmoded rituals will not do any good either to ourselves or to society....It is only when we devise ways of expressing our devotion in consonance with the Time Spirit that religion will be a reality. (B, 20.2.1957, 5)

Science and Religion

134. The subject matters of science and religion are different. The situation is similar to that of eyes and ears between whom there is no opposition because they have their independent fields. (VP, 14.5.1959)

135. Some hold that science is opposed to religion. They feel that religion would die because of science. But I think otherwise. Up to now there was no science and consequently, really speaking, religion had not come into existence. Now as science would advance, pure religion would come to be enunciated. (VP no. 422, of 1957)

136. Because of science only a true religion would survive and not the false one. Only a religion which is rational, which is not a figment of imagination, which has arisen above desires and has done away with all sorts of distinctions including that of worship, would be able to survive. (BY, 28.8.1958, 6)

Roles of Intelligence and Heart

137. In my opinion a man need have only intelligence, *buddhi*. ...The heart must be assimilated into the mind and lifted out of the unstable flux of uncertainty. The heart is a bundle of desires. Desires must move in tune with intelligence. There should be no hiatus between the head and the heart. There should be no conflict. The mind should speak and the heart must obey. The mind's work is to arrive at a decision. The mind is the legislator; it makes the rules. The work of the heart is to put the rules into practice, to enforce the laws, to act as the executive. The heart ought not to usurp the powers of the mind, nor encroach upon its jurisdiction. (SW, 12-13)

Reason and Feelings

138. Homeopaths pulverise their drugs. It adds to their efficacy. The finer an ingredient is ground the more efficacious it is; its strength increases. The strength of intelligence also increases as it is made finer. Little by little it is transformed. into *bhavana,* sensibility of feeling. (SW, 77)

Reason and Faith

139. Reason is not cripple like faith. Reason is not as powerful as faith. (RR, 123)

140. Intellect should be used in matters which come within its scope. But where it fails, faith is needed. It would be wrong to bring in faith in matters in which reasoning would work. (AD, 64)

Place of Faith in Life

141. No important work is ever accomplished without faith. Act (*kriti*) follows faith (*shraddha)* and conviction (*nishtha)* follows act. Before conviction grows in man, he works with faith. Conviction is faith affirmed by experience. Faith precedes conviction and has to be there before man commences any work. (B, 10.5.1952, 92)

Action, Knowledge and Devotion

142. I cannot cut up life into bits. I cannot separate *karma* (action), *jnana* (knowledge) and *bhakti* (devotion), nor are they separate. (Gita, 216)

143. The sweetness, the shape and the weight of a cake are not things apart. When we put it in our mouth, we eat up its form, absorb its weight and taste its sweetness. The three are mingled together. In every particle of the sweet cake is found its form, its weight and its sweetness. ... In the same way, the spirit should pervade every action of our life—every action should be full of service, full of love and full of knowledge. Every part of life should be filled to overflowing with *karma, bhakti* and *jnana.* (Gita, 231)

Karmayoga

144. There is fire on one side and flood on the other. There is disease at one place while people are crying at another. Under these circumstances how can one meditate ? Hence, the yoga of meditation is not timely. For this age the right thing is Karmayoga.

Karmayoga does not mean becoming less spiritual in attitude. It would not only result in fruits equal to those of Dhyanayoga but in something more. (PP, 31.1.1957)

145. I am aware of the existence of such Vedantists in India who say, "All pleasures and pains are unreal. Hence why worry about them ? We should always remain calm." .... This is not Vedanta. It is totally against it. I consider it to be an acme of deception. ... A Vedantist is one who, while himself remaining calm, constantly tries to remove the misery of society....A person who has truly realized himself, is always doing something. ... He does not desire anything for himself, feels satisfaction in serving others, does not wish for the fruits of actions and is constantly engaged in removing the misery of others with motherly affection. (BY, 13.12.1955)

146. In the path of action one is expected to utilise to the maximum this earthly sheath—this physical body with all its powers—for promoting good. All the organs of work and the senses of perception including the mind and the intellect, etc., have to be employed methodically with a view to purifying them in course of time. (SE, July 1970,5)

Action and Knowledge

147. Action is as fuel to knowledge. In order to keep the sacrificial fire of knowledge constantly burning, one must supply the fuel in the form of action. (RR, 36)

The Advantages of the Path of Action

148. The essence of the matter is that the *karmayogi,* by surrendering the desire for fruit, receives an infinite reward.

His life proceeds evenly. He is radiant in body and mind. The society in which he moves is happy. He attains inward purity and also *jnana.* (true knowledge). And society being rid of hypocrisy and deceit, the ideal of a perfect life comes within reach. This, experience shows, is the greatness of a *karmayogi.* (Gita, 38)

Desirelessness

149. If we give up our *svadharma* (one's own *dharma*) and take over another's *dharma,* it is quite impossible to attain the goal of desirelessness.

But in order to achieve freedom from desire through the practice of *svadharma,* something more is necessary—victory over *kama* and *krodha,* craving and agitation. As long as the mind is not as pure and peaceful as the water of the Ganga, desirelessness will not come to us. (Gita, 40 and 41)

Comparison between Karmayoga and Sannyas

150. Both the *sannyasi* (one who has completely renounced the world) and the *karmayogi* are *jnanis,* seers, and are entitled to the same high throne. Though the names are different, the substance is the same. They are two modes of the same reality. A wheel in rapid motion seems at rest. The state of the *sannyasi* is similar. From his *shanti,* his peace and steadiness, flows infinite power, endless movement.....Though all the endeavours of the *sannyasi* have ceased, and come to a rest, he does mighty deeds.

To do nothing, and yet to do all things, is possible for the *siddha,* the perfected one, not for the *sadhak,* the seeker.... *Karmayoga* is both the way and the goal, but *sannyas* is only the goal. From the point of view of the *sadhak, karmayoga* is preferable to *sannyasa.* (Gita, 63-64)

The Path of Devotion

151. After exploring various ways and means for spiritual enrichment of life, the saints all over the world came to the conclusion that *bhakti* (devoted surrender and prayer) of the Lord was the means pre-eminently the best of them.

(H, 28. 11.1948,336)

152. One should utter the name of God, use one's hands in doing God's work and see Him inside his own self. When all these three go on together, the path of devotion is accomplished in all its aspects. (VP, 9.1.1963)

153. In the path of devotion, remembering the name of God has been glorified. I do not understand it to mean repeated utterance of the name of God on beads. Its real meaning is to keep God always in mind and to regard any person one meets as the representative of God. (VP, 3.12.1959)

Why Devotion Needed ?

154. To attain purity of mind many *vikarmas* (special actions) are prescribed, like *yajna* and *dana* (sacrifice and gifts), *japa* and *tapas* (prayer and penance), *dhyana* and *dharana* (meditation and concentration.) These means I should compare with washing soda and soap. But *bhakti* (devotion) is the water. Without water these other things are useless; but even without these water can cleanse. (Gita, 85)

Devotion with a Motive

155. Whatever the excuse, enter the temple of *bhakti* (devotion). Though in the beginning you enter it with a motive, you will later become desireless. (Gita, 167)

Impersonal and Personal Devotion

156. *Nirguna* (the impersonal) and *saguna* (the personal) complement each other, they are not incompatible. Starting from *saguna,* one has to tread the path to the goal of *nirguna; nirguna* too needs the water of *saguna* to cleanse the subtle impurities of the mind. Each gains lustre from the other.

(Gita, 167)

157. It is true that the river of inspiration rises in the *saguna* (the personal) but it should reach perfection in fidelity to principle, it should flow into *nirguna* (the impersonal).

Lord Buddha knew this. Hence, he prescribed the three dedications* (Gita, 166)

---

* These are first to an individual (Buddha), then to an institution (Sangh) and finally to a principle (Dharma)—(Compiler)

The Yoga of Meditation

158. There are three important things in *dhyanayoga* (the yoga of meditation), namely (1) one-pointedness of mind, (2) setting bound to one's life, to help to achieve this, and (3) a state of equanimity or evenness of vision. One-pointedness of mind means controlling its movements. Setting bound to one's life means doing actions after weighing and measuring them. Evenness of vision means having the nobility to think in terms of the whole world. These three together make up *dhyanayoga*. To achieve these three, one needs the help of *abhyasa* (practice) and *vairagya* (detachment). (Gita, 70)

Perverted Detachment

159. If the qualities of an individual do not find expression in social dealings, their power becomes limited. In India there have been several men of knowledge, asceticism, detachment and greatness, but they kept aloof from society. Had they lived a social life, they would have acted as catalysts and the whole society would have been permeated with knowledge and the spirit of detachment.

A virtue which does not acquire a social value, ultimately turns into a defect. This has much happened in India.

(VP, 6.2.1963)

Meditation and Social Action

160. In olden times when there was no dearth of land, people had enough to eat. They had leisure. They could devote their time to worship and meditation. But times have changed now; the pattern of social life has altered materially. How can we remain content with the religion of temple worship and chant-ing ? Social action has become an urgent religious need... If a village is insanitary and infested with disease, how can you worship and meditate ? Is it not necessary that you take a broom in your hand and sweep the streets and clean the gutters of your village first ? Has not the Gita said that it is better to devote oneself to social action without any desire of personal return than to meditation ? Meditation has its importance but it is essentially individual. It brings an individual some return.

But a social action brings happiness to others. Meditation is as important as it was before but the people amongst whom we live must now be placed on the pedestal. They must become the object of our devotion and worship. Meditation has to be directed to the well-being of society.

My personal preference is for the way of meditation. I would be too happy if I could sit down and meditate instead of moving about like this. 1 have done it and know something of the happiness of sitting immersed in deep meditation. But I go about moving like this because I am convinced that religion will not evolve unless there are people who follow the path of social action. (B, 20. 2. 1957, 5)

161. I have always been of opinion that the traditional notion that action comes in the way of meditation is not correct, and it needs to be corrected. Just as a man can attain a state of *samadhi* by abstaining from all action, he should also be able to maintain his mental poise in the midst of action. I have some personal experience of this. Abstention from activity and retirement to some solitary place was usually regarded an essential condition for meditation. This may be necessary in preliminary stages, but it does not help further progress in meditation. The best meditation is achieved when one is constantly engaged in action without being conscious of its strain. Our breathing does not interfere with meditation. On the other hand, if it is controlled and well-balanced, it is a great help. In the same way, productive physical labour and silent, serene, sweet meditation done in a spirit of devotion and service of all, can easily go together. Such action need not interfere with meditation. A new orientation of *dhyanayoga* from this point of view is urgently called for. That will give new life to the traditional path of meditation.

(B, 23. 5.1956,2)

Nivritti, Cessation from Acts of Worldliness

162. In India the word *nivritti* (cessation from acts of worldliness) has been very much wrongly interpreted. It is so near to *tamoguna* (inertia) that the two ends of a circle have come very close. The virtuous and the sinner become one. (VP no. 321 of 1957)

163. The Gita considers *pravritti* (active life) and *apravritti* (inactivity) different from *nivritti* (cessation from worldly actions) ...Because of the lack of realisation of this, *nivritti* is generally taken to mean in India inactivity. The result has been that whosoever went in for self-realisation in India, he proceeded at once towards giving up of activity.

Inactivity is as strong an action as activity itself. ... To regard a strong activity as *nivritti,* to take a strong propensity as *nivritti* and to consider one-sided life as *nivritti,* all this is a delusion. *Nivritti* can never be one-sided. It is all inclusive. It cannot prohibit action. (AD, 25-26)

164. *By pravritti* is meant efforts for uplift based on *karmayoga,* an attempt to better society, to raise its standard of living equally for all. In short, it will be defined as the service of the people based on a disinterested performance of duties. Normally, the first half of everyone's life should be of this kind, and the second half should be that of *nivritti* (cessation from action of the world). In *nivritti* it is the thinking which predominates and its motive is people's education. If we say that by uplift is meant raising the standard of people's living, then *nivritti* connotes raising the level of the thinking of the people. It is through *karmayoga* devoted to public service that all actions for the material development of society take place, while it is thinking which plays part in all actions leading to the development of the finer aspects of society.

At present our *pravritti* is not of disinterested performance of duty devoted to public service, but of actions aiming at the satisfaction of the senses. Similarly, our *nivritti* today is not devoted to thinking or education but to ease and inertness. (BY, 11.11.1956)

Penance

165. Penance does not mean standing in the rains or the sun. It stands for the efforts made for the purification and uplift of society. (VP no. 4 of 1957)

Yajna, Dana and Tapas

166. At our birth we are born into three orders.. . .The first is the body that wraps us. The second is the vast universe that surrounds us, the boundless creation of which we are a part. The society into which we are born, our parents, our brothers and sisters, our neighbours—these form the third. Everyday we use these three orders, we wear them out. The Gita wishes that we should try unremittingly to replenish what is lost through us, and thus make our life fruitful.

To make up for the harm that has been caused to creation —that is *yajna* (sacrifice). We have been ploughing the earth for thousands of years and thus impoverishing it. *Yajna* says, "Return its strength to the soil. Plough the land and feed it with sunlight. Give it manure."

We are born in this world with a load of debt on our heads. Whatever we do to discharge this debt is *yajna* or service, not altruism. By this we must discharge our debt. At every step we use the order of creation. Therefore we have to do *yajna* to replenish loss, to purify things and to create new things.

The second order is our human society. Father; mother, teacher, friend, all these toil for our sake... .The service that we render to free ourselves from this debt to society, that is *dana* (the rite of giving). To help human society to progress is *dana.*

Besides these, there is the third order, that of the body. This too wears out day by day. We wear out by use of our mind, our knowledge, our senses. *Tapas,* penance, has been prescribed in order to remove the defects and distortions that arise in our body.

Here we have regarded *yajna, dana* and *tapas* as if they were three different things, but to tell the truth, there is no difference between them. For the three orders of Nature, society and the body are not absolutely distinct. Society is not an outside creation; not for that matter is the body. These three together make up the beautiful order of Nature. The creative effort we make, the *dana* we give and the *tapas* we perform, all these can be called *yajna* in the comprehensive sense. (Gita, 247-249)

Anashakti, Non-Attachment

167. *Anashakti* is an acme of love. None can love more than the man who is non-attached. (AD, 77)

Individual and Society

168. In the welfare of an individual lies the welfare of other individuals and of the whole society; in the welfare of society lies the welfare of every individual. Such is the faith of Sarvodaya. (SY, 113)

169. The human body has a lesson to teach us regarding the way society should organize its life so as to function efficiently. The body cannot work well if one of its limbs grows anaemic while another grows abnormally strong, because this disturbs its harmony. But it works well if all the limbs are nourished equally according to their needs.... Society is also an organism like the human body of which the individuals who compose it are constituent limbs. Some are its eyes, some others are the nose, still others are its hands and feet, and so on. And all of them must be equally well cared for to keep the body social in good health.

All the individuals constituting the society must work and render to the whole of which they are parts such service as they are capable of, then only can society be happy.

(H, 26.12.1953, 341)

170. Some give more importance to the individual, some to society. This is because of the spread in society of the concept of struggle for existence.

But in reality it is impossible to separate the individual and society. If a curtain is hung in the middle of a room to divide it into two and it is blown about by the wind, sometimes one part appears larger and sometimes the other. The size of the compartment is not fixed and permanent; it depends on the wind. (Gita, 257)

171. Society is an ocean while we are only drops. The welfare of the drop lies in entering the ocean. If it maintains a separate existence, it would dry up; if it merges in the ocean, it would acquire a greater size. We would only dwarf ourselves if we regard ourselves to be confined only to our individual bodies. (VP, 20.9.1959)

172. Man lives in society. Individual life is sustained by a network of social efforts. The difference between the individual and the social aspects of one's life is not distinct. They overlap and are intermixed. The individual part is small in dimension but has greater depth. The social part is large but lacks depth. There have been great men whose individual lives had depth which was greater than the total depth of the contemporary society. But such men are exceptions. The depth of the social life cannot be greater than the depth of the men who compose society. (B, 13.2.1957, 1)

173. There is no conflict between the individual and society. How can there be? Even between one individual and another there should be no conflict. If one is better endowed than another, what does it matter ? No one should suffer privation, and the riches of the rich should benefit society. That is enough. Does it make any difference whether my money is in my left pocket or in my right pocket ? After all, both are mine. When someone is rich, I am rich, the nation is rich—we can establish this in practice.

But we erect these walls of difference. If the body and head are separated, they both would die. Therefore do not separate the individual and society....Between the air in this room and the unbounded atmosphere without, there is neither difference nor conflict. If I imagine that there is conflict and shut the doors and windows, I shall only be suffocated to death. If, assuming that there is no conflict, I throw open the room, the boundless air flows into it. The moment I cut off my land and my house from those of others, that very moment I am cheated of infinite wealth. (Gita, 258-259)

Harmony of Interests

174. So far it has been held that one man's food is another man's poison. This is a wrong contention. We believe that a true gain of an individual implies a gain to an entire society and vice versa. The reason for the current false notion is that money has been given the place of God and manual labour is at a discount. Everybody seems to be anxious to earn maximum money by minimum endeavour.

(H, 13.11.1954, 295)

Society, A Bank

175. Work for the good of the society using all your physical and intellectual powers. Society is the best and the safest bank. Keep all your wealth with this bank and you can rest assured that it will offer help and protection to you whenever you need it. (H, 6.2.1954, 391)

Importance of the Individual

176. To determine the quality of the milk, we determine its butter-coefficient. The worth of a society is judged by its individuals.

(Gita, 258).

177. Everyone has a uniqueness. It is that which imparts a value to his life. The life of everyone has a social value and also an independent value. That independent value never diminishes.

(AD, 86).

178. Externally seen only society is real, the individual is unreal. Individuals will come and go, but society will go on for ever. Thus from the social point of view society is real and the individual is unreal. But from the standpoint of the individual, while an individual is today in one society, he may be in another the next day..... From that point of view all these institutions are false. Only his own individuality is real.

(AP, 79)

Individualistic Approach Not Sufficient

179. Science operates on a higher plane than that of the mind. The fact that science is higher than self-conscious mind has been known from ancient times. The Upanishads say that Brahma is the first vital principle (*prano brahma*), then that He is mind (*mano brahma)* and lastly that He is science (*vijnanam brahma).* The vital principle is the plane of animal life, the mental is that of man, the scientific is that of the sages. In those early times the scientific plane of living was known, but it was not then essential for all men. Some men attained to it in the course of striving for self-development, but it was thought of as an individual achievement only.

In the world of today this individualistic approach is no longer sufficient. It is now essential that all men should reach the plane of scientific thinking. Both spiritual insight and physical science call upon the mind to transcend itself.

(TP. 42-43)

180. This leads us to the third great quality which we urgently need today — that of devotion to society; that is, our thought and action must be aimed at the well-being of society. There must be free scope for individual development, no doubt, but the advancement of science in our times has made it quite easy for an individual to realise all its possibilities in full measure. What therefore requires to be stressed is not individual development but the dedication by every person of his developed abilities to the service of the society. It is not enough to develop one's qualities individually; all those qualities have now got to be cultivated and firmly implanted in the entire society. (H, 5.12 1953, 314)

Meaning of Spirituality

181. I would like to place before you the meaning of *adhyatma* (spirituality) in terms of Shankaracharya. In a small verse he has defined *adhyatma* for the common man. His first advice is to recite the Gita and the Vishnusahasranam regularly..... His second injunction is : Concentrate your thought ceaselessly on God. The third is : Keep your mind in noble company. The last and the fourth command is : Help the poor and the distressed. Thus helping the poor and the needy has been regarded as *adhyatma* by Shankaracharya. And not only by him but also by Ramanuja and all other Acharyas, by our Rishis and Munis, saints and seers, sages and holy men. All of them have placed service of the poor in the category of spirituality. (SE Jan-Feb. 1976, 226-227)

182. Spirituality is that science which enables you to perceive and recognize the whole infinite universe in your own self. It is impossible to comprehend fully the true nature of the universe and to find out who is its creator, for the universe is macrocosmic as well as microcosmic. And yet an effort can be made to comprehend its nature.

This effort can be made through observation which could be either outward or inward. Physics helps to understand the outward aspects of the universe, while metaphysics enables us to comprehend a little the inner nature of the universe. It is, however, not possible to attain to integral knowledge through the pursuit of physical sciences.

To try to know who is the Creator and to realize Him is again more difficult. That is why the only easy way of knowing and realizing Him is to try to find Him in the individual self. This itself is known as spirituality. (SE, July 1950, 4-5)

Spiritual Progress and Material Advance

183. It is wrong to separate spiritual progress and material advance. The two must coalesce. If the two are conceived separately, both will remain incomplete. It cannot be said that materially backward countries are spiritually advanced, while it is equally fallacious to think that materially developed countries like America are spiritually poor. Where there is only apparent material abundance, decay will be discernible; and where the emphasis is one-sidedly on spiritual progress, there too life will be lopsided. Thus, progress can only be all-sided.

(B, 26.11.1958, 252)

Science and Self-Knowledge

184. Science in itself is neither moral nor immoral; it is amoral and its standards of value must be supplied from elsewhere. Wrongly directed it leads to hell; rightly directed it may lead to heaven. The only power which can direct science aright is that of self-knowledge, spiritual knowledge. (TP, 45-46)

185. Man, like a bird, has two wings—science and spiritual knowledge—and he needs both together for his happiness. The design of every machine provides for two forces, one to generate energy for movement and the other to guide and control it. One cannot work without the other. A car has an engine and a steering wheel, so does a human being. We walk with our feet and not with our eyes, but the eyes show us where to go. Self- knowledge or wisdom is the eye, science is the feet...Nothing can be done in the world without science, but science cannot go in the right direction without self-knowledge. (TP, 47-48)

Self-Knowledge, Science and Faith

186. I have described how the greatest strength that a man can possess is his faith. If you want universal peace, happiness and prosperity, an end to suffering and hardship, you must hold fast to self-knowledge, science and faith. I have no magic formula in my possession except faith in men. In the armoury of Sarvodaya there is no greater weapon than the faith we place in our fellow-men.

Faith is the most miraculous thing in the world. The whole world depends on it. Without mutual faith the human race would have perished by mutual slaughter. Even thieves keep faith with one another. If we could only believe in the power of faith, realize its potential and act on it, it would not take long to stop the world's conflicts. They are caused mainly by lack of faith, and it is this that has to be overcome. Faith is the power of this age. People have faith in me; they have no guarantee that I shall not lie to them, but they have faith that I will not and I too have faith in them. Faith is my secret and it has great power. (ibid, 68)

The Ideal Man

187. A man of steadfast wisdom, *stithprajna,* is the ideal man of the Gita. Though there are also other ideals mentioned in it, they are not its ideal. My own ideal is that of the Gita. I have got it from it, but now it has become mine independently.

The highest ability of man lies in the power of his intellect, in his capacity to take decisions. The intellect cannot make any infallible decision unless it is free of attachment and hatred.

A *stithprajna* is free of them. There is no curtain before his intellect. Hence, his decisions are always correct. His intellect is like a clear mirror which reflects everything correctly. That is why he is capable of taking decisions on any issue.

Such a person is both a devotee as well as beyond attributes. He combines the essence and elements of all the other ideals, but his most important peculiarity lies in his capacity to decide. His decisions can never go wrong. In this respect he may well be compared to a thermometer.

To be a good man is one thing, to be a *stithprajna* is another. It may be said that while a good man wears such goggles which make him see only good everywhere, a bad man's goggles are of such a colour that he only finds evil everywhere. Both fail to understand the world as it really is. But a man of steadfast wisdom does it because he is completely objective.

All his actions would be fully scientific. Just as a moral man does not need any science of ethics and a poet need not study poesy, every action of a man of steadfast wisdom is scientific even if he has no knowledge of science.

His second special characteristic is that he is always in the state of *samadhi,* a state of inner equilibrium and tranquillity of mind. The concept of *samadhi* in the Gita differs from the prevailing concept. By it is understood a state in which there is no awareness of the outside world, no consciousness of it. Its intensity can vary in degree. I can imagine of a *samadhi* which is not disturbed even if the various parts of the body are amputated. Such a state is considered to be the ideal in meditation. But it is not necessary that one with such *samadhi* be a self-realized soul. The ideal of the Gita is higher. A man of steadfast wisdom will impart knowledge even when he is being amputated. He will be telling what veins and arteries are there, what nerves are there, and so on. Under an anaesthesia there is no consciousness of the self, while it is there in meditation. What happens in the latter is that due to the total concentration of mind, one does not feel the operation and its pain. But a man of steadfast wisdom remains fully conscious and goes on asking questions and acquiring knowledge as if somebody else was being operated upon.

A man of steadfast wisdom is always one with Brahma. It seems that he is so much engrossed in the Atma that he is not, in a way, aware of the world. Just as we constantly go on breathing and are not required to give up other activities for its sake, similarly he is ever engrossed in the Brahma. Even breathing is an activity, but the realization of the Brahma is not. His intellect, *prajna,* is fully integrated. That is why he has been called *stithprajna.* He sleeps, awakes, rises and sits. They indicate his physical existence. But these activities relate to his body, not to his self. He has no desires, no attachment, etc. Every moment of his is for service. He has no self-interest left. He actually lives for others. (Culled and arranged from 1943 unpublished talks on the Gita, nos. 29-32)

III
ETHICAL IDEAS

The Ethical Plane

188. I don't differentiate between moral and spiritual planes. Spiritual plane is higher, but the moral plane is not lower. It is nearer humanity. ...One is the ladder, the other, the destination. It is not possible for a man to be a spiritual being without first being a moral being. (SE, Jan. 1958, 201-202)

The Criterion of Morality

189. The criterion which is applied in the science of ethics for determining whether from the point of view of morals a principle is right or wrong, and whether from a practical point of view it is advantageous or disadvantageous, is to extend it to apply to all men and see what the result is. A principle which when thus extended tends to vanish, or not to hold good, or to destroy itself, should undoubtedly be regarded as invalid, both from the moral and practical points of view. (SS, 60)

190. A law of *dharma,* morality, to be true must be applicable to all. Any such rule which is applicable to some and not to others, is no *dharma* at all. To speak truth, to love all mankind, to be compassionate, all these rules are applicable to all. (PP, 29.4.1957)

General Principles of Morality

191. It is our duty to act in a manner conducive to a proper functioning of the creation, society and the physical body. We build up many good or bad institutions, but these three are no creations of ours. Hence, it is our inherent duty to make good the harm done to these three institutions through *yajna* (sacrifice), *dana* (gifts) and *tapa* (penance). (BYB, 21.8.1953)

192. The motto of "Live and let live" is in vogue these days. We have to replace it by another : First help others to live and then live. That makes a lot of difference. We must care for others first and for ourselves last. (H, 18.12.1954, 339)

193. A right action is one that gives us peace of mind; an unrighteous action is that which deprives us of it,

(VC no. 7, 32)

194. However unattractive a man's *svadharma* (one's own duty) may be, he has to find fulfilment by persisting in it, because it is only through such persistence that growth is possible.

However, superior another's *dharma* may appear to be, it is not good for me to adopt it. ...If someone were to say to a fish, "Milk is costlier than water; come and live in this milk", would it agree ? Fish can live only in water; they will die in milk. (Gita, 7 and 8)

Meaning of Svadharma

195. *Svadharma* implies that every person has his own independent duties. Such *svadharma* or one's special duties vary from individual to individual. But since a man is also a part of society, we may say that everyone should render service to society. However, each has his own special qualities and he should serve society by developing them well.

(Samyasutra, 49)

Svadharma of the Gita

196. What is *svadharma,* one's own dharma ? The Gita has no particular religion in view like Hinduism, Islam, Christianity or any other. Yet the *svadharma* of the Gita is so comprehensive that it is applicable to all. The fourfold caste system existed at that time and that is why it has been cited as an example. But it does not mean that any significance has been specially attached to it.

(Unpublished Gita lectures of 1943-44. Lecture dated 22.11.1943)*

---

* It may be mentioned that the word 'religion' does not convey the meaning of 'dharma'. See Glossary.

Various Elements of Svadharma

197. *Svadeshi dharma,* the national *dharma; svajatiya dharma,* communal *dharma ;* and *svakalin dharma,* the *dharma* of the age—all these come together in *svadharma,* one's own *dharma.* These three combine to make up *svadharma.* To determine one's *svadharma,* one should consider what is helpful and appropriate to one's nature and situation, and what duty falls to one. (Gita, 273-274)

Variability of Svadharma

198. Again in *svadharma* there are two parts. One changes, while the other does not. I am not today what I was yesterday, nor shall I be tomorrow what 1 am today. I am ever changing. The *svadharma* of childhood is just to grow. In youth, I am full of power of action, and should use it in the service of society. In maturity, others will get the benefit of my wisdom. While one part of *svadharma* is thus changing, the other part is unchanging. If we use the names of the old Sastras, we should say, "Man has a *varna-dharma* and an *ashram-dharma"* While *varna-dharma* does not change, *ashram-dharma* is constantly changing. (ibid, 274)

199. Different individuals may have different *svadharma.* Not only this, the *svadharma* of an individual may also vary from time to time. *Kul-dharma* (the family duties), *samaj-dharma* (the duties towards society), *yuga-dharma* (the duties of the age), etc. are some of the comprehensive duties. The *dharma* of an individual person varies according to the times and the development of his inclinations. The Gita teaches that the *svadharma* of an individual consists of his duties at a particular time.

(Unpublished Gita lectures of 1943-44. Lecture dated 22. 11.1943)

How to Determine Svadharma ?

200. "How then, is *svadharma* to be determined ?" If someone asks this, the easy answer would be, "It comes naturally, of it-self." It is born into the world with us. The very idea of going in search of it is strange. When a man is born, his *svadharma* too is born with him. As a child has no need to go in search of his mother, no one need go in search of *svadharma.* It is ours, right from the beginning. The world was there before we were born; it will be there when we are no more....The service of the parents to whom I was born, the service of the neighbours amongst whom I find myself, these duties come to me naturally. Then, my other obligations are matters of everyday experience. I feel hungry, I feel thirsty. So, to give food to the hungry and drink to the thirsty becomes my duty by nature. Hence, it is never necessary to go in search of the *svadharma,* of some form of service or compassion. (Gita, 205-206)

Relativism and Absolutism in Ethics

201. Dharma has two aspects, one changeless and the other changing. The observance of truth is as much a duty today as it was in days gone by, and as much in other countries as in India. The difference of time and space does not limit it. It is of the kind of eternal verities, which are the same always. So are love and compassion. But the rules of conduct through which they are sought to be expressed cannot last for all time. They change according to age and circumstances and country. Devotion is again an eternal Dharma and equally true for all, but form and ceremonial designed to express it will differ. What we must do therefore is to hold fast to this changeless soul of Dharma and keep it continually in our mind.

I am not concerned with the transitory forms. I am calling you to the changeless essence of Dharma. This changeless essence consists in the establishment of equality and unity, notwithstanding the diversity and differences of outward life. These differences will remain, but there will be equality and an inner unity. (H, 20.12.1952, 368)

202. Dharma is the name for those ethical principles which sustain life. It is unchanging. Its principles are permanent. Just as the rules of mathematics are the same for all countries, so is the case with the principles of Dharma...... The virtues of adherence to truth, love and kindness which have been characterised by Lord (Krishna) as divine attainments, constitute in reality the eternal Dharma. (BYB, 24.7.1953)

203. Socially accepted ideas of righteousness and unrighteous ness are mostly conventional. (VC no. 7, 31)

Observances or Vows

204. Bapu (Gandhiji) taught us that there are some values of life which are eternal and unchangeable. One should have complete faith in them.

Among them are on the one hand nonviolence, non-possession, truth, etc, and, on the other, Swadeshi and the removal of untouchability have been added to them. This leaves an impression that their texture is not uniform. Nonviolence, truth, etc. are basic observances, while Swadeshi and removal of untouchability are secondary ones derived from them, and equality of all religions, bread labour and such others are comparatively of less importance than truth, non-violence, etc. Thus, they are a mixture of both primary and secondary items. They are not in consonance with the thinking of those persons who think in the manner of Shastras. Yet, they embody a good deal of the essence of spirituality. (AP, 33-34)

205. The number of the observances can be less or more and it does vary, but nonviolence, truth and some others are eternal. (VP no. 422 of 1957)

206. They (the vows) have the capacity of protecting men and society. As a result of their observance, an individual like Bapu (Gandhiji) became a Mahatma. They embody the quintessence of the lives of all saints. They are not only meant for a recluse. They are for him and for the whole society. (VP, 17.2.1959)

207. It is said these days that 'vows' constitute a bondage, but it is a misleading idea.

The vows do not give trouble. ...They form a good straight path. When the road is good, we do not worry. Vows imply treading a straight path. They make it easy, they make men free. (MA, 28)

Importance of Truth

208. There is no inherent strength in untruth. Even for its existence, it has necessarily to depend upon truth. (RR, I)

209. The world is sustained by truth. It subsists because there is more truth in the world than untruth. If untruth acquires predominance over truth, the world would come to an end. (H, 25.8.1951, 222)

210. Four means have been suggested for the realization of self. The first among them is truth, and it is very important. If we put all the moral philosophy of the world on one side and truth on the other, the latter would outweigh. Truth is the highest principle of morality, while all others are secondary to it.

Truth here means the triple truth of thought, word and deed, not of the word alone. (VP, 26.2.1959)

Definition of Truth

211. Moral truth can be defined, but the idea of the Supreme Truth defies definition. Truth is that which makes us realize the existence of conscience and brings satisfaction to it. When the conscience does not feel satisfied or is shocked, there is untruth. That is, the conscience is witness to truth and untruth. . ..A dacoit may say, "I have done this thing for the sake of my children. I have done it out of a sense of duty." But this would not be correct, for there is a sense of evenness in truth. This is its second identifying characteristic. There is balance in it, no inclination this way or that. In truth all are looked upon with the same eye, there is contentment, there is inner satisfaction. (VC no. 7, 22-23)

212. Truth cannot be defined. It is self-evident. Nothing in the world is so obvious. (KP, 84)

Untruth, the Primary Evil

213. The prevailing social values stand in need of a very great change. These days some actions are reckoned among great sins, as for example, stealing gold, committing adultery, drinking, murder, etc. But it seems to me that we would not progress spiritually as long as we do not realize that all such evils as murder, adultery, etc., which the world takes very seriously, are only secondary evils, the primary one being that of untruth. It is the only moral evil, the rests are the faults of behaviour. (KP, 77)

Why Untruth ?

214. As a matter of fact man is essentially truthful by nature. Truth is more natural than untruth. We see this in children. Why then do we see so much dishonesty in society ? Obviously, the present social order is largely responsible for this. Its. accent is on money and cash nexus. We must change it radically and have a medium of exchange which will truthfully represent labour hours of men. ...Unless we are able to see the problem correctly, it is likely to become more insoluble by wrong remedies. (B, 20.8.1958, 140)

How to Attain Truth ?

215. I have composed a Sanskrit verse which says : "The essence of the Vedas, Vedanta and the Gita as extracted by Vinoba, is that Brahma is real, the world is a manifestation and life is the, discovery of truth." Gandhiji had talked of 'Experiments with Truth'. I prefer the phrase 'Discovery of Truth' to 'Experiments with Truth'. The word 'experiment' is a scientific term. Truth is discovered piecemeal. The whole truth is not attained at one time. Now the question arises how would one find truth. Gandhiji had said that truth could be attained by nonviolence. My idea is that truth can be attained by humility, objectivity and non-insistence. It is so in science. There is no dogmatism in it. Only that is considered as correct which is testified by experiment. (VC no. 7, 23-24)

Truth and Beauty

216. The principle that truth and beauty are not opposed to each other is correct. But we should not solely rely upon the test of beauty till we get accustomed to perceive non- duality between them. In a state of imperfection this criterion may prove deceptive. Hence, a seeker should not regard them as one and accept only truth as a criterion. This would do even if it is not beautiful. If he likes to accept non-duality between them, he must presume that what is truth must also be beautiful, even though it may not be so. He must not take this non-duality to mean that 'what is beautiful must be truth as well'. (KD, 188)

What Nonviolence is ?

217. What does nonviolence mean ? Love all beings to the same extent as you love your own self. (VP, 14.2.1959)

218. Nonviolence simply does not mean 'not to commit violence'. Its one meaning is to be fearless, the second is to cooperate lovingly, and the third is to have faith in constructive work. (KKO, 23)

219. Nonviolence is not merely an external activity. It is an inner faith. (S, June 1953, 721)

220. Nonviolence is the name for the maintenance of balance in thinking and not allowing the equanimity of mind to be disturbed. (ibid)

221. Nonviolence is that which keeps different persons together and which tries to seek non-difference in differences, while violence is that which creates divisions and increases differences. (SY, 110)

222. A life of nonviolence means not merely occasional sacrifice but perpetual sacrifice, not merely sacrifice but joy in sacrifice, (SS, 63-64)

223. In putting four lions at the top of his emblem, Ashoka has symbolically expressed the meaning of nonviolence. When bravery and love come together, there is nonviolence. (B, 13.3.1957, 5)

Essentials for Nonviolence

224. Non-attachment and universal love are necessary if we wish to practise nonviolence. It has to be continuous. It is a way of life. One has to be wide awake and distinguish between selfish interest and social good. We have to free our minds from all attachments and aversions (B, 13.6.1956, 5)

Complete Nonviolence

225. At present it is not possible to have a complete idea of nonviolence. What we can only think of at present is how far and by what methods we can progress towards nonviolence. Our idea of nonviolence has not yet proceeded beyond human society, though there is no reason why it should remain confined to it. Nor will it remain satisfied within this limit. It would only be satisfied when it has included the whole creation within its fold. (KD, 33)

Nonviolence and Truth

226. Truth without nonviolence would not be truth, and non- violence devoid of truth would not be nonviolence. Yet, for the sake of description and thinking they are sometimes treated temporarily as separate. Ultimately they are one and should be linked together. (AP, 14)

The Strength of Nonviolence

227. Balance in thinking, gentleness in words and restraint in actions, in these lies the strength of nonviolence. (S, Sep. 1954, 72)

The Working of Nonviolence

228. Nonviolence is an inner power. It works in several ways and much of it is invisible. It is this invisible working that does the whole thing. Such is the philosophy of nonviolence. In violence, it is the external activity which predominates greatly.

If nonviolence will counteract violence, it will do so in an imperceptible manner. Its main attack will be subtle. Its method will be of the change of heart. (VP no. 10 of 1963).

Nonviolence and Impatience

229. Impatience does not help in the growth of nonviolence. Lack of patience provides nourishment to violence. Hence, though I can draw up an extremist programme and know how to do so, I don't do it. (NA, 284)

Superiority of Nonviolence

230. Nonviolence is a straight line and quick acting. It leads to results which are undoubtedly substantial and lasting. The delay lies in the attainment of nonviolence, not in its results. (S, Sep. 1953, 105)

231. There is no dearth of weapons in the armoury of nonviolence. It can never fail. We may fail because of the lack of requisite nonviolence. (KKO, 47)

232. Nonviolence has such capacity that even if the whole world is drowning, a single individual can save himself by swimming. (KKO, 152)

The Power of Nonviolence

233. The power of nonviolence does not depend upon number but inner purity. Just as atom bomb has acquired impersonal power, similarly the impersonal factor will have to be developed in nonviolence. Only then will the power of nonviolence will be awakened. If man has acquired the power of annihilating the world sitting at home, he can also, develop the power of saving the world while sitting in his house. This power of nonviolence is an invisible power. It should be discovered, and this cannot happen unless he thinks deeply over it rising above our mind. (NA, 9-10)

234. Violence has the capacity to do immediate good. Only when nonviolence acquires that capacity, it will become a social force. (VP, 1.1.1959)

Two Warnings

235. If nonviolence is so defined that in it we have to proceed slowly and in such a manner that it does not change society greatly, I am of the view that such a definition would prove very dangerous to nonviolence and very favourable to violence. (KKO, 127)

236. There is a conception of nonviolence which is, I think, too negative. To cause least inconvenience or ill-will seems to be their criterion of nonviolence. This Fabian nonviolence is a dangerous doctrine. It is possible to go slow in matters which are not clearly concerned with violence or nonviolence. But if you are really serious about nonviolence, then there is no question of degrees and gradual progression. It should be immediate and whole-hearted. It has to move with speed. (SE, April 1955,312)

Nonviolence and Legislation

237. There is no conflict between nonviolence and legislation. A nonviolent movement prepares the minds of the people, and if a legislation is enacted in accordance with it, it comes within nonviolence. (KKO, 140)

238. Legislation does not necessarily belong to the category of violence. Only a law which has the moral sanction of the people is a nonviolent legislation.

Legislation, thus, can be nonviolent or violent. In the present condition of our country, I would advocate legal prohibition. I would also like to see that cow-slaughter is prohibited by law. But I would pay my attention solely to the educative side and would wish that the penal part is used as little as possible. (B, 17.4.1957, 1)

Nonviolence and Organisation

239. In his monumental work, *The Last Phase,* Shri Pyarelal has quoted Gandhiji's saying, 'Organisation is the test of nonviolence'. I have often raised my voice against organisation. Some think that the above phrase of Gandhiji denotes the importance of organisation. What Gandhiji wanted to say was that nonviolence can never build up an organisation in the manner of violence. The external aids available to violence cannot be used in a nonviolent order. But in spite of this, some technique must be evolved so that even in a nonviolent order when once a decision is taken, people will definitely carry it out. In a nonviolent organisation disciplinary actions will not be required, nor will it be necessary to enforce decisions by violent sanctions. Whatever is said or heard, is acted upon, not as a command, but as a reasoned advice. Execution of this advice should, therefore, be much more effective in a nonviolent organisation than in a violent one. While it is optional for the people to act upon the advice, in effect it will be much more imperative than a compulsory order.

(B, 28.10.1959,212)

240. A characteristic of nonviolence is that everyone has full freedom and yet everyone follows voluntarily all rules and regulations. In the military, compliance to rules is compulsory. There are three rules among the Catholics, viz., chastity, voluntary poverty and obedience. While the first two are acceptable to me, I would like obedience to be replaced by complete freedom. (SE, April-May 1972, 435-436)

Propagation of Nonviolence

241. The light of nonviolence cannot be spread by external and formal mechanisms of organizations. History shows that Jesus came alone and the light that he brought pervaded the world, not through church institutions or Christian governments, but in spite of them. That light inspires us even today. The same is true of Buddha. He was a prince but his message could not have been spread by the authority of the state. It spread because he threw his kingdom away like a blade of grass.

After all, what is it that will spread nonviolence? It is not the physical body that can do it, for it is an embodiment of violence. Nonviolence is assimilated to the extent one rises above one's body. It is the natural state of the soul. What nonviolence therefore needs is the quest of the spirit, the purification of mind, service of living creatures, love universal and fearlessness. This has become with me such an unshakeable conviction that I keep on telling in the words of St. Francis : "Do not get entangled in organizations."

(H, 8.1.1950, 380)

242. It is not enough to give sermons on nonviolence. Saints and philosophers have preached nonviolence for ages. That by itself can be of little use. We have a hundred and one problems before us. Unless we are able to solve them in a nonviolent way, the message of nonviolence will remain a cry in wilderness. (B, 26.9.1956, 5)

243. We shall have to work for nonviolence with the same faith, spirit of service and intelligence that have characterized the efforts to find solutions for the world problems through violence. Just as people devoted their lives to build up the instruments, the philosophy and an administration for violence, we have now to devote our lives to achieve the same for nonviolence. (BG, VI, 12-13)

Discipline in Nonviolence

244. Nonviolence needs discipline and planning much more than violence. (KKO, 162)

245. Nonviolence does not mean lenient tolerance; nor does it mean intolerable vigorous restraint. (RR, 111)

Nonviolence and Violence

246. Violence is not powerful enough to tolerate a nonviolent man, but nonviolence should have the strength of putting up with a violent man. (BG, VI, 65)

Nonviolence in Violence

247. The Gita has placed before us the idea that just as a man fasting out of anger can be violent, similarly a person who is physically violent can be nonviolent if he uses violence on special occasions thinking it to be absolutely essential because of the compulsions of circumstances, provided it is done with a calm and unruffled mind. This greatly deserves consideration. (S, June 1953, 722)

Nonviolence and Decentralization

248. Violence is inevitable in centralization. The political, social and economic organisations of Europe have provided ample proof of it. They have been unable to end war. India can become truly free only if it could avoid such centralization and thereby show to the world an example of true independence. (H, 12.9.1948, 239)

Nonviolence and External Aggression

249. Science has two aspects, the pure and the applied. Nonviolence also has two aspects, the theoretical and the practical.

I hold that only pure nonviolence is conducive to happiness, but when it is a matter of practising it several questions arise. Some say on the basis of the Bible that it need not be looked into as to what party has been in the wrong, who committed the aggression, what was the former situation, history, etc. All that one has to do is to ask one's own and other countries to stop violence. Despite all my sympathy for them, it has not been possible for me to adopt that position. Moreover, the question also arises whether nonviolence is an attitude of mind or an external technique, and the reply is that it is not only a technique but an attitude as well. And since the attitude is the main element, I am not yet clear that in case an occasion arises for external resistance and from the viewpoint of society it appears unavoidable, even then it should be avoided. (BY, 8.10.1965)

Nonviolence and Military Academies

250. Pandit (Jawaharlal) Nehru after laying the foundation stone of the National Defence Academy near Poona on his way to the USA delivered a speech. ...He said that the oddness of life was such that they were talking about nonviolence and at the same time starting military academies.

Such contradictions as Pandit Nehru referred to are found in mankind as a whole. Man is made up of spirit and body, both of which appear to be mutually contradictory. Since our life depends upon both we have to satisfy both and that is how it looks odd. This applies equally to our country, which also possesses a soul as well as a body. When the body adjusts itself to the spirit, then the conflict is the least. The spirit of India is nonviolence. The first expression to this spirit was given by the seers of old and the latest expression is by Mahatma Gandhi. We have to reach that stage of the spirit, but before that this restrained militarism becomes indispensable in many circumstances. We have, of course, to break this militarism and rise above it. Till our country acquires that strength, military training and our professions of non-violence, though patently contradictory, will stay. We need not be ashamed of it. (H, 23.10.1949, 285)

Nonviolence in Present-Day India

251. It is true that we obtained freedom by means of non-violence. But we must confess that it was not the magic of nonviolence alone (which did the work). Had it been so, we would not have been given to that inertia that we find rampant today. Nor would we have committed the black deeds that we did after freedom. World events, therefore, played a large part in our independence. That is why our people have not that glowing faith in the power of nonviolence which they ought to have. We do not feel we have given a new method or technique to the world. We have not realized the might of moral strength. (H, 18.9.1954, 234)

Nonviolence Suits India

252. Looking at the history and conditions of India one feels that we can never build her strength on violence. And unless nonviolence was firmly established here, even India's Swaraj or freedom will not be able to maintain itself. Billions of rupees will have to be spent for building up the strength of violence in India. She can never afford that expenditure. And even if India was able to do so, the consequence would be a great danger for the world. (H, 30.7.1955, 171)

How to Develop Nonviolent Strength in India ?

253. If we all agree that we have to develop this nonviolent strength, all the political parties in the country must give serious attention to this question. They must first agree that every trace of violence must be eliminated from our social life. Social life must become fully nonviolent. All the parties must sit together and devise ways and means of so ordering our public life that the army will not be needed for maintaining law and order in the country...... The more a nation depends on its police and army, the more does its government becomes totalitarian. A government which arms itself because of the fear of another country, begins to be afraid of its own people. (B, 25.4.1956, 4)

Nonviolence and Pacifism

254. Nonviolence is a positive force differing from pacifism which is a mere negation of the use of arms. (H, 2.1.1954, 350)

255. Nonviolence is not merely non-participation in destructive activities; its main manifestation is in the identification of constructive activities with the service of humanity.

The goddess of Ahimsa has very powerful weapons at her command. They are the weapons of love, and are, therefore, creative and not destructive. Yet they do destroy—they destroy hatred, iniquity, hunger and disease.

(Message to 1949 Pacifist Meet at Sevagram)

Real Love

256. What is there in declaring, "I will love you if you love me ?" Even the animals act like that. Real love goes out to love those who are full of hatred. (B, 9.7.1958, 96)

257. What passes for love these days is not love but lust. With the shackles of this lust we create around an 'appearance' of love. But it is an appearance only. As long as mutual love is not disinterested, the appearance of love is an obstacle, not an aid. (VP, 3.1.1959)

Unilateral Love

258. We must have the strength to possess this unilateral love and we must learn not to regulate our relations with others by looking to what they do or do not do. Our capacity to love should not be influenced by the conduct of others. If we dance to the tune of others, where is then our individuality ? Therefore, we should continue to love others and if we find there is want of love in them and their hearts are full of hatred, we must exhibit greater and greater love. If we do this, we may succeed. Even if we do not attain success in the worldly sense, we shall have a satisfaction which we can never lose.

(H, 17.1.1949, 160)

Love and Faith

259. Love is like electric power and faith is its switch. Put this switch on and thereafter the immense power is at you command. Love is there all throughout the world. What we lack in is faith. And this lack of faith is the reason behind the apparent inaction of the power of love. (B, 8.7.1961, 89)

The Power of Love

260. The power of the sword, money or intellect is only with a few, but that of love is with all. For everybody attends the God-designed school of love. There is universal education of love. (H, 20.11.1954, 305)

261. The power of love will be manifested when we attack even an enemy with love.

The power of hatred has already been organized very widely. The power of love too shall have to be made equally pervading. If we don't do that, society will be annihilated. (PP, 17.5.1957)

Compassion, God's Greatest Gift

262. The highest boon of God to man is the compassion in him. It is the inner light. (VP, 6.1.1957)

The Meaning of Compassion

263. Compassion does not signify merely love for others, but also implies an urge to do something for others. (VP, 27.1.1959)

Three Characteristics of Compassion

264. (a) It does not wait for anyone. It itself rushes (to help). (b) It knows no distinctions. (c) It keeps initiative with itself. (VP, 24.8.1957)

The Demerits of Violence

265. Violence admits of no limit being imposed on it. One cannot guide it along a predetermined course. One may fix a limit beyond which one would not go and may try to observe them, but occasions arise which call for an unhindered use of violence in the interest of victory and the limits are swept off. This is the lesson of the *Mahabharat* which, as I said, contains the quintessence of history. It is that that there can be no limits to violence once it is resorted to; that it brings destruction to all, and the safest course, therefore, is to abjure it altogether. (H, 24.4.1954, 67)

266. Of the various defects of violence, the basic one is that it does not have the wisdom to impose limits on itself. (BYB, 9.4.1954)

267. When we go to solve a problem by violence, several others are created. (Triveni, 10)

268. A violent means leaves the problem unsolved, though it may appear to provide a temporary solution.

(KW, April 1952, 219)

269. A chain of violent thought cannot be broken by violence. It can only be broken by nonviolence. (Shraddhanjali, 15)

270. A lion is not a maneater. But once it kills and eats a man, it becomes a maneater. In the same way, one, who attains freedom through sword, becomes later on an aggressor.

(VP, 29.9.1959)

271. A young Communist was discussing the subject with me..... I asked him, "Can violence be regarded as the weapon of the masses ?" He said, "Not as a general rule. But under particular circumstances and with adequate efforts, the masses can be prepared for using the weapon of violence."

I observed : "Granting that violence can be generated among the people for a particular purpose, how can it help them ? Surely you do not suppose that a revolution once brought about will continue to give its results for all times to come, like an endowed fund. The artificial cultivation for a short period of a quality which is not natural to the masses is like a borrowed capital. Ultimately, it will transfer the power to those few who possess that quality—the capital—as a natural aptitude. And, if you feel, that it might be possible to bring about a permanent change in the nature of a people as a whole, I say, even if it were possible, it would be a great calamity. For, in that case, it means that man is to be made a ferocious animal. Its results would be more dangerous than you imagine."

To this my young friend replied : "Let the results be what they will. Let us first change the present condition. One step is enough."

"You might get a momentary illusion of having changed the present condition. But the reaction will be worse than the present evil." (KGM, 30-31)

272. The power of violence is not natural to the people. It is not even necessary that it shall only be at the disposal of a wise man. It can be in the hands of wicked persons as well as good ones. (VP, 12. 12. 1959)

Minor Violence

273. Faith in minor violence is still there. Minor violence is more dangerous than major violence. When major violence manifests itself in the form of war, it also purifies society. Minor violence only does harm. It increases hatred and solves no problem. It checks the progress of society.

(VP no. 236 of 1957)

Purity of Means

274. We have always been taught that evil should be conquered by good, that it is only light which can prevail over darkness and that water alone can extinguish fire. (VP no. 3 of 1957)

275. Many a saint have preached the path of righteousness. Man is not, however, yet fully convinced that good alone begets good. He is still experimenting to see if good can come out of evil as well. He does not doubt that Babul tree cannot produce a mango fruit and vice versa. May be, in ancient days even this might not have been so clear to him. But the present age is convinced that so far as the material world is concerned, the law of relation between the seed and the fruit holds good. In the moral sphere, however, he has not yet shed his doubts. He, of course, realizes that goodness generally pays, but he lacks the conviction that unadulterated goodness has the power to do good.

He who works for the ideal must be more careful about the means than about the ends. Correct pursuit of means is the achievement of the end. The distinction between means and ends is therefore imaginary. Means not only lead to the end but also shape it. (H, 27.2.1949, 442-443)

276. Nowadays the purity of means signifies that neither the means employed should lead to any kind of mental perturbation in us nor should it be so with the opponent. Only those changes, psychological or societal, be brought about in society which do not lead to any perturbation. That is, they should be done after mutual deliberations. While this age of science welcomes difference of opinion, it forbids any ill-will or hatred. The problems will always be there. We cannot imagine of any time when they would not be there. But the means adopted for their solution must be pure. Formerly, purity of means only implied that none should be abused or assaulted, but its scope has become wider today due to science. It now includes 'methods which do not create any perturbation or agitation', (VP, 24.1.1959)

The Meaning of Brahmacharya

277. 'Brahmacharya' means that a man directs the path of his life to the search for Brahma. Brahmacharya is a positive, not a negative concept. It does not merely mean that we have to avoid any particular thing, but that there is something tangible, positive, to be done. Brahmacharya means the greatest aim of all is achieving the realization of the Lord. Nothing less than this has been said. It has such a vast and comprehensive aim. (WP, 71-72)

278. Two things are important in Brahmacharya. 1. The aim should be high and it should develop into devotion to Brahma. 2. There should be control of all the senses and the mind. In Brahmacharya it is important to lead the senses and the mind into the right direction. If we think in terms of suppressing them, our evolution will be hindered. That is a negative method. Therefore, all the senses should be rightly used. They should be correctly restrained; this will be very helpful to aspirants. (ibid, 73-74)

Brahmacharya, An Endeavour for Completeness

279. The spiritual endeavour of Brahmacharya is an endeavour for completeness. Usually women are soft and gentle, less acrid and adventurous. Men have more of acridity. Hence, a man engaged in the spiritual endeavour of Brahmacharya will need to develop the highest compassion. Jesus Christ is an example of one who combined compassion with celibacy. A woman engaged in this endeavour has already a great deal of compassion in her, and hence she will have to develop in her intense asceticism and acridity. Then only she can acquire completeness. But I have also seen men who are mild and women who are hard and cruel. Hence, there is no rule that men are always hard-hearted and women, tenderhearted. Yet, it is usually so, and the above observation has been made with this in view. (MA, 26)

Brahmacharya, A Social Need

280. Today, in the age of science, world population is increasing rapidly and the available land is decreasing. Therefore people are saying that we should have small families. This means that Brahmacharya now has a new social context. ... Previously it had a personal value. That value lay in controlling the body to give priority to the growth of the spirit. This is a permanent value belonging to all the three ages—past, present and future. But a new social dimension has arisen in that now the public does not need many offsprings. (WP, 5-6)

Brahmacharya, Truth and Nonviolence

281. As long as the vow of Brahmacharya is not observed, the observance of the vows of truth and nonviolence is well-nigh impossible. (AD, 42)

Aids to Brahmacharya

282. The reading of sacred books, and the company of saintly men, is certainly a great help towards a life of Brahmacharya. But to live a natural life in the open air, and to work bare bodied in the sunlight, is an even greater help. (TE, 40)

283. On the basis of experience I have come to the conclusion that if someone wants to observe Brahmacharya to live in a pious manner throughout his whole life, the negative way of Brahmacharya would not be helpful to him.... It is easier to observe Brahmacharya if its concept is a comprehensive one. (VV, I, 103)

Attitude towards Women in Brahmacharya

284. It is a wrong idea that a *brahmachari* should avoid coming in contact with women. It leads to the imposition of unnecessary artificial restrictions. (SH, 64)

285. If a *brahmachari* feels that he should not look at any woman who may have come before him, we should regard that as his shortcoming. (WP, 80)

Brahmacharya and Intellectual Power

286. The power of the intellect is like a flame, but it is Brahmacharya which is the oil inside helping it to burn. Brahmacharya imparts greater acuteness to intelligence. Hence they, who have to work in the intellectual field and to do high thinking, should not use their procreative power for the ordinary purpose of producing children. (SH, 71)

Family Planning : Opposition to Contraceptives

287. Not only I do not find any good of the country in family planning, I also hold that it is a defeat for spiritual and moral values. (TKS, 70)

288. These days attempts are being made that while the means and the urge for indulgence may well continue, there should be external methods of controlling the population. These methods, are greatly in vogue, specially in the cities. Some of them are even entering villages. It is doing something of great consequence, without realizing its moral, spiritual and social implications. (NA, 240)

289. I have coined a maxim: "The earth is burdened by sin, not by virtue." Progeny can increase or decrease both due to sin or virtue. If it increases by the observance of virtue, it would not burden the earth. If it decreases because of it, there would be no harm. But if it increases because of the commitment of sin, it would certainly be a burden on the earth, and if it declines due to it, it would also be harmful. This is my personal view. (TKS, 33-34)

290. It is a matter of regret that we are given to superficial thinking. None ponders going deep into life and it is also not taken into account that there are certain basic things pertaining to life, which if not preserved, we shall be nowhere. It is an accepted fact that the Mother Earth can provide for all who are born on it. (KSP, 33)

291. It has been a world experience that when people do hard labour, their sexual desire and passion diminish. If all get opportunity for hard labour, there would naturally be control over sexual desire and passion. Moreover, the more enterprising we shall be in India, the more food we shall produce. When people are under-nourished, their sexual desire is increased. It has been observed in the animals. Stronger animals are less prone to passion than the weaker ones, and the offsprings of these weaker ones are impotent and good for nothing. Hence, I say that this subject is both sociological and spiritual. It should not be trifled with. Let such a climate be built up which is congenial to self-restraint. Let hard work and enterprise be encouraged, let there be a reform of literature and let obscene literature and cine posters be prohibited.

(S H, 89)

Control of the Palate

292. The observance of Brahmacharya is found difficult because we are not able to control our palate. An important measure of success in that spiritual endeavour is the degree of victory over palate. That is why control of the palate is reckoned as a vow and therefore an aspirant should take care that his diet becomes purer... .Food is only a means to maintain the physical body. It should not be accorded greater importance.

(AD, 44)

293. If we are slave to the palate, we consume more than we need. ...This makes society suffer. One fond of tasty food is a slave and he undermines his strength. It we overeat, our sexual passion is excited. Consequently, we do harm to society. (ibid, 57)

294. For true service, purity in food is necessary. As is the food so is the mind. The food we eat should be regulated. Not what food we take, but how much we take, is the more important question. It does matter what food we choose to eat, but it matters even more that it is in right measure. (Gita, 253)

The Meaning of Non-Stealing

295. It is theft to use foodgrains, cloth and other things without directly participating in their production. ...Non-stealing does not merely mean taking a thing not given by others, but also accepting something without giving anything to others. Consumption without sacrifice is theft. (AD, 43)

Various Forms of Stealing

296. Take *asteya* or non-stealing. This we have tried to practise up to a point. A thief is put into jail. But there are other forms of stealing which do not find mention in law. We do not take any notice of these. What are fat salaries, rich dividends, exorbitant interests and the commissions of middlemen, if not a form of stealing ? We must eradicate all these different forms of stealing and put a limit on the amassing and possession of wealth. (H, 3. 7. 1954,143)

The Meaning of Non-Possession or Non-Accumulation

297. 'Non-Possession' stands for 'liberality', though people understand it differently. They hold that non-possession stands for poverty. But it is not so. In fact it means that no sooner there is accumulation, it is to be passed on to another. Where wealth flows, it is non-possession. (BG, IV, 13)

298. The true meaning of *aparigraha,* the vow of non-accumulation, is to discard the sense of identity with one's body. For, the body itself is the main thing among one's accumulation. (RR, 94-95)

Why Non-Possession ?

299. There is no accumulation in the creation for tomorrow. Man should follow suit. If I preserve today what would be needed in the next twenty-five days, it will mean an accumulation made by committing theft affecting twenty-five persons, and I shall be committing the sin of keeping them more or less hungry. At the same time, since the creation does not accumulate much, I shall have to resort to dubious methods. To accumulate that much will also put a strain on me and thereby lower my vitality. Moreover, I shall be worried about the safety of that accumulation, and it will make me secretive. Thus, accumulation leads to the violation of the five vows of truth, nonviolence, non-stealing, Brahmacharya and non-possession. Hence, there should be minimum accumulation with the purpose of maintaining the physical body, and no accumulation at all of things not required for it. There should be constant efforts to make living increasingly simple by continuously bestowing thought on the question as to how requirements can be lessened in life. (AD, 43.44)

Five Features of a Non-Possessive Society

300. A non-possessive society has following five features, namely an abundance of wealth, equal distribution* of it among the members of society, no accumulation of such injurious articles as liquor and cigarettes, accumulation of foodgrains, cloth, housing, agricultural implements, means of knowledge and recreation etc. in the above order of priority, with minimum accumulation of money. (KKO, 67).

Non-Stealing and Non-Possession, Their Relationship

301. The Vow of Non-thieving regulates the mode of acquiring wealth, while the Vow of Non-accumulation regulates the quantity. In consequence, both are one and the same. (RR, 119)

302. Misers create thieves. ... If there is no possessiveness, there will be no thieving. (B, 11.7.1956, 2)

303. What one has to realize is that one cannot profess a virtue without being vigilant about such other virtues as are complementary and concomitant to it; otherwise it can only result either in confusion or self-deception. For example, in the Shastras non-possession is considered as a necessary concomitant of non-stealing. If theft is regarded as a crime, accumulation of property and inequality also must be regarded as sinful, whereas at present one is punished and the other is praised. (B, 10.10.1956, 4-5)

304. Non-stealing and non-possession supplement each other in making economic dealings moral, without which *dharma* (morality) cannot be established in individual and social life. Truth and non-violence are basic, but in the economic field

---

* By "equal distribution", Vinoba means "equitable distribution," (See 463 above)

they can only find expression in non-stealing and non-possession. Economic matters play a very big role in life and the science of morality cannot be indifferent to it. On the contrary, it is the responsibility of ethics to regulate and control it. (Triveni, 46)

How to Measure Non-Possession ?

305. There is no external measurement for non-possession. I hold that one may even be observing it though living in great splendour. Hence, there can be no external measurement. Let everyone find answer by asking oneself.
(VP, 19.12.1959)

How to Practise Non-Possession ?

306. Gandhiji held that not only in the present condition of society, but in every condition whatsoever, the only practical way of practising non-possession is to use one's (tangible and intangible) powers as a trustee. (KGM, 24)

307. When a man deals in the world, he comes to acquire possessions, however less they are. Hence the way to be free of that sin is to surrender a part of it to society.
(BY, 9.12.1955)

Non-Possession and Political Power

308. When non-possession comes to be recognized as the basic principle of social order, there will be minimum need of power to coerce for the government to rule. People living in a village will look to their administration and the government at the top will be there more or less in name. It will be a government which will guide by advice and not govern. Persons constituting such a government will be men and women of good character and of clean behaviour. Therefore, the power they will exercise will be moral and not physical. This is the sort of Sarvodaya social order which we seek to establish. (H, 16.7.1955, 154)

Non-Possession, A Force for Social Good

309. We have long known that non-possession brings about individual purification. We have now to realize that it can also serve as a powerful means of social well-being. We have to prove that it is not only spiritually efficacious, but it can also help us in constructing a richer and better worldly life.

(H, 10.10.1953, 256)

Non-Possession and Ownership

310. Instead of saying non-possession, say possession by all. I may possess this watch but I may not exclusively claim its ownership. If I need it, I shall keep it with me. When I am not using it, it should be available for others' use. Anybody should be free to ask for it and I should be free to give it. There should be no exclusive ownership. (B, 16.1.1957, 6)

The Word 'Trusteeship'

311. 'Trusteeship'is a very odd word, a word which could be used by Churchill, Truman, Tojo, Hitler and others. This unlucky word has become so worthless that it is almost impossible to give it a new meaning. Even then Gandhiji did so.

(Khadi Jagat, Aug. 1946, 497)

312. The word and its abuse seem to have been born together. But it has a good connotation in law, and Gandhiji having been a student of law, the word seems to have clung to him. Also being a votary of truth, he associated with it only the higher side of its meaning and use. As I have not been a student of law, despite the use of this word by Gandhiji, it has failed to stick to or attract me. However, it does not come in the way of my understanding and appreciating the idea which Gandhiji sought to express through it...

Even if inequality of wealth is abolished as being the result of an unjust social order, the inequality of the intellectual and physical powers cannot be wholly done away with. Let us assume that with education and regulation even these inequalities will be greatly reduced. Still, even, in an ideal state we cannot conceive of their total abolition. The conclusion is that whatever talents, physical strength, wealth, or other capacities a person might possess, he should take them as having been given to him as a trustee, for the benefit of the world. This is the noble idea of trusteeship. But selfish people have so debased the word that it seems nearly impossible to restore it to its pristine purity. I have, therefore, substituted for it another word, *Vishwastavritti,* i.e. the attitude of confidence, a word which is free of any undesirable associations. (KGM, 24 and 25)

The Need of Trusteeship

313. If we want to build up a nonviolent society, we have to keep non-possession in mind, i. e. those who have property should become its trustees in a real sense. Only then will non-violence be realized. Otherwise, there will be increasing unrest. (SY, 100)

314. Acceptance of the trusteeship ideal will transform our entire thinking in regard to wealth and the relationship between the individual and society. (H, 7.11.1.53, 285)

Implications of Trusteeship

315. The first implication of trusteeship is that just as a father maintains and protects his son better than himself, a trustee should care more for his employees than for himself. The second is that just as a father wishes his son to become as capable as he himself is as early as possible and to stand on his own legs, in the same way a trustee should be anxious that the labour acquires ability at the earliest and becomes self-dependent. (KKR, 112)

316. Trusteeship implies complete renunciation of ownership. (BY, 9.12.1955)

317. The whole property should be looked upon as public and there should be rules and regulations regarding its management. If a trustee does not look after it in accordance with them, the people should have the right to remove him from trusteeship. If he who presently controls a property does not use it for public purposes, he should be deprived of that control. This is my interpretation of trusteeship. However,this expropriation has nothing to do with violence. (Khadi Jagat, Aug. 1946, 497)

Legacy Is Undesirable

318. I regard such a father to be an enemy of his son who maintains an estate for him. The boy should be educated, he should be taught how to keep himself physically fit, he should be trained in some craft, but no estate should be left for him. ....Only then, he will turn out to be intelligent and enterprising

(VP, 17.1.1957)

The Vow of Physical or Bread Labour

319. We should start doing physical labour as a worship. It should be a daily rule with us not to take food without doing some physical labour. (PP, 19.6.1957).

320. I shall not give food to anyone, be he even a professor or a judge, unless he has done physical work for two to four hours. Nonviolence cannot be attained without physical labour. In doing it lies the humaneness of man. We cannot serve others by riding on their shoulders.

(Khadi Jagat, July 1946, 495-496)

321. Today bodily labour commands no prestige in society.The peasant works hard but he likes to see his son on some job in an office. In other words, the field labourer too has no respect for his bodily labour. It is, therefore, very imperative for us that bodily labour should be daily performed as worship. It will result in the production of wealth, wiping out differences and forging unity. (H, 19.2.1955, 412)

Bread Labour and Other Vows

322. Bread labour alone is a mode prescribed by nature for man to earn his living. ...An observance of this vow makes the observance of others easy. If one gets bored by physical labour, it is a sign of degeneration. (AD, 46)

323. Our main shortcoming is that we have not been able to fully identify ourselves with the poor around us. As far as I can see, this is not possible so long as we do not give up our dependence on money and do not rely completely on body labour. We do perform a certain amount of body labour, but it is not enough. We should take a pledge to earn our bread through body labour alone, and free ourselves from dependence on money. Without it, nonviolence can never manifest itself as a great force. I believe to the very letter of what Jesus Christ said, "It is easier for a camel to pass through the eye of a needle than for the rich to enter heaven (i.e. to realize nonviolence)." (H, 8.1.1950, 388)

The Real Purpose of Physical Labour

324. Ordinarily we should do some productive physical labour as a matter of vow. But I have observed that it becomes something mechanical. We do have to produce, but I ask if the composition of the Ramayan by Valmiki will be reckoned as physical labour. It was composed some two thousand years back, and yet it inspires people today. He even made monkeys perform physical labour. This shows that he had become one with the creation. The source of his compassion was the creation itself. The very purpose of physical labour is to be one with the creation. (VP no. 3 of 1957)

325. What Sri Aurobindo wrote is so comprehensive that none could have written it without becoming one with the universe. It is physical labour. Metaphysically physical labour signifies full contact with nature and the capacity to be one with it, and an attempt to identify oneself with the life of the people and to feel for them. (VP no. 4 of 1957)

All to do both Physical and Mental Work

326. It (the Varna system) does not mean, however, that some should be absolutely exempt from physical labour. It only means that everyone should contribute his share to the society in accordance with his capacities. But even while so engaged in one's own way in some useful work, one cannot ignore those responsibilities which are common to all. Professors, students, judges and others have all their own places in society, but just as air, water and food are quite essential for one and all, so too both mental and physical work are essential for everyone. It is wrong to say that some may do only physical work while others do only mental work.... It is a different matter if someone does more of one type of labour than another. But everyone must perform some physical labour. If we forget this principle, society falls into pieces and the distinction of high and low also comes into existence.

(H, 31.7.1949, 176)

327. God has created us with brains, hands and also hunger. If He had desired that only a few persons should produce things and others should do only intellectual work, He would have given only brains to some and only hands to others, for He is omnipotent. But He has not done so. He has given hunger to all and so also hands. It is, therefore, against His will that some persons do only intellectual work like reading,writing etc. and the rest merely do the physical labour of production. (H, 16.2.1952, 431)

The Need of Fearlessness

328. Within us there are good qualities on one side and bad ones on the other. And both armies are well arranged. An army needs a commander. The good qualities have their own commander named *abhaya,* fearlessness.... Without truth, good qualities have no value; but then, for truth, fearlessness is essential. In an atmosphere charged with fear, good qualities cannot grow; in fact they themselves become bad qualities, and good efforts and tendencies get weakened. (Gita, 233)

329. In the twin qualities of *ahimsa* and *satya,* nonviolence and truth, all good qualities are included; they are the essence of them all. But the case of fearlessness and humility is different. Fearlessness makes advance possible and humility ensures safety. (ibid, 233-234)

330. Fear and morality are mutually contradictory. A disposition to fearlessness is the basis of divine virtues. (AD, 44)

Fearlessness, its Varieties

331. Fearlessness is of three kinds—fearlessness based on knowledge, fearlessness based on God and fearlessness based on discernment. Fearlessness based on knowledge is that fearlessness which results from the knowledge of dangers and their remedies.

The second one, i.e. fearlessness based on God, makes one fully fearless. But it cannot be acquired without prolonged efforts, devotion and continued practice. But once it is acquired, it would need no external aid.

Then there is the third kind of fearlessness based on discernment. It restrains one from needless and reckless daring, and if one has no option but to face a danger, it makes him do so keeping his mind calm out of discernment.

(VV, I, 183)

What Does Fearlessness Require ?

332. Fearlessness represents a state of mind which can be brought about only by a change in the way of man's thinking.

(SE, June 1958, 378)

333. Fearlessness can only be derived from the inner self.

(VP, 19.12.1959)

334. If one has the inner strength to die rather than to live with indignity, even a child can face any danger fearlessly.

(KD, 67)

When is Fear Desirable ?

335. If one leads a virtuous life in constant fear of temptations, death would lose its dreadfulness. (RR, 70)

336. Even fear is good. If we do not do any evil out of fear,it is good. (Triveni, 58)

The Vow of Swadeshi

337. Swadeshi is an inherent duty of man. Swadeshi means self-reliance in a comprehensive sense, i.e., Swadharma, one's own duty.

Just as nonviolence is an established rule of Dharma, similarly Swadeshi is a rule of conduct. Things nearer to us, be it the neighbours, prevailing customs or morality, are inherited by us, and therefore are dear to us. In this lies the secret of Swadeshi or Swadharma. (AD, 45)

338. Bapu (Gandhiji) had taught us that just as truth is one moral duty and nonviolence is another, similarly it is also our moral duty to go in for goods produced by our neighbours. If discarding them, we go in for those produced in far-off places, then our approach is not of compassion but of profit. If it be that of compassion, we shall consider it our duty to remove the distress of those who are our neighbours. It does not imply any hatred for those who live far-off. (BG, V, 277)

Some Misconceptions about Swadeshi

339. If we boycott articles giving an extreme interpretation to the moral duty of Swadeshi, we shall prove ourselves to be men of a long past world. We shall be antiquated. It is all right to produce our food and cloth, but if we try to produce everything, it will be reverting to a past world. However, if we so wish, we may try to go back, but it would not be possible. (NA, 52)

340. It is not that Swadeshi forbids dealings with outsiders. There is good scope in it for reciprocal dealings. But it is wrong to burden others with work we can well do ourselves. (BG, V, 280)

Swadeshi, No Narrow Attitude

341. Some have even begun to ask, "Is not the ideal of Swadeshi a narrow and exclusive attitude of mind ? We must think on international level. We must consider the entire world as ours." I am surprised to find these people coming to teach us Vedanta. When we observe the Swadeshi Dharma, how do other nations suffer thereby ? How does it affect the international friendship ?

In short the plan should be one which will make each village a self-sufficient unit with regard to food, cloth, education, etc. This will not in any way militate against the interests of any nation in the world. (SE, May 1956, 371)

Equality of All Religions

342. I am of the view that there are four essential ingredients of Sarva-Dharma-Samabhava, the feeling of equality for all religions. One of them is faith in one's own religion; the second is respect for all religions; the third is the reformation of one's religion; and the fourth one, which naturally follows from the three, is opposition to irreligiousness. When all these four ingredients are found together, there is Sarva-Dharma-Samabhava. (HS, 18.7. 1948)

343. The idea of having equal feelings for all religions also implies the acknowledgement that one's own religion is imperfect. It is what follows the worship of truth and is the touchstone of nonviolence.

If we are imperfect, the religions conceived by us are also imperfect. (AD, 47)

344. All religions are partial embodiments of truth. (RR, 15)

Why Religious Toleration ?

345. The various religions should be understood as different forms of worship. God has innumerable attributes. Hence His worship too can take innumerable forms. But that should not lead to any feeling of hatred in us. (SV, 103)

Hindu Temples and the Non-Hindus

346. Friends, please understand why I am anxious that non-Hindus be allowed to visit Hindu shrines. If you don't allow them, you lower the Hindu religion. I have been allowed to enter mosques and churches. I have been allowed to speak in them... Religion must be broad and all-comprehensive. It must reconcile the various viewpoints. I am a believer in philosophic reconciliation. ...Tukaram has said that he had four companions in life—Jnanadeva, Namadeva, Ekanath and Kabir. Is it wrong, then, for me to wish that the gates of the temple should be opened to the Harijans, Muslims, Buddhists, Christians and men of all faiths? Opening the gates of temples to all means opening the doors of one's own heart. (B, 4.6.1958, 53)

Need to Follow One's Religion Better

347. I would say that every Hindu should try to be a better Hindu, a Muslim a better Muslim and a Christian a better Christian, and thus give rise to a grand symphony of religions in India. Let each follow his particular way of worshipping the Lord. God has infinite names and attributes. There are several approaches to a city. Why should not then there be countless ways of approaching the Lord. This will enable us not only to be better Hindus, better Muslims and better Christians but also better men, and thus create a very rich social and national life in India, based on love and goodwill.

(H, 29.8.1953, 202)

The Feeling of Touchability

348. I have coined the word *sparsha-bhavana* (the feeling of touchability), which is different from the word used by Gandhiji, which was *asprishyata-nivaran (*eradication of untouchability). The word *sparsha-bhavana* is comprehensive.The feeling should be that we should have touch with the whole world. (AD, 56)

How to Eradicate Untouchability ?

349. The task of eradicating untouchability has got to be done by us in two ways : (1) By improving the economic condition and mentality of the Harijans, and (2) by purifying the Hindu religion, i. e., by restoring it to its pristine form. (KD, 139)

Great Men and Scavenger's Work

350. There were times when Swami Ramakrishna Paramhansa used to wake up early in the morning and clean the latrines in the residential area. On being questioned, he used to reply that he did it to weaken his ego and to acquire humility. In other words, he looked upon scavenging as a Sadhana, a spiritual endeavour. Gandhiji too did it. Several great men have been doing it and that is why Hinduism has retained its glory. (SY, 226)

Eradicate Scavenger's Work

351. To earn money, man has taken to tanning and shoemaking but not to scavenging. This only shows that it is not regarded as man's job. It should, therefore, disappear. And 1 want that the Bhangis of India should get land for cultivation and lead a prosperous life. The only possible reform in this profession is to eradicate it altogether. (H, 22.1.1955, 378)

Not to Speak Ill of Others

352. These days I am talking of the vow of *aninda,* not to speak ill of others. In a way, it is included in the observance of nonviolence, but the need of according it an independent place is being felt. (VP no. 422, of 1957)

353. We should only talk of the good qualities of a man in his absence. If we have to point out his shortcomings, it should be done to him in private or in the presence of friends before whom it would not be improper to do so.

If we hear something praiseworthy about someone, we should be inclined to agree with it immediately. If we hear something evil, our heart and mind should not be prone to accept it.

We should not look upon anybody with suspicion. It acts as a great obstacle in the way of devotion and service.

(KP, 69-71)

354. The evil that one finds in oneself is not really his. It is something linked up with the physical body. Then why talk of that which does not pertain to us ? Similarly, the evils in others are not theirs, they are of their physical bodies. Then why should we look to their defects ? We should only speak of the good present in them, and this also applies to one's own self.

(AD, 52)

Humility, Its Importance

355. In Sanskrit, the word used for education is *vinaya,* a word also used for humility. The reason is that humility is the gateway to all other virtues. It leads to them. A man who is modest, humble and gentle will immediately grasp and hold fast to a virtue,wisdom and any other good thing, wherever it may be found.This capacity to get hold of virtues is the chief distinguishing quality of humility. (SY, 73)

356. There can be no search for truth without humility. That is why all scientists are humble. There can be no purification of mind and heart without humility, and that is why all spiritual persons are humble. (REC, 11)

357. Fearlessness is the commander of all good qualities; but the army has to be watched front and rear, and on both sides.The direct attack will of course be in front, but one may also be stealthily set upon from behind. While, in front, Fearlessness stands alert, Humility guards the rear. (Gita, 233)

Real Humility

358. Humility is no doubt an essential virtue. But a humility mixed with fear is no real humility. (B, 15.5.1957, 5)

IV

IDEAS ON HISTORY AND REVOLUTION

The Meaning of Progress

359. Progress has come to mean power over others. But this is all wrong. Progress really means rising above the self. Progress is progress in charity. (B, 11.7.1956, 6)

The Cultural Evolution of Man

360. Mankind has been continually moving forward ever since it came into existence. It has been taking up and developing one quality after another in accordance with the call of the age. The spirit has innumerable qualities, as innumerable as the stars in the sky or the grains of sand on the earth. Every age draws forth, as it were, one of these according to its needs and tries to put in into practice with all the ardour it can command.

For example, there was a time when people realized the importance of cleanliness. They then raised it to the position of a supreme virtue and tried to implement it in their lives. At another time their attention was drawn to the need for control of the carnal passion. There were, so we are told, eight different forms of marriage prevailing in those days, and it was a question which of them to choose and adopt. Finally, they chose one of them and vested it with great sanctity, so that it became the generally accepted form of marriage and has remained so since then. This was a great step forward in the direction of the control of the carnal passion.

Thus human society, in the course of its onward march, took up many diverse qualities for its practice and evolved many different social institutions as useful means to the end they had in view. Some of these, it is true, have outlived their usefulness and need to be scrapped now. But in the days when they were devised and introduced, they did help humanity to cultivate and realize the qualities of the spirit, the qualities which were of the utmost importance in their respective ages. (H, 5.12.1953, 313)

361. Just as experiments are done in social and physical sciences, similarly sociological experiments have been carried out since eternity. On an idea proving harmful, man gave it up and accepted a new one. This happened in sociology, spiritual science, political science etc. That is what happens in various aspects of life. (Triveni, 65)

362. Human mentality has been considerably changing and now even children are not prepared to put up with punishment for the sake of education. It is apparent that the old mentality no more exists in education now. It has all changed and man has come to realize the need of independent development to a greater degree. (BG, III, 73)

363. There is an episode in the Mahabharat. Draupadi was forcibly brought before a crowded assembly. She enquired if a woman could be put on stake in a game of dice. Had a man proprietory rights over a woman ? Even our boys and girls will say that it is not a difficult question. But Bhisma and Drona did not have the answer. As a line of a poem says, "Bhisma, Drona and Vidur felt puzzled." They were wise persons, but they could not answer whether a woman was personal property of a man or not. They found it difficult to decide.

When we think on these lines, it strikes us how advanced is our thinking in this age. In olden times even petty problems seemed difficult to men and they were unable to arrive at any decision.

The people used to say then that if a Kshatriya was invited to play dice, it would be morally wrong on his part not to go. When Dharmaraj was invited, that pious ruler accepted it out of a sense of duty. I do not want to laugh at that man of great knowledge. His times were different and he had his problems.

If today we possess greater knowledge and wider vision, the reason is that we are standing on his shoulders. If a child sits on the shoulders of his father, he is able to see to a much greater distance. If we are able to decide on matters on which Bhisma and Drona could not, it does not mean that we have greater knowledge. It only signifies that the society of today has greatly progressed in ideas since then. (SKA, 45-46)

364. The social order has ever been changing with progress in moral ideas. For instance, in ancient days polyandry was in vogue in our country. That custom has now disappeared.... Similarly, in ancient days, inhuman punishments were awarded. Chopping of hands or legs of the accused was once considered as just by courts of law. But that concept of justice has now changed and disappeared, and the laws of justice have begun to become humane. In this way the evolution of society and of its ideas of morality and justice is continuously going on. (SE, Oct. 1952, 76)

Growth of Nonviolence in Indian History

365. It is worth studying how nonviolence has developed. We would then understand how the life of religion has developed step by step and what scope there is for further growth. In the beginning the nonviolent man had to consider how to save himself from the attacks of the violent. At first the Kshatriya class was set up for the protection of society, but it went too far and started devouring society itself. Then the nonviolent Brahmins began to consider how society could be saved from these power-mad Kshatriyas. Parasuram, though a devotee of nonviolence himself, resorted to violence. He set out to destroy the Kshatriyas. For removing the violence of the Kshatriyas, he himself adopted violence. Though this was an effort of Ahimsa, the attempt did not succeed. Twenty-one times he destroyed the Kshatriyas, still they survived, because the method was wrong in its very basis. He who set out to destroy the Kshatriyas became a Kshatriya himself and added to their numbers.

Then came the age of Rama. Then the Brahmins began to think about it again. They had already given up violence; they had resolved never to commit violence themselves. How then to escape the attack of the Rakshasas? They thought, "Here are these Kshatriyas who practise violence anyhow; why should not the Rakshasas be destroyed through them ? One uses a thorn to remove a thorn. We shall stand aside." That is why to protect his Yajna, sacrifice, Visvamitra took Rama and Lakshmana and had the Rakshasas destroyed by them. Now we think, "The Ahimsa that cannot protect itself, that cannot stand on its own legs, this lame Ahimsa, how can it sustain itself ?" But men like Vasishtha and Visvamitra saw nothing wrong in finding protection in the strength of the Kshatriyas. But what if there was no Kshatriya like Rama? Then Visvamitra would have said, "I would rather die than commit violence." If they could not find a Kshatriya, they would prefer to die. To that extent the ground had been prepared. In the Aranyakanda of the Ramayan, there is an episode. Walking in the Dandak forest, Rama asks, "What are these heaps ?" The Rishis answer, "These heaps are made up of the bones of the Brahmins, of nonviolent Brahmins. When the violent Rakshasas attacked them, they did not resist. They lost their lives. It is their bones that are piled up here." In this nonviolence one sees the sacrifice of the Brahmins; but at the same time, they had a wish that others would protect them. Where there is such a weakness, nonviolence cannot reach perfection.

In later times, good men went further and tried a third method. They resolved, "We shall never seek the help of others to save ourselves. Our Ahimsa is enough to protect us. That is the only true defence." But this experiment was conducted on the individual plane. They perfected this individual method, but it stopped with the individual. If violent men attacked society and men went and appealed to those saints and asked, "What shall we do now?", it is doubtful whether they would have given a definite answer....It would not be true to say that they were never moved to use the method of Ahimsa on the social plane. It may be that the conditions of the time did not seem propitious. And so they never experimented individually, by themselves. But it is out of such experiments, conducted separately by individuals, that a science is born. Science arises from the combined experience of many.

After these individual experiments of saints, today we are conducting the fourth experiment. And that is, the whole of society joining together to oppose violence with the methods of Ahimsa. Thus, there have been four experiments so far. In each of them there have been and there are imperfections. But it must be said that each method was perfect for its time. And ten thousand years later, people will see even in our nonviolent struggle an element of violence. Many more experiments in pure Ahimsa will of course take place yet.

(Gita, 234-238)

366. There was a time when man lived on animals only. But even then, the more intelligent, the nobler ones, did not like this. They laid down a restriction that, if they had to eat meat,they would only eat the flesh of animals offered in sacrifice. The intention behind this was to limit violence. Many people gave up meat altogether; but those who would not do so were permitted to offer it to the Lord in sacrifice, do a little penance and then eat it. It was thought then that, as a result of the condition that one could only eat meat in a Yajna, a sacrifice, violence would be controlled. But later on, Yajna became common and whoever felt like it performed a sacrifice and ate the meat. Then the Lord Buddha went a step further. He said, "If you want to eat meat, eat it. But don't bring the name of God into it." The aim of both these statements is the same, that violence should be controlled, that somehow people should be drawn into the path of self-control. Both from the performance of Yajnas and from non-performance of them, we learnt to give up meat. Thus, little by little, we gave up eating meat. (Gita, 239)

If Progress, Why Conflicts Then ?

367. All the efforts made by men in this world are aimed at becoming one in love. Some conflicts, and some disputes too,appear to be there, and some have built up an elaborate philosophy of struggle, but these conflicts and struggles do not last long. They come and go, but man's life, full of love, goes on.

If man struggles, it is for peace; if he quarrels, it is also for love. (BY, 4.11.1955)

Another Objection to the Idea of Progress

368. **Question :** Probably so much of injustice, atrocity,violence and untruth never existed before as we find today. Is it progress or regress ?

Vinoba : That is what it looks to us. But the human society is advancing towards its goal through these injustices and atrocities. The greater prevalence of violence only establishes the need of nonviolence, and only by passing through it, society will attain nonviolence. (VS, 71)

Symptoms of Decay in a Society

369. When a society is in decay, there is no high aspiration or goal before it. The life of man becomes like that of ordinary living beings. It cannot be said that if a society aims at higher production it is leading a higher kind of life.

(VP, 6.2.1957)

The Causes of Societal Decay

370. When indifference to wordly things grows less and sense enjoyments increase, greatness declines. (NA, 209)

371. When those considered *Jnanis,* men of knowledge, feel bored by actions or are ashamed of doing anything, the nation begins to decline. (VV, II, 7)

372. In his *Fall of the Roman Empire* Gibbon has explained how the Roman Empire fell. The people of Rome were at their height when efforts, inspiration and enthusiasm were there. But when there was an increase in sex indulgence and sensuousness, when physical labour came to be looked down upon and the people acquired the feeling that their hands should not get dirty, Rome declined. (VP no 144 of 1958)

Have the Indians Declined Morally ?

373. The moral standard of our people has not fallen down as often repeated by many. Their very consciousness that they are dropping down from the high pedestal of spiritual life, itself would help them to maintain and improve their moral standard. The real cause of this dissatisfaction with one's own self and society is the improper economic structure of society which is based on money economy which has no relationship whatsoever to the labour spent and the production turned out. Money rules the life of individuals, society, governments and even nations. It is but natural that such a state of affairs should lead to glaring inequalities, greed, jealousy and wars among peoples. Until that is set right and inequalities between man and man removed, no man can dream of a happier society. (SE, Aug. 1952, 29-30)

A Revolution Needed

374. I believe that Swaraj has not brought about any revolution. It has merely been a change of masters in India. This is not to belittle the value of Swaraj. I know that it is after a lapse of two thousand years that we have obtained the opportunity to build up our country on the basis of Lokniti or strength of the people. Nevertheless 1 maintain that there has been no revolution as yet. Those who talked of revolution till yesterday talk of development today. I welcome development, but I ask what should be its basis ? Should official power continue to serve as basis ? That would fail to do away with our ills. What is required is to change the standing values. The social structure has to be recast. From the President down to the scavenger, all services must be regarded of the same class. I worry little about what you pay them. But I insist that the same moral value be accorded to the standard work of the two. This is not happening in our country today.

(H, 11.9.1954, 227)

Revolution Must Be Peaceful

375. I want revolution but I also want peace. Without peace, India cannot survive. And without revolution, the poor of India would know no end of their misery. If we adhere to aggressive or violent methods, we are bound to seek shelter, like Pakistan, of some expert military Guru. Hence, I insist on peaceful and nonviolent revolution. (H, 14.8.1954, 196)

His Objective

376. My object is not to avoid a revolution. I want to save the country from a violent revolution and to bring about a nonviolent one. (S, Dec. 1951, 1127)

377. My aim is to bring about a threefold revolution. First,I want a change in people's hearts; secondly, I want to create a change in their lives; and thirdly, I want to change the social structure. (H, 8.12.1951, 350)

Peace and Change

378. There are critics who seem to think that peace-loving, people are by nature submissive and that they cannot fight injustice until they abandon the ways of peace. But this is not true as was partly demonstrated in our fight against the British imperialism through peaceful methods.

And yet this example, striking though it is, does not fully reveal the power of peace as an effective solvent of all our difficulties. The achievement of Swaraj has brought us face to face with several others and in some ways more formidable difficulties, especially those arising from the existence of poverty and social and economic difficulties. Now, if we can tackle these difficulties through peaceful methods, then we will surely be said to have demonstrated the power of peace quite satisfactorily. (H, 9.1.1954, 357-358).

The Meaning of Revolution

379. In a revolution, there is a change of heart, a change of values. (NA, 95)

380. Merely a very big change does not make for a revolution. As long as there is no revolution inside, there can be no revolution outside. Change in mental attitude is termed as revolution. (BG, V, 98)

381. Nowadays it is violence which is termed as revolution. But where there is no revolution in basic things, it will be wrong to term superficial changes as revolution. Revolution only takes place when we change our moral life. (BYB, 9.10.1953)

Evolution and Revolution

382. A Revolution does not occur gradually and gradually like an evolution. Hence, it is imperceptible. When there is a revolution, it occurs all of a sudden. It goes on imperceptibly developing inside. The birth of a child is a revolution. He goes on growing throughout his whole life. That is evolution. Then he dies and it is a revolution. In a revolution there is a sudden change. (BY, 4.4.1958)

The Roots of a Revolution

383. All revolutions which take place, whether they are social or economic, have their roots in spiritual ideas. At first there is a change in spiritual values and later on social, political and economic values undergo changes. (VP, 11.7.1957)

The Process of a Revolution

384. A revolution cannot be confined for all times to any fixed technique. By its very nature, a revolution is bound to throw up newer and newer technique for its success. A revolution with a fixed technique would be a contradiction in terms. In that case it would be no revolution at all. (H, 24.7.1954,165)

385. It is not that the science of revolution has been worked out. It is still in the making. (AG, 14)

386. Four processes are involved in social change, namely a change of heart, a change in conditions, a change of ideas, and service. It is God who brings about a change of heart. It is society which changes conditions. The change of ideas is wrought by thinkers, and it is servants who serve. The capacity to change heart is derived from God. For that there should be devotion and the utmost purification of heart.

A thinker prepares the ground for change in social conditions. All sorts of ideas, favourable and unfavourable, should be studied. Those which appear to be correct should be acted upon and placed before society. It will derive strength from them in tune with the situation. Immediate results cannot be expected. The function of a thinker is only to put the ideas acted upon by him in the background of a pure life. It is the work of society to change social conditions.

Then there is the person who serves. He does not worry about the change in conditions. He goes on serving society in the manner of a doctor who repeatedly treats a patient falling ill again and again because of his mistakes. He does not think of apportioning blame. A patient visiting a doctor is conscious of his mistakes but he has faith that he would get love from the doctor. Such should also be the faith of the people in one who serves them.

If these four elements duly discharge their roles in the scheme of social change, society continues to evolve in the right direction, irrespective of the fact whether the progress appears to be slow or rapid. (BY, 18.5.1961)

387. The fundamental idea of a revolution first of all occurs to a man of knowledge given to contemplation. Then it is communicated to the people. After that, the people examine it minutely and adopt it. Later on, the government also accepts it and a law is enacted accordingly. (BYB, 22.1.1954)

The Possibility of a Change of Heart

388. If God dwells in the hearts of all beings and controls every movement of theirs, even their breathing, and if He is the source of all inspiration, a change of heart is always possible. The Lord of the Ages is eternally present, and if He desires a change, that change has to be. When a man falls into a stream, it is not only his own capacity of swimming but also the force of the current that helps him, and it does so whether he likes it or not. Similarly, when the current of the age flows this way, it will help in changing his heart. (H, 29.9.1951, 260)

389. The power of the Spirit is not confined in its action to one physical body. It pervades the entire universe. Hence, the belief that the Spirit can work only in the domain of individual and private life is erroneous ...... Just as it works in the heart of an individual, it similarly works in the hearts of all beings. (H, 1.3.1952, 6)

Change of Heart and Moral Pressure

390. There is no practical difference between moral pressure and change of heart.....So even when a man acts due to the fear of public disapprobation, *lokalajja,* his sincerity should not be doubted, because it is also a form of the change of heart. (H, 22.8.1953, 193)

391. Pressure is of three kinds. They are (1) pressure by threat of violence, (2) pressure by the sanction of law, and (3) moral pressure by the force of good public opinion. The last I welcome. (SE, April 1954, 260)

The Die-Hards

392. God creates some people who put saints to test. Some are pure die-hards. We leave them to God. But the hearts of the common people can be changed. (PMV, 74)

The Place of Fear in the Process of Revolution

393. It does not matter if somebody donates (land) out of fear. It does not mean that gifts be obtained under threat that "either donate land or you will be killed". That would be wrong. But if we tell somebody that "leave your bed since there is a serpent on it," the fear involved in it is legitimate...One should be aware of a real danger. (Triveni, 58)

Social Conditions and Change of Heart

394. Social conditions have to be changed for a change of heart.But it is itself a part of the change of heart. It is an error to regard it as something different. If we wish to give up a particular attachment, we must also so mould the external environment that that attachment may disappear.

It is correct to say that change in social conditions can only result from a change of heart itself. There can be no meditation without concentration. Even if it be done in a lonely place, the mind can roam hither and thither. Hence, while solitude is only an external means, concentration is the primary thing. Similarly, the change of heart is primary for the power of nonviolence. (S, July 1953, 795-796)

The Importance of a Change in Ideas

395. Believe me, I have an absolute faith in the efficacy of thought. Beyond explaining the new ideas to the people, I want to do nothing else. If they are understood, the people will follow them without any outside effort. (B, 21. 11. 1956, 2)

396. Thought is the basis of human life. Even in the material life of humanity, thought is responsible for change and progress. Ideas start movements, build up strength and create new life. Then the social structure changes, the pattern of life changes. The French Revolution was brought about by an idea. Marx lived, and a nation was shaped in Russia by his thought....Thought is the foundation upon which the house of life is built. (DV, 17)

When Does an Idea Spread ?

397. The resurgence and the renaissance that we come across in intervals of our long history were brought about by men of God who saw truth and worked strenuously to realize it. Religion cannot spread if it is only confined to the realm of thought. It needs to be lived. Austerity and penance are necessary if a new thought is to be communicated.

(B, 16.1.1957, 4)

398. Only that idea will spread in society which has been tested in a laboratory and which is in accordance with the needs of the times. (S, Nov. 1953, 203)

Revolution and Discontent

399. **Question :** Would not your movement, by relieving the woes of the poor to some extent, result in delaying the prospects of a revolution in the country ?

Vinoba : You know thirty lakhs of people died of starvation in Bengal in 1943, yet there could be no revolution. Why ? I believe that a revolution requires two forces for its fulfilment: (1) *vichar-shakti* (thought-force) and (2) *pran-shakti* (vital force). Discontent alone is meaningless. (H, 13.11.1954, 294)

Change of Individual and Revolution

400. We do not hold that mere change in individual will lead to change in society. Change of ideas, change of life and then change in society, such is the triangle of revolution. To bring about change in individual is the first function of ideas. The saints worked for change in individual lives. As you see, their work has not been in vain. Had they not done what they did, we would still have been beasts. (VP, 26.5.1959)

401. Even if independent-minded persons do not become slaves to conditions, they are at least moulded by them.

(VV, II, 16)

Political Power and Revolution

402. No revolutionary thought has ever been propagated through the power of the State. ... The great Buddha gave us a revolutionary thought, but he did not use political power for the propagation of his thought. On the contrary, he had to bid good bye to political power. Gandhiji also did not want the power to rule for the propagation of his ideals.

(H, 26.12.1948, 361)

403. The authority of the government is incapable of bringing about any revolutionary change among the people, such as the reform of their social life. ... The decline of the Buddhist faith in India dates from the day when it received the backing of government power. When the Christian faith was backed by the imperial power of Constantine, it became Christian only in name. The pure religion practised by the first disciples of Christ was seen no more. In our own country the history of the Vaishnavites, the Shaivites and the Jains shows that when their movements won royal favour they were joined by thousands who were not real Vaishnavites, Shaivites or Jains at all, but merely loyal devotees of the ruling king.

No, do not allow yourselves to imagine that right thinking or righteous conduct can be propagated by governmental power. On the contrary, if there should be any genuine encounter between them, religion would destroy the power of the state. The two can no more exist together than darkness and the sun. (DV, 18.19)

404. Shri Kripalani had said that without taking power into our hands, it was not possible to establish the social order of our conception. But is not power in our hands today ? If we think that by taking power from the hands of those who are wielding it today, we shall be able to do better, we are very much mistaken....If I myself had the power in my hands, I would not be able to do very much, because government reflects only public opinion and is never revolutionary. A democratic government represents the outlook of the common people. A government is what its people are.

Hence, social revolutionaries have to give up political power and carry on their work. The work creates the power needed to bring about a political revolution.

(H, 19.6.1949, 126)

405. Everyone recognizes that love brings happiness. But they do not know that it is also a power which can change society. Politicians and students of political science are strong votaries of power. They believe that power is the only effective lever with which they can bring about a social change. 1 think that this is an illusion. We were discussing the land problem of Kerala and we saw that legislation is both a help and hindrance to a happy solution of the land problem. Legislation has a contradictory effect. It is an illusion to depend entirely on law in bringing about a social change. We have to demonstrate the power of love in order to bring about radical change in our society.

Many doubt if this can be practicable. They feel that coercion is indispensable. I ask what holds a family together? Love or coercion ?...Sarvodaya believes in the power of love. It is the most effective force which can create a radical change in society. But for that we need workers who have realized this and who have dedicated themselves to social service.

(B, 1.5.1957, 7)

406. To say that we can bring about a revolution only with the help of governmental authority is to abandon one's faith in nonviolence, for then one accepts that it is force and not ideas which brings about changes. (H, 19.6.1949, 127)

Institutions and Revolutions

407. The work of revolution cannot be done by ready-made institutions. (Purnea, 121)

Constructive Work and Revolution

408. Constructive work will only be revolutionary when it will be carried out with a revolutionary outlook. And then only that capability will develop in it. (HS, 26.6.1949, 142)

Violence and Revolution

409. People want a revolutionary programme and think that a revolution cannot be brought about without bloodshed. Let me tell you that I do not accept it. Those who hold that there can be no revolution without shedding blood are not, really speaking, revolutionists at all. They are status qou-ists. Their aim is not revolution, but only exchange of places. They wish to give the place of the present happy ones to the unhappy ones and to put the happy in the place of the unhappy. But it is no revolution. It will not lead to any change in the present system. What a revolution must imply is that all become happy without exception. (HS, 15.12.1951, 362-363)

410. Changing the basic values and replacing them by the new ones means revolution from the roots, revolution in the means as well as in the end. This cannot be brought about with the aid of the sword. Such revolutions took place in other countries and we have seen their results. (VP, 9.5.1959)

411. How did the ideas of Marx spread among the people ? Was it through violence ? Not at all. People understood them to some extent and they put them into practice to the extent they could grasp. (SAS, 61)

Individual and Revolution

412. The source of every revolutionary idea is in the heart and mind of an individual. Christ, Buddha, Muhammad and a host of others who gave some great ideas to the world, first conceived them in their own minds. Lofty peaks of mountains catch drops of rains first. It is from them that rain water percolates below. (B, 29.5.1957, 5)

413. It (Bhoodan) began with an individual. There was no previous plan or blueprint. It had no organisation behind it. Its appeal was to the individual. All religious mevements throughout the ages have had similar beginnings. A creative revolution has a mass effect, but the individual is its centre and circumference. As the wind carries the fragrance of a flower to far and near places, a new thought gets communicated from man to man. (B, 20.2.1957, 4)

414. Both as a principle and in theory we hold that if there is even one fully pure individual who has realized nonviolence, he can have perceptible impact on society. (S, July 1953, 795)

415. We should have in our lives hundred times that measure of equality which we desire in society. Only then we can establish equality in society through our ideas, actions, hopes and resolves. (S, May 1951, 618)

Scientific Materialism

416. There was a school in European philosophy which said that the whole creation was a product of the mind. As against it, Marx argued that the creation was so vast and our mind so small that it would be wrong to say that the creation was a product of the mind. It is the mind which is a product of the creation. Marx made use of it. It is called 'scientific materialism', i.e., the main factor is not the mind but the creation.

We have accorded primacy to the soul which is beyond mind, and have looked upon mind as secondary.

Thus both the materialist and spiritual philosophers consider mind to be secondary. (KP, 16 and 17)

Dialectical Materialism

417. I term dialectical materialism as 'dialectical conditionism'. The word 'materialism' does not suit it. Materialists are those whose life consists only of eating, drinking and making merry. Dialectics is only a method of thinking. It can lead to revolution as well as to counter-revolution. If to a tree of sour lemon we graft a plant of sweet lemon, the resultant fruit will be both sweet and sour. Such is also the process of thesis, antithesis and synthesis. I could not understand how this theory creates a zeal for revolution and how it follows from it that haves must be extirpated. (SAS, 40)

The Concept of Classes

418. The class divisions of upper, lower and middle are purely arbitrary. Castes, whether they be three or four or more, are of our own making. Therefore any theory of organization based on them is also arbitrary in the sense that even if they are related to facts, still they are certainly not fundamental. Similarly, though it may be difficult to say that the difference between the rich and poor is arbitrary, we cannot regard that distinction as fundamental. That is, it does not belong to the very nature of things, but is merely the effect of special circumstances. Thus if we call the wealthy wealthy because of money, and the poor for lack of it, the poor can, on the contrary, be said to be wealthy from the point of view of capacity for labour, and those called wealthy today can with reference to their capacity for labour be said to be poor. Thus, wealthy and poor are alike merely arbitrary distinctions.

(SS, 14-15)

419. We must realize that everybody has got something which he can give. The division of society into 'haves' and 'have-nots' is wrong. (B, 11.4.1959, 341)

The Concept of Class Conflict

420. They (the Marxists) view life as a conflict. Even a mother suckling her child (the most sacred example of love) is for them a conflict between the breasts of the mother on one side and the child on the other. But this is an error. The world runs not on conflict but on love. A dying man feels consoled to see his dear ones. Are we to believe that it is an outcome of a conflict between his eyes and the dear ones ?

(H, 6.12.1952, 346)

The Drawbacks of Class Struggle

421. Churning produces butter, but struggle or friction produces fire. Hence, our attempt should be to produce only butter. A movement or agitation should be so conducted in society that while there is a good churning of ideas, there is no friction. The idea of conflict does not belong to this land. It is Western and destructive in every way. (VP, 29.1.1959)

422. It is better to strike at the root of classes than to achieve what we want through class struggle. For by accepting class struggle, you strengthen classes and form them. It is not necessary for an owner to have affection for another owner, but they unite when we declare all of them to be our enemies.

In other words, we create a bond between them which did not exist before. Thus you strengthen them.

(A Conversation on 16.10.1957)

423. Communism declares that equality can never be achieved unless the present upper class is totally abolished. Class war and extirpation of those who hold power offer the only way to this cherished goal. This much violence is inevitable and even obligatory for us.

It is obvious that such an outlook can never make for peace, because violence produces counter-violence. Not only that, it also results in the depreciation of human virtues, which are ultimately the only real foundation for any programme worth the name. (H, 7.11.1953, 285)

Sarvodaya and Class Reconciliation

424. It must be understood that what I want is not class reconciliation but class disappearance. Eradication of classes is surely not the same thing as reconciliation of classes. It is true that we, who believe in Gandhiji's teachings, do not subscribe to or want class struggle, but it is wrong to assume that we want to give a lease of life to the existing classes by reconciling their differences. (B, 11.4.1959, 340)

How to Abolish Classes ?

425. It (class transformation) presupposes that each class shall have to put aside its own narrow interests which are supposed to conflict with one another. For example, there would not be mutually exclusive and separate organizations of employers and employees, of teachers and pupils. But there would be common organizations including both workers and employers having the good of society as a whole as their objective.

(ibid)

426. If we desire a classless social structure, some ten or twenty of us acquainted with each other should join together, equally distribute our wealth and successfully demonstrate in our own lives the experiments of a classless social structure.

Such experiments should be conducted at many places. They should be conducted in Ashrams. They should be conducted alongwith a few farmers. They should be conducted along with our friends and fellow-workers. If enterprising persons were to conduct such experiments, society would follow them. (S, Dec. 1949, 293 and 294)

The Programme for Societal Transformation

427. The programme for transforming society will be as follows :

1. Decentralization of power so that there are maximum powers at the lowest level, minimum powers at higher levels and only moral power at the highest level.
2. Cooperation.
3. Full opportunity for individual development.
4. Spirit of dedication for society.
5. Combining knowledge and activity in education.(SAS, 62)

The Experience of History

428. **Someone :** History and psychology point out that vested interests will never easily forego their interests.

Vinoba : You should realise that in future many things are going to happen which never occurred in history. As regards psychology, I think that your impression is not correct. In a family some members earn more and some earn less, yet all the members live together and share with each other. My idea is that a village too can likewise constitute a family. This idea is in keeping with the times through which we are passing.You should know that the communist ideas too had never been expressed before, and yet they were tried in Russia. In the same way, there is scope for nonviolent revolution as well.

(RKSM, 68)

V
SARVODAYA

What Sarvodaya Is ?

429. Sarvodaya is a new thought. It avows the indivisible unity of life. It refuses to divide life into watertight compartments. It does not split life into opposite categories like individual versus society, society versus state, national versus international, secular versus religious, individual salvation versus social progress. These divisions are unreal and mischievous. They have created the present chaos. There is one law and one way which is universally valid. What is good for the individual is good for society. There is no real conflict of interests. Well-being is indivisible. (B, 26. 9. 1956, 5)

430. Sarvodaya does not believe in double standards. It lays down that there can be no conflict between individual and social good. Progress means progress of all. One man's loss cannot become another man's gain. We are so linked up together that there is no private universe. We create an illusion of a personal or private existence. But all existence is one. (ibid, 6)

431. Sarvodaya is a word pregnant with so much meaning that the more we ponder on it and practise it, the more meaning we discover in it. It will dawn on us gradually and gradually. However, one thing is clear. When God has created human society, he must not have created conflict in the interests (of individuals and groups). No father desires clash in the interests of his sons. There may be difference of views among them but no conflict of interests. It is not possible for a human being to have a complete idea. Some part (of it) would dawn on one, some on another and some on a third one, and they would all go to constitute the whole. Hence differences in views are necessary. It is a gain and no disadvantage.

(SV, 32-33)

432. The Western idea of the greatest good of the greatest number contains in it the germs of minority and majority problems. But the idea of Sarvodaya as preached by the Gita, is to merge oneself in the good of all. This, of course,demands an absolute faith in truth and nonviolence. Never should people resort to untruth in their private and public life, nor in their business and other occupations. They should try their best not to allow violence a place in their life. The constructive programme which was meant for the uplift of society, should be carried out in part or full, individually or with the cooperation of friends or colleagues, as also by establishing local institutions wherever necessary. (H, 13.2 1949, 422)

433. The roots of Sarvodaya lie in the idea of the welfare of the last. (SV, 43)

The Sarvodaya Attitude

434. We desire the welfare of all, and also our own. But the question is as to which of them we give priority. If we give it to the good of others, our attitude is that of Sarvodaya. If it is otherwise, then it is not.

The sum and substance of it is that we should be prepared to make sacrifices for the good of others, and the external suffering involved in it should give us inner satisfaction. Externally we would suffer but internally we would be happy.

(SV, 105,107)

The Basis of Sarvodaya

435. The spiritual basis of Sarvodaya thought is nothing short of *Advaita,* non-duality. It is even more, and this is not only to be kept in mind but is also to be realized in this world.

(VP, 22. 9. 1958)

The Peculiarities of Sarvodaya

436. The philosophy of Sarvodaya is, on the whole, a harmonizing one, and has the capacity of bringing all ideologies closer.

(SV, 83)

437. Sarvodaya is not a reaction to any 'ism'. It is India's own thought and her own system but not something that cannot be applied to any other time or country. Its external form may vary according to the needs of particular times and places. (This non-insistence on a specific form is a fundamental element of Sarvodaya philosophy.) But its inner core is eternal.

I am firmly convinced that the various one-sided ideologies, groping towards their own fullness will ultimately merge in the ocean of Sarvodaya.

(Introduction to Jayaprakash Narayan: From Socialism to Sarvodaya)

438. A virtue of Sarvodaya is that the self-interest, the interests of others and the supreme interest become one in it. No contradictions are left. All conflicts, internal or external, are resolved. (VP, 29. 1. 1959)

439. No revolution is possible now unless it is peaceful, and no peace will be stable without a revolution. Only those will be able to hold out now who are peaceful revolutionaries. The thought which assures a peaceful revolution, is called Sarvodaya. (VP, 19. 2. 1959)

440. In Sarvodaya, the two currents of the heroes and the saints become one. The distinction between them vanishes. The hero becomes a saint and the saint becomes a hero. The preserver of society himself plays the role of a social revolutionary and the enactor of a social revolution preserves it. (VP, 10.11. 1957)

441. Sarvodaya is a philosophy of life. That is why it has enough depth. It has economic, political, social and ethical aspects. (VP, 7.6 1957)

442. I never hold that our ideas are the last words. They can be further improved upon. As man would advance in spiritual practice and gain experience, he would feel that his present vision had been a limited one. (VP, 10.11. 1957)

No 'Sarvodayis'

443. We are neither a sect nor a party. Therefore the word 'Sarvodayi' often used to designate us, is misleading. We are simply men, human beings like other men. Political parties have their different labels which may continue because they are useful to them. But we are not a party. If anything, we are a 'third power', not the third power of political phraseology, which some political-minded persons desire to bring about as the way out from being entangled in the American or Russian Bloc, but the third power which is opposed to violence and is different from the power of the state. (H, 16.5. 1953, 87)

The Pattern of Sarvodaya

444. In the (U. S. A.) the land-man ratio is different. They have more land and less people. So the pattern of Sarvodaya experiment in America is bound to be different from the one in India. (B, 23.1.1957, 2)

The Four Pillars of a Sarvodaya Order

445. Let me tell very clearly that all will have to do manual labour in a Sarvodaya order. We desire to improve implements, but they must remain in the hands of the peasant and must be owned by him. Productive labour is always required. It provides perennial employment. The raw produce of the village must be turned into finished products in the village itself. We shall not allow the children of the village to be deprived of milk and butter. All production will primarily be for local consumption. Only the surplus will be exported to the cities.

Secondly, Sarvodaya believes that private ownership of land must end. Everyone who desires to work on land should have land to till as a matter of right. The village must learn to live as one family.

Thirdly, Sarvodaya believes that there must be Nai Talim for all the children of the village.

Fourthly, Sarvodaya means a classless and casteless society.

These are the four pillars of a Sarvodaya order.

(B, 17.10.1956, 2)

The New Ideal of Sarvodaya

446. Just as formerly we had the ideal of Swaraj to work for, we have now the ideal of Sarvodaya. Without such ideals to inspire us, life will not progress. As a matter of fact, this new ideal of Sarvodaya has developed out of the old ideal of Swaraj, because the concept of Swaraj contained within itself the urge for social reform. We have, therefore, to take this new mission of Sarvodaya to every village. This is the new mission we have to work for, live for and die for.

(B, 25.2.1959, 356)

The Aim of the Sarvodaya Movement

447. We want a Kingdom of Kindness. Christ spoke of the Kingdom of God, but the word 'God' is beyond us. There is some kindness in the present society also, but what we want is a Kingdom of Kindness. We want kindness to be the dominant force in society. (B, 25.2.1955, 418)

448. We must remember what we are engaged in is a movement for the complete regeneration of society.(B, 25.2.1959, 356)

Sarvodaya and Science

449. Many are of the view that Sarvodaya is an out-dated ideology with an aversion for science. But it is totally wrong. I have repeatedly said that it is Sarvodaya alone, and no other ideology, which has a claim on science. If others acquire the power of science, it would lead to the annihilation of man. If that power gets linked with Sarvodaya, it would lead to the development of humane feelings and to the good of mankind.

In Sarvodaya planning, science would be made use of to the greatest extent possible. (VP, 19.12.1959)

Samyayoga, The Basis of Sarvodaya

450. I propose to speak to you about the basic idea behind the Bhoodan. We call this idea 'Samyayoga'. It consists in accepting the belief that the Spirit is equally immanent in all beings. It is on the foundation of this principle that we want to build up the Sarvodaya society, that is, a society which provides for the full and free development of one and all.

(H, 7.11.1953, 285)

The Basis of Samyayoga

451. Samyayoga takes its stand on the inner unity of man. It recognizes the great principle that all life is one. And on the foundation of that spiritual unity, it seeks to build an equitable order in which everything will have its right place.....Samyayoga is opposed to inequalities; it is not opposed to right discrimination. As a mother loves all her children equally, nevertheless she feeds her weaker darling on milk, which she may not give to others. This is an instance of wise discrimination....And because Samyayoga makes use of the light of discrimination, it provides scope for development to every individual. (H, 19.4.1952, 68)

Implications of Samyayoga

452. Let us see how the application of Samyayoga revolutionizes our economic life. According to it, every man who works for society to the best of his ability, has a right to livelihood. A blind man, for example, has as much right to it as any other, if he exerts himself fully within his capacity.

Therefore all work which is an act of service to society must have equal value. The prevailing practice is just the reverse of it. Intellectual work is regarded as superior to physical labour and paid more than the latter. This distinction between intellectual and physical labours is entirely baseless.

Everyone must get full opportunity for development. The students will acquire training and knowledge according to their receptive capacity. But we cannot allow the present state of affairs which provides for the education of a son of a rich man but not for the son of a poor man.

The implication of this view (Samyayoga) in the economic sphere will help the building up of self-sufficiency in the villages.

Samyayoga will produce equally revolutionary changes in the political sphere also. We want a social order which will be free not only from every form of exploitation but also from every form of governmental authority. The powers of the Government will be decentralized and distributed among the villages. Every village will be a state in itself; the centre will have only a nominal authority over them. In this way, gradually, we shall reach a stage when authority in every form will have become unnecessary and will therefore fade away giving rise to a perfectly free society.

In the social sphere also there will be no caste or any other variety of invidious distinctions. He who has the qualities of a Brahmin may be entrusted with a work suited to his capacity, but this will not give him a superior status. In the same way, sweepers, scavengers and cobblers also cannot be regarded as inferior to others because they render to society services which are no less valuable than that of the Brahmins.

Thus, Samyayoga will transform the entire life of society in every field. This is what we call revolution.

(H, 7.11.1953, 285-286)

Future of Sarvodaya

453. I have not the least doubt that the world will either have to accept Sarvodaya or annihilation. There is no third alternative, and it is certain that in this age of science the world will accept Sarvodaya. It may take time, but that is beside the point. (VP, 1.10.1959)

VI
SOCIAL IDEAS

The Present Day Society

454. We observe that though the means of comfort have greatly increased, no country in the world is happy today. This signifies that there is something wrong somewhere.
(Triveni, 26)

455. The society of today is like a heap of wheat grains. There are some grains which move to fill up a depression, but their number is small. The other ones remain where they are. But the human society we have to build up would be like water.
(NA, 164)

456. The tasks of defence and reconstruction of society have got into the clutches of violence and competition. The goddess of defence has taken the form of violence and that of reconstruction the form of competition. (JJ, 54)

The Distinctive Feature of a Living Society

457. The distinctive feature of a living society is that the pain experienced at one place is communicated to the other. When the sensitivity of a physical body begins to decline, it is presumed that it is moving towards death. The same is exactly with society. (KKK, 89)

The Aim Concerning Society

458. We have to transform the present society into a Sarvodaya one. We have to abolish castes, sects, classes etc. existing in the society of today. (BAC, 19)

459. The society of today is based on competition. We wish to build up the future society on cooperation. The society stands today on the foundation of ownership. Tomorrow we have to abolish ownership. There are ineqalities in the present society. We have to abolish inequalities. Thus, we want to build up a new society. (PP, 3.11.1957)

460. We want to do away with the owner-labour distinction. In other words, we desire to make use of both the intelligence and the capacity for manual labour of the two. We want to bring about equality without sacrificing efficiency. (VP,14.4.1959)

461. The life of society can be built upon competition as well as compassion, but, ultimately, it is only a compassionate social structure which is conducive to good. (ibid)

Equality, The Demand of the Age

462. The age demands the establishment of equality. The age is yearning for equality. When there is such an intense longing, it is bound to come. The only question is of the method to be adopted for it, so that on being established, it may prove to be stable, beneficial, conducive to well-being and satisfying. This method would be that of compassion. (NA, 66)

The Meaning of Equality

463. I do not want arithmetical equality, but I do want equity, or such equality as, for instance, the five fingers of the hand have. These five fingers are not equal in dimensions, but they all work in full cooperation and together perform innumerable tasks. (H, 26.1.1952, 408)

464. We want equality tempered with right discrimination. The attempts made in other countries to bring about equality by force lacked the insight of proper discrimination. That is why the idea of equality in those countries is proving abortive. A mother does not distribute food among her children on the basis of mathematical equality. To the youngest one she gives only milk, to the next one some milk and some bread, and to the grown-ups only bread. In the same way, in society also we will exercise discrimination and take into account the intensity of hunger and the power of digestion of each in the distribution of food. Where equality is brought about by force, all are compelled to conform to the same pattern. We are totally against this kind of regimentation. We aim at spiritual equality based on proper discrimination.

(H, 20.12.1952, 368)

465. We thus stand for the abolition of all the differences which make for inequality between the different members of society, such as those between men and women, between the rich and the poor, as also between the masters and the servants. Not that we dislike all differences. There are natural differences of various kinds between different individuals...... They make for variety, but they do not produce inequality. We have to do the same in regard to society. All differences which make for inequality and disharmony have to be abolished.

(H, 6.2.1954, 391)

Differences, God-made and Man-made

466. We can neither obliterate God-made differences, nor is there any need to do so. The man-made or artificial differences lead to unhappiness and do harm.

The differences of rich and poor, of high and low, have been created by man himself. (BYB, 13.1.1954)

The Nature of Friendship

467. Friendship is the best relationship, and it also constitutes the basis of society. There is no rivalry between friends.When a friend helps another, the other is obliged. On the contrary, the kiths and kins are always quarrelling over their rights and never consider the good turns done to them. (JJ, 55)

Varnashram

468. Amongst us the term *varnashram* is in vogue, but it contains two ideas—*varna* and *ashram.* They are not identical. *Varna* is concerned with social order, which may undergo change. The *varna* system signifies that everybody should discharge his duties in accordance with the social order prevailing at that time.

The *ashram* system is not so much concerned with society as with individuals. Hence, it is applicable to all societies and all times. There may be some outward changes, but its basic form will remain the same. Though other religions have not prescribed anything like the *ashram* system of Hinduism, the idea behind it is present in all religions.

(Khadi Jagat, Oct 1948)

The Varna System

469. From this viewpoint, the organisation of society in terms of hereditary occupational groups is a very great experiment made by Hinduism. But because of the ideas of superiority and inferiority coming into it, its original pure form became contaminated and later through attraction for the principle of economic competition, it became altogether destroyed. That the individual should do the work allotted to him by society, that society should allot him work in view of his fitness, that his inherited dispositions should be taken advantage of in training him into fitness, that having acquired fitness the individual should regard it his duty to take up the work for which he has been trained, that no other should compete with him in his work, that all should receive adequate equal protection and commensurate wages, that all, who do their allotted work with devotion and with a sense of responsibility, should be esteemed equally, and that every individual should work and God be pleased with his worship in the form of doing his own appointed task—such in short is the institution of the hereditary occupational groups.

An ideal state will have need for some such social organisation. (SS, 56-57)

470. Varna does not mean 'caste'. There are innumerable castes today in the country and this goes against the original concept of Varnas. How did these castes come into existence ? Its history too is very interesting. Co-existence also is one of its causes. When people came here from other countries, these castes were formed so that they could co-exist together. They are not needed now. (VP, 29.1.1959)

471. **Dada (Dharmadhikari) :** I don't like your word 'Varnavyavastha' at all. It will help the caste system to thrive again.

Baba (Vinoba) : Not at all. On the contrary, the moment we pronounce the word 'Varnavyavastha' it is an attack on castes. In the original concept of Varnavyavastha there were neither caste differences nor the sense of high and low. There was in it the idea of equal payment and of equal social, moral and spiritual prestige. (KKR, 148-449)

472. There was a very good idea underlying the four Varnas formed in India......The idea was that in every person there should be all the four Varnas. In other words, every person should be a Brahmin, a Kshatriya, a Vaishya and a Shudra, and thus be a complete individual. But he should take up the work of one of them only as his social activity. For instance, if Kshatriyas had been assigned a particular function, it did not follow that the quality of courage had been made their monopoly. That quality was to be possessed by all. Only the particular function of defence had been entrusted to the Kshatriyas. Similarly, the function of management had been made the responsibility of the Vaishyas, but the managerial quality was to be in all. Particular persons had been entrusted with various functions. Each function had been assigned to particular persons as specialists, but the idea was that these qualities must be in all. However, what happened was that both functions and qualities came to be divided.

(Vyaparion Se, 9-10)

The Distinguishing Traits of Various Varnas

473. I want to say that where there is peace of mind and heart, it is a mark of a Brahmin.

The true mark of a Kshatriya is fearlessness.

The third is the Varna of the Vaishyas. Jf we have to describe their trait in one word, it will be 'Kindness'.

The fourth Varna is that of the Shudras. ...If their trait is to be given in a single word, it will be *shraddha* or faith. In Shudras, it is the element of service which predominates, and there can be no service without faith and devotion.

(BG, VI, 265-267)

The Idea Underlying the Ashram System

474. The idea underlying the Ashram system is that the purpose of man's life is not the enjoyment of the senses but the service of the world. One has to perceive God by practising self-control. (Khadi Jagat, Oct. 1948)

The Importance of the Ashram System

475. If someone were to ask me, "What is the reason of your being proud of Hinduism ?" I would say that the Ashram system is for me the top pride of Hinduism. There can be no better scheme for society than this. (NA, 306)

476. Life is a continuous adventure. Like the flowing water of a river we must be ever on the move. Stagnation is death. Our ancient Rishis understood the secret of life. They created the fourfold division of life in order to keep man on the move and save him from becoming a contented pig or a repetitive machine. I have been fascinated by this idea of four Ashramas. The last one, namely of a Sannyasi or a homeless wanderer, has always thrilled me.

In the modern society all this has changed. We have lost the sense of thrill and adventure. The stream of social service has become dry. People continue to be householders almost to their last breath. We must get out of it and devote ourselves. to some selfless service. That will give us a new vision and strength. (B, 8.5.1957, 4)

477. I feel that we need to revive this ancient division of life in the four well-marked stages. (ibid)

The Traits of Various Ashramas

478. Let us first take the Sannyas Ashram. The trait of a Sannyasi is tranquillity or calmness. Where there is no peace of mind and heart, there is no Sannyas. One does not become a Sannyasi by getting his head shaved or by allowing his beard to grow. The test of a Sannyasi lies in his peace of mind.

The next is the stage of Vanaprastha. Its trait is control over the senses. We have to control them by penance, austerity. We have to attain complete conquest over ourselves.

Then comes Grihasthashram, the stage of the householder. Its trait is kindness. Tirukural also says that the highest quality of a householder is kindness, compassion and love.

Lastly there is the stage of Brahmacharya. Its trait is faith. (BG, VI, 267-268)

Grihasthashram, the Householder Stage

479. If the householder stage is well-ordered, it results in the proper observance of all the stages of life. (VP, 16.6.1959)

480. A householder needs stability of mind and vital force. It is not that he has a license for sex indulgence. On the contrary, this Ashram signifies an endeavour for the purification of mind and heart in an ordered manner and for acquiring training in social service. (AP, 17)

481. Love, compassion and tenderness are developed at the stage of a householder. It is needed for these qualities. (MA, 25)

Vanaprastha, the Stage of a Hermit

482. Vanaprastha is a find of spiritual India. Thus far it has been the life of an householder. The sense organs have been calmed down a bit. Now one should take to retirement. If one would wait for it till they have been completely calmed down, the desires would not even end till death. (PP, 24.8.1975)

483. At a certain period of life, both husband and wife must give up the responsibility of the house, entrust the same to grown-up children, live like brother and sister, and take to life of public service. If they do not do so, the evolution of the soul is blocked up....The Shastras enjoin all, who attain the grand-fatherly status, to abandon their homes and to devote themselves to educating the society. There is plenty of education in our country today, but good and experienced teachers are not available. In case we have Vanaprasthi teachers, who have had profound experience in the domain of trade or industry, administration or political affairs, political parties or social organizations, who have glorious attainments to their credit, they would impart such training to children and

youths as none else can....Society progresses when people after relinquishing their burden take to universal service.
(H, 1.1.1955, 350)

Sannyasa, the Stage of Renunciation

484. Sannyasa means the complete elimination of self-regard or selfhood and a sense of unity and harmony with the whole world. A Sannyasi has no interest of his own; in fact, the words 'I' and 'mine' are not to be found in his dictionary.

In subsequent times, however, Sannyasa acquired a very differrent meaning. It meant turning away from the common people and even despising them. Ramakrishna led the believers of Advaita away from this unhealthy development. He introduced in their practice of religion love of all beings and the realization of God through the service of the poor and the distressed. (B, 13.6.1956, 6)

485. One takes to Sannyasa to make that love universal which had been developed in the family and which had remained confined to some persons in particular. A Sannyasi does not give up love. He develops love but gives up jealousy and vices. He relinquishes the house to seek how to make his love universal. One who leaves it out of boredom or hatred, is not a Sannyasi. (PP, 24.12.1959)

The Object of Marriage

486. We solemnize marriage with auspicious rites so that it does not become a plaything of lust. The sex desire is present in all living creatures. When it gets perverted, it results in adultery, bloodshed, lack of restraint, indulgence etc. All these are perversions. There should not only be no perversions, the sex desire should also be sublimated. (By, 11.7.1958)

Parents and Marriages

487. Parents can advise about marriage, they can help, but it is the decision of the girl herself which must be respected. If the advice of the parents appeals to her, it is all right. If it does not, parents feel distressed over it. Even then, in spite of their unhappiness, I am not prepared to accept that there is something wrong with the girl. She should not agree to it merely to satisfy the parents. To do so would be to deceive oneself. (Stri-Shakti, 75)

The Condition of Women Today

488. Sometimes I wish I were a women ! Not only in India but in the whole world the condition of women is unbearable.

This state will persist till they have freedom for spiritual efforts. (BY, 13.6.1958)

489. Our present condition is that those whom we love are not our fellow-companions in work, and those who are fellow-companions in work are not love-fellows. This should go.

(Prerna Pravah, 136)

490. In the Hindu society women are far behind. Besides legal and social hurdles, they also face hindrances created by spiritual notions. There was a time when it was said that they were not entitled to study the Vedas. Even the males of today are not interested in this right for themselves. It commands no value. But when it was considered as valuable, women did not have a right to it. Even highly religious persons and the learned ones were of the view that women had no right to observe lifelong Bramacharya. All this has created a very big spiritual obstacle for them. The result is that the ideal before every girl is, and it is also inculcated in her, that she has to leave her father's house for another. Their whole education is based on it. Their attitude too is moulded accordingly. India does not conceive of independent enterprising women.

(BG, II, 169-170)

His Desire to Serve Women

491. I prepared some young men in my youth for service. Let this advanced age serve sisters now. I want to spend the rest of my life in their uplift. (LY, 6-7)

The Causes of Women's Bondage

492. Men have shackled the hands and feet of women. They have pierced their noses and their ears. If God had so willed, could He not have created woman with holes in her nose and ears?

But this has been the work of man. Since the fetters are of gold, they are not called as such. Had they been of iron, they would have been 'fetters'. The result is that women cannot move out alone and cannot do anything with courage. ...From childhood they are turned into decorated dolls, so that they may become cowards. Since they are thus decorated with costly jewels, they themselves are frightened. Men have converted them into their bank. Poets also proudly write that women are timid. They should take it as an insult. ...They should abandon all these shackles and become fearless.

(WP, 34)

493. The ornaments have made prisoners of women, and society regards them as blessed symbols of being married...The importance of a wife is no less than that of her husband, but society did not feel the need of prescribing some blessed symbols for him as well. (BY, 13.6.1958)

494. Just as machines have destroyed village industries, foreign countries have destroyed the trade of our cities and our cities have destroyed our village industries, in the same way men have made an organized effort to destroy women's industries. From the Vedas we learn that in those days only women did weaving. ...But later on man took up the work of weaving and gave the woman the work of filling bobbin. That is, man took up the important work and left the less important for the woman. ...Thus, women were given an inferior place.

(WP, 103)

Women Must Rebel

495. Had I been a woman, I would have revolted a great deal. I do want women to rise in revolt. But only she would be capable of it who is a personification of Vairagya, asceticism. Only when this attitude will find expression, motherhood will be realized. That is why I hold that women will have deliverance only when someone like Shankaracharya is born among them. If they want freedom, they should not allow themselves to be driven away by the current of (sex) desire. (SH, 14)

Women Should Be Self-Protected

496. Today we have made the relationship between man and woman artificial. We think that women are protected and men are their protectors. This is a mistake. In our society, woman should not be merely protected, she should be capable of self-protection as well. (WP, 32)

The Present Discrimination Between Men and Women Wrong

497. I am not inclined to recognize any difference between man and woman. I consider that women's social, family and political rights and responsibilities are exactly the same as men's. Both have equal economic rights, and both have equal moral capacities. They should be educated together and should study the same subjects. Their differences are external, not basic. I am aware of the existence of a different opinion, but I am expressing here my own view. They have the same human soul and, therefore, even if there are apparent external differences, there is no need to emphasize them. Because of these external differences, it is natural that there may be some difference in their fields of work, but the differences which are at present accepted are not justifiable. (ibid, 17-18)

498. Besides the school of thought which holds that women are-attached to the world while men are detached and desirous of *Moksha,* liberation, there is another and different school which says that women are superior to men. By nature, she has more of kindness. If the education of children and the government of society are handed over to her, it will be easy to realize a non-violent society. I also want women to participate in all these activities. They have been generally confined to men so far. Hence, I hold that the entry of women into those areas will impart some freshness to them. But I cannot agree with the new thinkers, since kindness and other such qualities are neither dependent on caste nor on sex. External differences may result in their varying modes of expression, but to hold that their qualities also vary is both against thought and experience. (SH, 2-3)

499. There is a popular notion that women are more passionate than men, but this is a mistaken idea. Women have to suffer the pains of childbirth and have to face great difficulties for their children's sake. Hence it does not seem that they would have greater liking for that passion because of which they have to undergo so much suffering. ...But people say that women have a strong wish for children, that they have a natural inclination for motherhood. It is possible that a woman may have a desire for a child, and that it may be more difficult for her than for a man to follow completely the ideal of not having any child at all, but after the birth of the first child, she should not be desirous of another because of the great suffering at childbirth. This is my analysis. I do not know how far it is correct. (WP, 77-78)

The Education of Men and Women

500. There are some common and some special factors in the education of men and women. The common factors outnumber special factors. Let us first look at the common ones.

The spirit of both men and women is equally pure. In this respect there is no difference between them. This is the first common factor. The second common factor is about 'desires'. Both have common desires like those of hunger and greed. They both bear the same relationship to nature. It is not that nature appears to them differently. This is the third common factor.

Thus it is clear that in the education of men and women a greater part should be common. The laws of the development of qualities apply to them equally. Taking these things into consideration, I say that they should get the same education and both should be educated together. (SH, 95)

Mixing of Boys and Girls

501. Many object to boys and girls mixing together. They say that such an experiment will prove dangerous. But the thing that will be proved will be what we ourselves want to prove. It all depends on our strength. However, the mixing of any two persons has both good points as well as some dangers. Some ask me, "Will the Brahmin and Harijan boys be kept in the same room ? Will they not be spoiled due to such association?"

I reply that I too have the same fear. In keeping them together the danger is that the Harijans will also acquire the false vanity which had been confined to the Brahmins so far. But we have to undertake such risks when we have taken up the work of education. Without risk, there is no experiment, and without experiment, there is no education. (ibid, 4-5)

502. Many questions are raised in this country on the mixing of men and women. They are simply based on the anxiety as to how the purity of social climate will be maintained then. I too am anxious about its purity. I want it to be thousand times more than what it is at present. For I know that our existing purity is only superficial.

Purity is something inner. I even hold that the living together of men and women should help them in becoming purer. However, the present social climate is against it. The reason for it lies in our literature. (ibid, 12)

503. I consider that even between man and man it is not good to be too closely acquainted physically. They should be mentally and spiritually acquainted, and physical acquaintance should not exceed that which is necessary for service. (WP, 81)

The Real Meaning of Pativratya, Loyalty to Husband

504. Today the term 'Pativratya' has been taken to mean that howsoever the husband be, good or bad, his wife should become one with him. She has no independent existence of her own. But the real meaning of Pativratya is to cooperate in the vows of one's husband. If a husband is a drunkard, he should not be helped to drink. On the contrary, taking hold of his hand, his drinking cup is to be thrown away. She should tell him, "If you do not give up drinking, I shall not cook for you." If at this he says, "1 shall beat you", then say to him, "You beat me. This will hurt your hand, but I shall not cook for you." This is the Dharma of a Pativrata. I think it to be a duty of women to keep men under control. (SH, 79)

Opposition to Dowry, Not to Gift

505. Gift or *dahej* is given in marriage. In other words, when you give away the daughter, you also give some gold and other things alongwith her. None else has a right over it. It is considered as *Stridhan,* the girl's property. I am not opposed to such a gift. I am against *dahej,* demand, taking money from the girl's family on the plea that the boy has done M.A. and so much money has been incurred on it.

(M, April 1974, 209)

Divorce in Special Circumstances

506. If there is injustice, cruelty and hatred between husband and wife, children suffer. Under such conditions, there is no harm in recognizing the right of divorce. The whole of morality is based on free will, not on compulsion. It does not ordain, it permits. Therefore a provision for divorce in special circumstances would be considered as justifiable. (SH, 24)

Women and Violence

507. As long as violence is your weapon, the women will have a second place no matter how lofty the principles may be. However much we may try, they cannot have the first place. If that is to be accorded to them, it is essential that the means of protection must be nonviolent. (SH, 35)

Women and Army

508. At one time it was held that a women's field was her house. Even today, its management is bound to remain in her hands. But during the last twenty-five years men have so managed the world that it is today in a state of total perplexity and distress. This management led to two wars and the third may occur at any time. They now want to give guns into the hands of women and to raise their regiments on the plea of equality between men and women, instead of handing over to them such control that they may be able to turn back men from such actions and to bring into action their own motherly strength. ... All this goes on in the name of fearlessness and women too think that they would perhaps become fearless if they have guns in their hands. But the gun has nothing to do with fearlessness. Had it been the case, the Americans and the Russians would have been fearless.

Though they are so strongly armed, their hearts beat fast. They are afraid of each other. (SH, 126-127)

Women and Public Life

509. So far, whenever there has been any effort to bring women into public life, it has been according to the wishes of men. They have been told, "Come and fight elections, join the army, march forward, prove your skill in marksmanship on that flying bird and so on!" ...This won't advance them in public field. They will only become henchmen (henchperson) and nothing else. (WP, 51-52)

Women Are Not Weak

510. It was later that women were called *Abala,* powerless, in our society. The original term for them is not *Abala*, but *Mahila,* that is, great, powerful. It is only the female idol that has been accepted as a symbol of Shakti, power, not the male idol. (VP, 1.1.1959)

No Exaggerated Respect for Women

511. Just as it is wrong to discriminate against women, it is equally so to show exaggerated respect for them. (WP, 83)

Let Man and Woman Supplement Each Other

512. Man and woman can also become the protector of each other. Let woman save man, and man woman. It is necessary that they become man and woman by supplementing each other and thereby removing each other's deficiencies. This means that a man will have to become a woman and every woman, a man, and both will have to become complete. (SH, 14-15)

The Area of Woman's Work

513. It may be that women may have to do more of housework, but they should also get an opportunity to work outside. Such a division that outside work for men and housework for women is wrong. Both should find places in both. (Purnea, 143)

514. Women should take into their hands all those fields which are considered as cultural. Till now they have been mostly in the hands of men. All the epics of the world, be it Valmiki's Ramayan, Vyas' Mahabharat or the epics of Homer, Dante or

Milton, were works of men. In the Vedas, there are a few hymns composed by women and in the later period we find the names of Akka Mahadevi of Karnatak, Mira of Rajasthan and of a few others, but, on the whole, women have not much influenced literature. Today even the social work of educating children is in the hands of men. They have no aptitude for it. They may have the ability to educate grown-up boys and girls, but what do they know about treating primary school children? The whole of this field should be in the hands of women. They should have place in the fields of literature, education, religious matters, etc. (BG, VII, 139-140)

Vinoba's Expectations from Women

515. Menfolk are today running like horses. You must hold their reins. (H, 4.6.1955, 105)

516. Social and political life the world over has all these years been led and moulded by men. It is now time that women enter this field because the way men have done it proves their utter incompetence for the task.

With the discovery of the atom bomb, violence has reached a stage when it has to be abandoned and nonviolence accepted in its place as the governing principle of human conduct in all its forms.

Women, in view of their inherent qualities of love and capacity for sacrifice, are naturally expected to play a major part in working out this change. (H, 6.2.1954, 391)

Attempts for the Advancement of Women in India

517. With regards to the efforts made for the advancement of women in India, we have, in ancient times, the names of Shri Krishna and Lord Mahavira, and, in modern times, we have the name of Gandhi. It is not that the intervening period was absolutely blank. It has its own history. But these three names can never be forgotten.

Whatever Lord Krishna did for women is being sung for the last five thousand years....The love of Shri Krishna for the shepherdesses, the respect in which he held womenfolk, and all that he did for women as their friend, these stories are unrivalled in the history of India.

The story of Lord Mahavira is extraordinary. He did not recognize any difference in spiritual rights. As a result of it, amongst his disciples there were more nuns than monks. That tradition is still alive in the Jain religion.

Shri Krishna's work was not that of initiation, but rather that men and women should be equal from the point of devotion and that due to detachment and purity they should feel no embarrassment in their mutual relations. This is a basic principle of life. Even if women are accorded the right to Sannyasa, we need not fear that many of them will take to it. It is, however, a different matter. In a way, there is a danger in accepting equal right to Sannyasa. But Shri Krishna showed us that in ordinary family life we should not be embarrassed, we should meet like brothers and sisters. He demonstrated it through his own life.

Gandhiji revealed the whole power of women. The weapon of nonviolence came to the fore. Women can use it with greater efficiency than men. (WP, 22-25)

The Importance of the Rural Areas

518. The rural areas constitute our foundation. Even today our culture can be observed there. They are our backbone, our soul. (S, Sept. 1951, 603)

Villages, Then and Now

519. Men in India have always lived in villages and the village has been held in high esteem. A Vedic text, for example, says, "May our villages grow and prosper and be strong." We thus find the village ideal upheld in India from very old times. Every village in those days was a State in itself. It was ruled by a Panchayat, that is a village council consisting of five elders representing the five Varnas.The members of the Panchayat worked with one accord like the five fingers of a hand. What the five said was for the people, as the proverb has it even today, the word of God.

The village provided for all its needs, both intellectual and material, locally. It was for all practical purposes a self-contained unit. Every village had its carpenters, cobblers and weavers. They served the peasants in their various ways and received an adequate share in the produce. The share increased or decreased according to increase in the year's production. The artisans were thus members of the village community on the same level as the peasants. The land and the produce was owned and shared by the community as a whole.

The things have changed since then and today we find that though the villages still produce all the raw material, they depend for most of their wants on cities.

(H, 21.11.1953, 297)

Agrarianism

520. Agriculture is an extremely old profession. It is the highest worship. It is a wonderful remedy for all our ills. Rishis (seers) and Krishi (agriculture) are intimately related.

(BY, 28.11.1958)

521. The most dangerous thing for man is to get uprooted from soil. Just as every tree is rooted in the soil, in the same way everyman should be connected with it. To disconnect a man from agriculture is to cut him off from soil.

Everyone should get an opportunity to work in the field for two to three hours. In the remaining time, he may take to some other work. Agriculture is a basic activity. Field is a fine place for worship, a fine gymnasium and a good school for knowledge. (BG, VI, 106, 107)

522. We want to create a society wherein the ideal will be that every person is associated with agriculture.

Agriculture is indispensable for the development of life. I would not, however, go to the extent of saying that none can be a 'man' unless he is a farmer. The soul has many potentialities and it is not impossible for one to develop oneself fully without any association with agriculture. Yet, it may normally be said that full development is not possible without it.

I am of the view that cultivation will help in the observance of Brahmacharya. If all people take to it, there will be greater self-control in the country. (KP, 51, 52)

What Are Cities ?

523. I have defined city as a place where a man does not recognize his neighbours. (Sarvodaya Yatra, 104)

City People and Villagers Compared

524. We city people lack devotion. Faith and devotion are found in villages. There are several evils and defects in the cities. They can be pointed out, they can be told. They are observed less in villages. Hence on seeing villagers, I feel much satisfaction. On the whole, the Indian villagers are somewhat more dynamic and less indolent than those of other lands. But the city people here are seen to be comparatively more indolent, weaker and duller. There (in the West) they are more resourceful and are always engaged in one thing or another. The intelligence of the city people of this country appears to have lost its acuteness.

It does not, however, mean that Indian villagers do not stand in need of reforms. They are acquiring the evils of the city people. (BY, 25.7.1958)

City Life Rejected

525. I fail to understand why people live in cities and what happiness they get there. They mistake for real happiness what is an appearance only, and, on the whole, they suffer more and get less happiness. In other words, they are at a loss.

(BY, 9.3.1956)

The Two Worlds of Cities and Villages

526. They (cities and villages) are two worlds, between whom there is hardly any communication. Their faces are turned in opposite directions and as a result both are drying up. The cities are soulless, village life is nothing but an unrelieved tale of drudgery and monotony. Their implements and their way of life are untouched by any scientific knowledge.

(B, 9.5.1956, 4)

Advice to Villagers

527. The small and expensive houses in the cities in congested localities are no good. It is much better for you to live in your village hut and enjoy fresh air under the radiant sun. Of course, you should improve your existing houses and plan for better ventilation and better sanitation. But do not try to rush to the cities in search for higher standard of living.

Who enjoys a higher standard of living, the so-called rich person who lives in the city in a crowded locality and hangs on his walls paintings depicting various natural scenes or he who lives in a village under healthy conditions and is in direct contact with nature ?

Which is a higher standard of living ? To live a normal life, to work for one's own livelihood in open air conditions, or to live in cities on the labour of others and then to take physical exercises to improve one's digestion and appetite ? I will any day prefer the former. (WV, 37 and 38)

How to Re-Invigorate the Villages ?

528. We need to do three things for re-invigorating the village life. First, we must change the system of education; next, we must start village industries; and, thirdly, land must be redistributed. (H, 21.11.1953, 298)

Relationship between Cities and Villages

529. I do not want to destroy the industries that already exist in the towns and they certainly should have the right to go on working for the town population and perhaps for export. But the industrial goods should not be forced on any one. The villagers should be free to put barriers against the import of industrial textiles and food stuffs into the villages.

(H, 10.4.1954, 47)

530. If we wish that the houses be strong, it would not do to have a weak ground-floor. All of our articles of food come from rural areas. The life of the city people is dependent on them.In other words, the peasants of rural areas serve the whole country and then only the life of all is maintained. Hence the city people should think about their benefactors.

Just as different organs of the body cooperate with and are sensitive to each other, similarly there should be cooperation and affection between the rural and urban peoples.

(PP, 11.7.1957)

531. Since the attainment of Swaraj they (the townsmen) have forgotten the distinction between Swadeshi and foreign articles.They purchase whatever looks cheap, good and attractive.......

Such is the picture of the towns. On the other side, the villages have become depleted of all their industries. Their petty vocations have been snatched away from them by the cities. ... The proper thing for cities to do is to maintain village industries in the village itself, and to establish only such industries in the cities as will stop the influx of foreign goods. If they do this, the towns and the villages can work together in concord and raise the prosperity of the country. Just as they declare some forest as 'reserved', so the need is to declare some of the industries as 'reserved for the villages'.

If this is not done, the very existence of the towns will be in danger. On the one side, they would be exploited by foreigners and, on the other, they would be attacked and looted by hungry and unemployed villagers. What I ask townsmen to practise is merely enlightened self-interest.

(H, 12.5.1951, 86)

Future of the Cities

532. I hold that as man will come to have a more developed attitude towards life, everyone will maintain contact with nature. Then the cities will be so built that from one's house one will be able to have a view of the fields and the sky.

(BY, 13.7.1958)

533. Houses with fifty storeys have now been constructed.There are 12.5 million people in New York and 8 million in London. Thus men have been brought to live in giant cities. They have no contact with Nature....When innumerable people live under such artificial conditions, I prophesy that all these cities are going to be depopulated. They will be facing hard times. They will be destroyed by those very hands which built them. As human perspective will develop, mankind will get more farsighted. Society will be re-planned. (Ambar Charkha, 4)

VII
ECONOMIC IDEAS

Principles of Economics

534. An economics which goes against humanity, is not a human economics but a demoniac economics. (PP, 27.5.1957)

535. Mathematical calculations are universally applicable but it is not so with the theories of economics. They are variable in so far as time and place are concerned. Principles of economics which can be suitably applied in India, may not suit America or Russia. Even in India, the suitability of certain principles of economics may vary from time to time. (B, 15.4.1959, 404)

The Defect of Modern Economics

536. In modern economics, the human factor has been reduced and greater attention has been paid to the increase of mechanical power. (Ambar Charkha, 3)

The Approach of Sarvodaya Economics

537. We do not attach importance to the principles of the so-called general economics since they often signify greed. We have to apply the same logic to a village which we apply to a family. ...Hence the incentives accepted by the society so far, are not acceptable to us. The basis of our incentive will be spiritual, and this work (of Gramdan) is based on it. That is why we have to see that people develop day by day greater and greater propensity for morality and they come to feel joy in continuous sacrifice. It would not matter then whether they get more money or not. ... We are of the view that 'wealth' differs from 'money' as much as a god differs from a demon. (BG, III, 289-290)

The Money Incentive

538. The exponents of the theory of incentives forget that if higher gains goad me to greater efforts, they may also goad someone else to rob me. The theory of incentives is bound to create inequality and conflict. Security and peace can only prevail when there is equality. (B, 16.1.1957, 3)

Money Economy

539. I want to discard money economy, i.e., a social order based on money and to establish in its place an order based on labour. (HS, 16.1.1957)

540. At least I, for one, see the salvation of India through only the double-edged weapon, namely, freedom from the lure of money and performance of body-labour. In it I see the acme of Gandhiji's philosophy, a synthesis with Communism and an antidote to both Communism and Capitalism. (KGM, 34)

541. All Rajas (monarchs) have gone away for good in democracy, but money continues to be on the throne. It rules our life. It is at the basis of our dealings. But it is thoroughly a rogue or villain by character. It resembles a knave through and through. A knave's word cannot be relied upon. So also money's. Sometimes it fetches eight seers of wheat, other times five and hardly two seers at still other times. ... Consequently, its integrity is at a discount. Man has exalted money to the highest status. Hence the more he gets it, the more secure he feels. And since the value of money, like knave's words, is undependable, his passion for money knows no bounds. The higher the passion, the greater the avidity.

Thus in all walks of life money enjoys ascendancy. Everybody, from peasant to the trader and on to the Brahmin, is mad after it. The Government is equally mad after it. Hence, it realizes revenue in cash and not in kind. It also encourages money crops like tobacco, jute, etc. We have to break this vicious circle and bring down money from the pedestal it enjoys today. Bringing down money, we have to raise the dignity of Lakshmi (wealth), which is born of productive bodily labour. Money is made at the press in Nasik. You can print any amount of it. But Lakshmi is produced by hard work, toil and sweat.

(H, 8.1.1955, 364)

Preference for Labour Currency

542. Question : You have denounced money. If you despise it, how can there be a compromise between your thinking and the practical viewpoint ?

Vinoba : It is a good question. I did not say that money is something to be despised. What I said was that money is something unstable whose value is always changing and we have to avoid it. I want to save the country from the prevailing money economy, which has ruined the villages. If the rural people fulfil their primary needs themselves, they will be able to avoid (the use of) money.

Question : Will you prefer some currency with fixed value ?

Vinoba : Of course. I have already said that I don't favour barter. I prefer paper currency provided there is a reference to labour hours on it and not to the money.

Question : But when there will be variation between one work and another, there will also be qualitative difference between them. Then how will your currency be able to maintain the same value ?

Vinoba : This problem is a creation of the capitalist society. The method advocated by me is that the value of one hour of honest labour, whether the person concerned is male or female, should be the same. I want to implement in the whole society the system prevailing in a family. All get food in a family though they do not do the same work. The females cook food, the children sweep and the men work in the field. All these works are necessary and they have equal value. If we take the whole society as one unit and decide to build it up anew, the question of this equality and inequality will not arise.

(S, Jan. 1952, 1240)

Revenue Realization in Kind Favoured

543. When there was control on cereals, there was blackmarketing. On it having been lifted, the prices shot up. In my opinion, there can be only one way out of it. This difficulty can be solved if the Government realizes its land revenue in kind. If it has a good stock of cereals, the rates in the open market will get automatically controlled. (HS, 22.8.1948, 217)

Charging Interest, A Sin

544. To charge interest is a great sin. It has been assailed by all religions. (L. 197)

Economic Equality

545. As long as economic equality is not established in the country, there would be no peace. (S, Nov. 1951, 1056)

546. It is the economic inequality among the people that is making India unhappy. Political independence would be complete only when it is followed by economic independence. It is therefore the duty of the people to establish economic equality. By equality I do not mean absolute equality. Our aim should be to give people all things that are necessary for the maintenance of the body. The luxurious life of the West, which led to greed and wars after wars among nations and created dissatisfaction and unhappiness, should not be the ideal for India. (SE. Aug, 1952, 30)

The Ownership and Management of Industry

547. What is true about land is also true about the factories and other property. Nobody can own them because of the investment of certain capital. As these investors are the products of the society, they, as also their wealth, belong to the society. No doubt, they apply their intellect to the task, but there are others also who labour therein. So, all of them, whether they contribute intellectual or bodily labour, should draw like amounts. And in times to come, the factory owner would get only as much as others in the factory. It would be owned by the society. In the transitory stage, there would be a partnership of both the owners and the labourers. What is required to be done is that the labourers must be equipped intellectually so that they may participate in its management. (H, 11.12.1954, 327)

Why the Present Attachment to Private Property ?

548. The development of the attachment for private property in the people is due to the present social structure and laws. (BY, 27.5.1956)

549. A man wants ownership because he desires to live on the labour of others. (VP, 19.1.1958)

Abolition of Private Ownership

550. Private ownership is now being assailed at on one side by self-knowledge and on the other by science. (BY, 2.11.1956)

551. **Question :** Do you then want to abolish private property totally ?

Vinoba : The answer depends on what you understand by 'private property'. Instead of abolishing private property, I want that the emotional involvement with it should go.

Questioner : It is getting very difficult to understand what you say.

Vinoba : For example, there is my physical body. I should not have the feeling that this body is only meant for me, but it is for the whole society. However, its growth is my responsibility.

It is only nominally my personal property. It is not for my enjoyment. Thus my effort is to instil into the minds of the people the idea that 'private property' does not belong to any of us, but to all. (BY, 19.11.1956)

552. I also hold that if someone has earned something by his honest efforts, none should attack it. Its expropriation would be wrong. But as the word 'property' denotes, one has to see as to how it was acquired, whether the means were proper or improper. If they were not proper, the term 'property' does not apply to it. But if it has been acquired by moral means, it is something sacrosanct. However, if a father earns something by honest labour, we tell him that you are entitled to your earnings but relinquish that right as far as your progeny is concerned. And if he agrees to it, it would not be deemed immoral but moral. (PP, 8.5.1957)

Decentralization and Ownership

553. If power is decentralized while ownership is being maintained, it shall only be a scheme of decentralized exploitation. It should be a prior condition for the membership of cooperative societies that ownership must be relinquished.

(BY, 17.10.1958)

Expropriation Not Favoured

554. I agree that there is no sacredness in private property. But it is equally necessary to understand that forcible expropriation can never end the attachment and greed of man for wealth. The Muslims were great iconoclasts. They broke idols. But what happened ? Idolatry has not vanished from our land. If anything, it has become stronger. If they had explained to the people why idolatry was wrong and convinced them that it was meaningless, the result would have been different.

(B, 10.4.1957, 5)

How to Achieve the Results of Expropriation ?

555. When the question as to how the city people can be made to relinquish their property was raised before me, I offered two suggestions :

(1) There should be so many Gramdans that they may be able to exert moral pressure on the cities.

(2) Form Shanti Sena. When businessmen will find that it is of service to them, they will come to like it and thus the purpose will be served. (VP, 27.2.1958)

The Safest Bank

556. If there is any bank safest for man, it is society.

(BY, 2.11.1956)

Nationalization Not Favoured

557. **Question :** Why does the India Government not nationalize big industries ?

Vinoba : The reason why they do not is that they do not believe in it. There is a strain of capitalism in their economic outlook. Moreover, it is not true that nationalization is bound to solve problems. Railways have been nationalized but that has not brought any remarkable advantage to the people. If the Government cannot use their present powers to the best account, what is the use of vesting it with more power ? We cannot do much until people develop character. For example, there is a great deal of bribery going on in the administrative offices. If now we put more powers into the hands of the officers, things may deteriorate still further. What we need therefore as a condition precedent to our success in our efforts is the mental and moral purification of the people so that their conduct may improve. (H, 1.8.1953, 170)

Increase in Productivity and Social Progress

558. A society without vision is a decadent society. Vision gives vitality and strength and inspires a people to noble adventure. It creates the national ethos. Society progresses when its members have a sense of social purpose. No society can survive or hold its head high unless its members have a sense of purpose.

Increasing production or the doubling of national income may be necessary but it cannot be called a national objective. Industrial nations of the West have done it. We see that some insects and animals also show an acquisitive instinct. In a poor country like India it is obvious that we need higher production urgently. No one can belittle its importance. And yet it cannot take the place of a national purpose. In spite of economic plenty there is fear and a sense of insecurity in the countries of the West. (B, 20.2.1957, 1)

Production and Distribution Must Go Together

559. It is argued that the 'first thing' necessary being full production, the problem of distribution may well wait for the present. But this is a mechanical way of reasoning. Mechanical methods might be good in processes of production, but their application in logic leads to fallacious thinking. If there were no production at all, there would be no problem of distribution. But since there is some production, the question of proper distribution automatically arises alongwith it. If,again, distribution could be postponed until full production was reached, perhaps it would be possible to put off its consi- deration to a later stage. But we do consume day after day whatever is produced. And while some secure far more than what is just, others don't get enough. And it is the producers who almost invariably get less. If unequal distribution adversely affected non-producers only, there could be perhaps some justification for it. Even if it had been the case that though the non-producers got a larger share, producers were able to get sufficient enough, the consideration of equitable distribution could be deferred. But the present condition does not admit of patient awaiting.

Under these circumstances, the issue whether production or distribution should be regarded as more important, is irrelevant and one cannot be preferred to another without harm.

Another error involved in such compartmental consideration about the problems of production and distribution is that it might lead to the adoption of such methods of production as to make equitable distribution impossible later on. Our methods of production must be such as to solve the problem of equitable distribution simultaneously with increased production. (H. 12.2.1950, 427)

Life of Simplicity, Its Advantages

560. Simplicity highly becomes of man. It is specially so when the people are poor. No matter whether there be poverty or affluence, simplicity is a must. For, when we lead a simple life, we do not have to devote much attention to the externals. We can concentrate on inner things, we can think more. (PP, 16.6.1957)

561. More attention should be paid to raising the level of thinking than to that of living. No doubt, in a country like India, where people do not even get the necessities of life, the standard of living will have to be raised. But higher thinking is only possible with simple living. Wherever the standard of living rises too high, the level of thinking goes down. (BY, 7.9.1956)

What is Meant by Simple Life ?

562. By simple life is meant ordering of one's life in accordance with the standard prevailing in the society as a whole.

We do not want the people to revert to the past ages. The necessities of the present age must be fulfilled, but it should be done taking into consideration the level of the country.
(Pravachan no. 344 of 1957)

Happiness and Standard of Living

563. Wherever the standard of living is very low, it must be raised, but it should also be realized that happiness does not increase by merely increasing material conveniences or gadgets. It is wrong to think that we shall be happier if there are more goods in the house. Attempt should be made to raise the standard of living while also developing spiritual attitude.
(BY,14.10.1955)

564. Some have presumed that higher the standard of living, the greater will be the happiness. But God has not so constituted man. He is only happy in the middle position. It is, however, difficult to know where it lies. Extreme poverty leads to the sins of various types. The same is true of much affluence. Hence, man only derives peace and satisfaction when he keeps away both from comforts and misery. (BG, V, 43)

Economic Decentralization, Its Real Meaning

565. Both the word (decentralization) and its meaning, or the idea behind it are new. But, one may ask, was it all not decentralized before the advent of the machine age ? What is new in it then ? Well, the fact is that prior to the machine age it was not a decentralized order. The fact that industries were carried on in villages in independent small units or plants does not constitute decentralization. Decentralization presupposes a comprehensive all-pervading idea behind the various village industries. In the absence of any such idea, small non-centralized industrial units mean merely scattered industries. There were plenty of them before the machine age. But they were easily swept off with the first impact of the machine age. Decentralization (that is intelligent non-centralization) will stand on firm foundation. Not only will it not be blown off, but will disintegrate the machine age itself..... When we affirm that decentralization will disintegrate the machine age, what I mean to convey is that we shall disintegrate it after we have drawn out all that is good in it. Indeed, it will not be disintegrated until then. The former non-centralized village industries lacked this power of digesting and assimilating the advantage of the machine age. This is the fundamental difference between the purposeful decentralized industries and the old non-centralized village industries. Hence, both the word *decentralization* and the idea which it expresses are new. If this distinction is borne in mind, most of the objections which are brought against decentralization will become as blunt as a sword struck against a rock. (KGM, 26-28)

Science is Welcome

566. Some think that Baba (Vinoba) prefers Ambar (Ambar spinning wheel) to a mill, small spinning wheel to Ambar and Takli to the spinning wheel. He would be happy if the Takli is made of wood, and he would feel like being in heaven if he could spin with fingers instead of a Takli. Those who think like this are under a misconception. Not only this, I can even claim that during the last ten years I did not come across any person who had been so much insisting on science as I had been doing. (VP, 5.12.1959)

567. If the introduction of science and technology helps small tools, I need it. I am in favour of it. The only conditions are that neither should they be monopolized by any particular individual, nor should they result in the exploitation of others. That much precaution would have to be taken. Therefore when you say that the industrial civilization is going to have a comprehensive impact on life, I have a feeling that it too is an advance in the same way as there had been from the Greek culture onwards. Such developments always create some problems, and it has also happened in this case. However, its solution lies in finding out the purposes for which it can be advantageously used and not in rejecting it altogether, (VC no. 5, 38)

Industrialism, No Curse

568. What is to be understood is that though in the beginning the new technology has resulted in the exploitation of man, yet I hold that it has a purpose to serve in the world, which is to liberate man from the unnecessary labour he has been compelled to do so far. It is possible to achieve it if proper use is made of technology. Hence I have faith that the prevailing concept of industrialism will lose its hold after it has done good. I do not consider it to be a curse. It has many demerits but the next step will only follow when its good points have been assimilated. (ibid, 35)

Science and Technology Not Identical

569. It should be comprehended that science and technology are not identical. A misconception prevails in this country that science stands for big machines. But this wrong impression should be removed by us. Science means the knowledge of nature. Hence, just as it is utilised in big machines, it can also be used in small ones. (VP, 2.6.1959)

General Attitude towards Machinery

570. I am not an irrationalist. Machine lacks intelligence. I shall accept those machines which are necessary and reject those which are not. (KD, 133)

571. The importance of the implements should not exceed that of the sense organs. How will it do if a cycle acquires greater importance than legs. Spectacles are important, but they have their place (as aids to the eyes). (SKA, 31)

572. Let us remember that a machine is made for man and must ever remain subservient to him. It must never be permitted to ride over him. (B, 7. 5. 1958, 20)

573. Machines are of three categories, time-saving, destructive and productive. I am not against time-saving machines, such as trains, aeroplanes etc. Though they do not add to the production of the country, they save time.

Destructive machines, such as guns, bombs etc., have no place in nonviolence. We are, therefore, opposed to them.

Productive machines are of two varieties, those that are helpful and those that are harmful. Machines that reduce employment are harmful to human beings. Whether a particular machine is harmful or helpful depends upon time, place and circumstance in which it is used. A machine which might be harmful in one country might be helpful in another. A machine which might be helpful at one time might become harmful at another time. So also with change in circumstances. No set formula can be laid down to judge whether a machine is harmful or helpful. We, therefore, have neither a blind infatuation for machinery nor an irrational opposition to it. Service of man will be the sole criterion for acceptance or rejection of a machine. (H, 5.9.1953, 209)

Agricultural Machinery

574. We are not against the use of machinery or scientific improvements for better cultivation, but mechanical energy should only supplement human energy and not altogether liquidate human power, resulting in unemployment and unequal distribution of wealth. (SE, May 1958, 370)

575. People ask why do you not use tractors ? I reply that it has two big drawbacks. We sow maize and then we get both maize and fodder. Your tractor neither eats fodder nor it gives manure. My bullock does both. (SKA, 32)

576. A scheme to provide ten-hour work to all is bound to fail, and it would also not be correct. Therefore the work load on men should be lightened, production should be increased and none should be unemployed. We should use such instruments as correspond to our view. At present very good implements are available, which, if properly used, can easily increase agricultural yield four or five times. (AAV, 141)

Attitude towards the Use of Power

577. Electricity and gas may be used for housework.

(BY, 31.7.1959)

578. Today the boys of the Paramdham Ashram had come. Paramdham has been electrified. I told them that full use be made of electricity. I do not want it for light at night. It should mainly be used for industries. It may be used to draw water, to run the press etc. (AAV, 141)

579. There is a Gujarati gentleman of Hubli. At his place he operates his Magan Charkha with electric power. By spinning on it, a single person is able to spin enough yarn for the cloth needed by the family. He asked me if that cloth would be considered Khadi. I replied, "Yes. If you don't sell it, it will certainly be reckoned as Khadi. You can use electricity for self-reliance." Thus, machines and science can be utilised for repairing tools and operating them with the aid of power. But there are some limits too. It should neither lead to external nor to internal exploitation. Secondly, improvements be made in a planned manner. (ibid, 144)

580. I do not want to eschew any kind of power. Only the Spirit should be in control of it. Power should serve man and not become his master. It is not enough that it is cheap, even if it is available for cooking. It must be owned by the villagers. If you want to fix priorities in power distribution, it should first be received by Koraput, not by Bombay.
(B, 26.11.1958, 252)

The Importance of Village Industries

581. I am quite clear that if anyone left village industries aside and yet wished to follow nonviolence, he would be pursuing an impossible ideal..Like Uma and Shiva, village economy and nonviolence are wedded together and would always stay together. Their mutual relationship could be stated as under :

(a) Where there is nonviolence, there will always be village economy; and (b) where there is no village economy, there will be no nonviolence.

Readers will note that I have not said that where there is village economy, there will definitely be nonviolence.That would be a wrong statement. (H, 27.5.1950, 113)

582. In a vast country like India, the peasantry cannot survive by relying on agriculture alone. Village industries are indispensable for the peasant's survival. (H, 10.9.1955, 219)

583. If I am satisfied that any other scheme can provide full employment to my people without exploiting them, I would unhesitatingly burn my wooden Charkha and use it for cooking my own meal. (WV, 32)

What Kind of Village Industries ?

584. My principle in this regard is that all those industries whose raw material is produced in the villages and finished articles are used in consumption, should be reserved for villages. (The Khadi World. Vol. 1, 83)

585. It is not at all proper to compel a man to undertake physical labour for eight hours a day to earn his living. If such is the condition of village industries, they should be given up. If a strong healthy man cannot maintain himself properly by working for four hours, it is something which cannot be put up with. (BY, 31.7.1959)

Village Industries Defended

586. Some people remark that this is an age of large-scale producton. What use can it have for our small toy-like instruments ? I tell them that I am not satisfied with production only on a large-scale. Let us, however, be clear as to what we mean by this production on the largest scale. In my judgement, it is only these small instruments which are capable of production on the largest scale because they need millions of people to use them. In your large-scale industries you can employ only a million or two million hands, you can feed at the most a million or two million mouths. But these small instruments require hundreds of millions to handle them. They feed countless millions. Will you call it small-scale production ?...The man who compares a drop of rain with water stored in a cistern and belittles the value of the tiny drop betrays poor understanding. The tiny drop of rain irrigates the entire earth giving fresh life to every blade of corn that grows. Therefore it is mighty in spite of its littleness... The economy of village industries is the plan of universal production on the largest scale in its true sense. (H, 26.12.1948, 360-361)

587. To say that village industries cannot be adopted as they cannot compete with mills in point of efficiency discloses a wrong approach to the question. The way the West went should not be copied blindly by us. Gandhiji has already warned us that that way lies a disaster for us. When we advocate equality, its opponents cannot of course argue for inequality, but they speak of inefficiency. We surely want efficiency, but in the name of efficiency millions of mouths cannot be starved. I desire full employment for all. If village industries help us achieve this, we will adopt them. It does not deserve the name of efficiency which makes millions starve for want of employment. (H, 5.9.1953, 210)

588. Khadi seems to cost more than mill-made cloth, but one must think more realistically in terms of social costs. In India textile mills have led to an increase in unemployment; those who are out of work have to be fed at least at a subsistence level. If the cost of maintaining them were to be borne by the mills, would mill-made cloth be cheaper than Khadi ? ...There is something spurious and deceptive about the comparative cheapness of mill-made cloth. (B, 10.10.1956, 6)

589. People go on talking about high prices and low prices as if they were more important than consideration for the country as a whole and concern for the poor people in it. Low prices are not a panacea. If attempts are made to cheapen food grains or cloth in villages, the low prices will, at a certain stage, prove disastrous to the cultivator or the weaver by reducing his income below the starvation level. In this preoccupation with the price level, lives of the multitudes are also treated like commodities. (ibid)

Reservation Advocated for Village Industries

590. In a big country like India there is scope both for large-scale and village industries. But their spheres should be clearly demarcated. I want that some industries should be reserved for villages, specially those for which raw material was there in the villages, e.g., cotton.....If we demarcate like this, there can be some big industries in the cities. (H, 11.9.1954, 227)

Village Industries and Government

591. In fact they (the Government) have not a clear mind on the subject. It is said that the report of the Planning Commission is subject to improvement. This may mean that village industries will gradually prosper. It may also mean that they will gradually disappear. Yet, due to the pressure of the public opinion, they seem to realize the place of village industries more and more. ...But in no case they regard them of more than auxiliary help, fit for so-called transitory period.They do not find them essential for a new order. They are there for want of any alternative. (H, 18.12.1954, 338)

592. You want village industries to stand on their own feet! First you cut off my feet and then you ask me to stand on my own legs. You should rather admire my ability to walk even then with the support of my hands. You must recognize the fact that Gandhiji carried out Khadi and village industries programme in the face of the vehement opposition offered by an alien government, both by its policy and intent. Far from admitting it, you tell us now about its impractibility on the ground that it could not succeed in spite of twenty-five years' work of such an eminent person as Gandhiji. I ask you whether Khadi has or has not contributed, say even ten per cent, to our freedom movement ? If you admit it, why should you not support it ? It is very much like an ungrateful son abandoning his old mother after coming into his own.

(Talk with a Planning Commission Member, KW, Vol. I, 81-82)

Khadi and Other Village Industries

593. Other village industries are joined to Khadi. Khadi alone will not survive without them. (SE, March-April, 1976, 333)

Khadi, A Symbol of Revolution

594. I am not surprised that the spinning wheel does not spread rapidly. It is not a new kind of cigarette or tea to attract people. It is a new and revolutionary idea which goes counter to the prevailing currents of thought. He alone can spin who has the courage to go against the modern world currents. I do not, therefore, lose hope at the slow progress of the spinning wheel; rather I feel all the more earnest in its cause.

(H, 17.10. 1948, 277)

595. The other items (other than Khadi) of constructive programme are good, and have to be worked out. But they are not representative of the Sarvodaya ideal, because other items are not inconsistent with other conceptions. For instance, no one would doubt that the service of lepers is a necessary item; and so too village sanitation and health. It is not so with Khadi.There is opposition to it. It is said to be inconsistent with the modern age, which in common parlance is called the age of 'mechanized industrialization'. The older generation called it the age of *Kali* (strife). Ours is a rebellion against *Kali.* Khadi must, therefore, occupy the central place in our thought and services; all the rest would adjust themselves around it. We might and should render other services also, but if we admit defeat in Khadi, then I have personally no doubt that the rest of our programme becomes one of secondary importance only. (H, 3.4.1949, 40)

Feelings Associated with the Spinning Wheel

596. Among the feelings associated with the spinning wheel those of sympathy for the poor, respect for (voluntary) poverty and finding joy in it, are the important ones. Nothing else has the capability of the Charkha to bring about unity between the rich and the poor.

Just as a man has a tendency to get violent if he keeps a sword with him, similarly he acquires composure of mind by plying a spinning wheel. (KV, 12, 13)

Spinning, Not for Money but Cloth

597. One thing is obvious. If one plants a mango tree, one should not expect to get bananas from it. Thus from yarn one can get cloth, not money. It is wrong to think of earning money from yarn. (B, 23.5.1956, 6)

Khadi and Gram Swaraj

598. Khadi cannot survive apart from the concept of Gram Swaraj.

(KV, 90)

599. Khadi is as indispensable for Gram Swaraj as it was for country's independence. (ibid, 91)

How Can Khadi Survive ?

600. I wonder when the Government will understand the basic facts! But it is all the more important that our Khadi programme should not be dependent on the Government. It must stand on its own legs. If the villagers resolve that they will use nothing but cloth made in their own village, Khadi will never die out. (B, 18.7.1956, 5)

601. I personally think that now it would not be wise to insist on the plying of the old Charkha. (VC no. 6, 46)

People's Cloth

602. Half a century after its discovery in 1921 where does Khadi stand today ? ... In fact, Khadi is playing a vanishing trick.

So I placed an idea before the Khadi workers. This is about Lok Vastra (people's cloth). It would be produced and consumed in the village itself. There would be no sale and purchase of it outside the village. If a village decides, a unit of 8 to 10-spindle Charkhas could be operated by electric power. To clothe a population of one thousand, it would need a capital of six thousand rupees and a work-force of forty people. They will have to work full-time for different processes—carding, slivering, weaving, bleaching and so on. Since the Charkhas and looms would be operated by power, the cloth produced may not be Khadi in the strict traditional definition. That is why I have called it Lok Vastra or people's cloth.

The capital investment for this should come from the government. But no more government subsidy, as given in Khadi, would be necessary to run Lok Vastra. .. .If villages comprising a population of 250 millions decide to go in for Lok Vastra, ten million people will find full-time employment in it. The Lok Vastra produced in this manner will be cheaper than Khadi but costlier than mill cloth of the same quality. ...Its employment potential would be tremendous.

But it is not its employment potential alone that is important. More important is the emergence of a village community, self-sufficient in cloth. This will be the basis for building up a self-reliant village community. This self-reliant village community will be built on three pillars—Gramdan, Gram Sabha and Lok Vastra. This, I think, will be quite revolutionary. (SE, March 1973, 364)

Khadi and the Government

603. Today the Government is giving some help to Khadi,but it makes no secret of the fact that it looks on Khadi as a relief measure. It does not believe in the principle that Khadi stands for a way of life. (B, 8.10.1958, 194)

604. The Khadi work going on at present is an action preliminary to its death, and I call the Government aid 'oxygen'. (VP, 17.2.1959)

The Meaning of Self-Sufficiency

605. The idea of self-sufficiency is often misunderstood. It is certainly not opposed to wider cooperation. It need not be an isolating factor. I desire that the people should cooperate consciously on as wide a scale as possible. Self-sufficiency enables man to cooperate intelligently with as many groups in the world as he can. From the village republic to the world government there can be a continuous and widening sphere of intelligent cooperation in which all will help one another. (B, 22.8.1956, 5)

606. Our concept is not of narrow self-sufficiency, but of kindness and compassion. (BG, V, 283)

607. We want to build up a society in which the villages will be self-sufficient. Their daily needs like food, cloth etc. will be produced in the village itself through small industries. The big industries which have dealings not only all over the country but also with other parts of the world, will not be owned by any individual but by the society. (Triveni, 53)

608. We would also like mutual cooperation. We would not grow wheat where a good quality one is not produced. We would not insist on eating wheat everyday. We would eat rice and millet daily if our soil produces them. And then if on some occasions we feel like taking wheat, we shall not say that doing so is a sin. We shall purchase it from outside. But we should not put our burden on others for our daily needs without which we cannot do for a moment. (BG, V, 280)

Self-Sufficiency, A Truly Modern Concept

609. In this age of science, decentralization is easy. Power can be decentralized and distributed to villages. ...The ideal of village self-sufficiency can, therefore, now be accepted as a truly modern concept. (B, 26.11.1958, 252)

The Principle of Cooperation

610. Cooperation is an eternal principle of life. But it is only when it is given voluntarily and with full knowledge that it is useful and that it is nonviolent, and only then it is true cooperation. On the other hand, a cooperation given because of helplessness or ignorance is not of any use to a good state, for though it may look outwardly like cooperation it cannot last long because of its unreality. It will develop first into hidden violence and then assuredly into open violence. (SS, 45)

Cooperation in Agricultural Activities

611. Let there be cooperation wherever it is required. People are putting forth a plea for full cooperation. But I see that the country has not yet reached that stage; but partial cooperation is possible in matters like ploughing, irrigation, night-watching, etc. (H, 2.8.1952, 166)

612. I have often expressed my views on cooperative farming. Almost every big town puts me this question and 1 have to repeat my reply. The truth is that when I think on a problem, I firmly hold my feet on earth and do not allow myself to soar high in the air. I hold that if we really want to do something in the present distressful plight of the country and bring immediate relief to the poor, we should not get involved in the jugglery of words. We should understand that our country has been predominantly agricultural for at least ten thousand years, and the people have therefore evolved a definite way of life which has become their second nature.

Keeping this in mind, I say that the only practical and fruitful way for India is, for the present, to allow small holdings which individual families of peasants can concentrate their efforts on and produce maximum foodgrains through intensive cultivation.

Peasants can and in fact practise today a partial cooperation in matters such as the use of bullocks, irrigation, night-watch etc. At present this cooperation is unorganized. It needs to be properly organized. (H, 30.8.1952, 233)

Collective Farming

613. I do not insist on collective farming. Let all meet and draw up schemes and let them be implemented. Nothing should be imposed. Even a good thing imposed brings bad results. Therefore in the beginning small cooperatives, if not big ones, should be formed. It should also not be considered wrong if some persons do not join them. Hence, let there be no insistence on cooperative and collective farming.

(VP, 24.2.1959)

Economic Holdings

614. 'Economic holding' is a relative term. In Madhya Pradesh, a pair of bullocks ploughs twenty acres, which perhaps makes Shri R. K. Patil think that twenty acres are needed to constitute an economic holding. But the U.P. Government has fixed 6.25 acres for economic holdings. I have no objection against distributing 6.25 acres in place of five.If you donate more, I shall distribute more. (H, 2.8.1952,186)

615. We should not forget the deplorable economic condition of the country when we discuss economic holding. We have very limited land in our country. The right remedy, therefore, lies not in increasing the size of holdings, but in resorting to intensive cultivation in small plots of land and increasing yield per acre. There are small holdings in China and Japan.

(ibid)

Fragmentation of Land

616. I even say that I do not mind if (due to Bhoodan) the production in the country goes down. However, where hearts get joined, the production will go up hundred times. Our object is not to fragment land but to join hearts. (BYB, 4.9.1953)

Ownership over Land

617. There can be no peace if the existing conditions are maintained in society. We wish to preserve our ownership over land, but no matter how hard we may try, it cannot be done, for the whole trend is against it. (PP, 15.1.1957)

Compensation for Land

618. The Constitution stipulates payment of compensation. But what compensation will have to be paid to those who have all along owned as much as ten thousand acres of land ? They have recovered enough return from land. But they too are our countrymen and we cannot be indifferent to their means of livelihood. Hence, it is a different thing that they should be given something for that purpose. But all such people will not need it. I therefore ask them to donate their compensation. as well. (H, 23.8.1952, 212)

Inheritance Not Favoured

619. Everyone should resolve that the estate earned by his father is for the whole society. He has no exclusive right over it. It is the responsibility of a father to educate his son properly up to a certain age. Thereafter he must be made free to live and remain like any other friend. (KW,Vol. I, 140)

Ideal Economic Order

620. In the ideal state, the method of estimating the value of labour cannot be purely mechanical and irresponsible as it is today. The ideal state will feel responsible for maintaining and protecting all its members, whatever their "physical strength, intellectual capacity, or fitness or lack of fitness for work. All cannot work in the same way. Besides, there is also undoubtedly a difference between physical and mental work. And even in physical work there is a difference between skilled and unskilled work. But in spite of all these differences, whoever works without shirking, honestly and to the best of his ability, at something which is useful to society, should be regarded as deserving of equal right to maintenance.

When we adopt the principle of providing a maintenance, the extreme differences we find in wages today will automatically disappear. Sometimes it happens in families that expenditure over children is even more than over those who are earners. These children have of course done no service at all; it may be that they will render service later. Even then one does not first calculate how much service they can do in the future and on the basis of that spend money on them. Instead, parents think it their responsibility to bring up their children. Similarly, the state should regard such responsibility in regard to every individual as its duty and the individual in his turn should, as a matter of duty, dedicate all his talents to the service of society. But there should be no weighing of service rendered by the individual as over against the protection given by the state.

Further, it is necessary here to understand the difference between protection and wages. Every individual will receive absolutely equal protection. But that does not mean that he will receive equal wages or salary, for equal wages do not result in equal protection. A man should be given only that much wage as is necessary to fulfill the state's responsibility to give him equal protection. The result may be that a very capable individual whose needs are few will get less wages and an individual of meagre capacity whose needs are many will receive more wages.

Briefly, all the principles mentioned above may be enumerated as follows :—(1) Every individual will receive equal protection. (2) Service from each will be according to his ability and will therefore be unequal. (3) To obtain equal protection is not the same as receiving equal wages. (4) But the inequality which prevails in wages today will under no circumstances exist. (5) Wages will be as little unequal as possible, or to put it positively,will be commensurate. (6) Inequality of wages will not be in proportion to inequality of service, but in proportion to inequality of need. (7) The total amount of service rendered by in dividuals and the total amount of protection given to them by the state will be equal to each other. (SS, 52-54)

The Ideal Village

621. Just as there is a code of conduct called *Kuldharma* for a family, and for a clan called *Jatidharma* which helps to maintain these social units, so there has to be a code of conduct to be observed by a village community for the proper maintenance of the village life which we call *gramdharma* or villagism. I shall tell you what I suppose should be considered as the leading characteristics of this code.

First, the dispute in the village should be settled locally in the village.

Secondly, you must arrange for providing medical help to all those who may be out of health. Medicines are not to be purchased from outside. Herbs with medicinal properties should be grown in the village and patients should be given their fresh juice and treated with other nature cure methods to restore them to health.

Thirdly, we must provide for the education of the village children. All the children in the village should be enabled to receive education and not only those, as at present, who can afford.

The fourth constituent of *gramdharma* is agriculture or the service of land. Land will not be owned privately inasmuch as it belongs to God. All must live and work in cooperation with one another for the good of life. They should lift up the declining village industries and make them prosperous. Every need of the village must be produced or manufactured in the village. Nothing should be brought from outside.

Fifthly, there should not be any privately owned shop in the village. All village shops will be held jointly by all the villagers who will have each a share in its capital. The poor who have no money will contribute their labour. For example, if he puts in eight hours' labour, he will be entitled to a share worth a rupee. Thus, the village shop should be a cooperative undertaking owned by all the villagers. Naturally it will be managed and run in the interest of all.

These are some of the principles of *gramdharma.* Observance of these principles will lead to the enrichment and prosperity of our villages. (H, 5.6.1954, 109-110)

VIII
POLITICAL IDEAS

The Meaning of Swaraj, Self-Government

622. Self-government means ruling over oneself. It follows that we shall have Swaraj when all people have acquired the strength of self-control and have realized their duties. Until then we have only government. (DV, 13)

623. It is one mark of Swaraj not to allow any outside power in the world to exercise control over oneself. And the second mark of Swaraj is not to exercise power over any other. These two things together make Swaraj—no submission and no exploitation. (DV, 13-14)

624. Under Swaraj the smallest child will have the strength to stand against the whole society to declare its resolve not to suffer injustice. The society in which even a person who lacks physical strength stands firmly to express his independent opinion against the whole of it for the protection of morality, is free. (H, 3.12.1955, 320)

625. Every adult person, whether great or small, has now one vote for himself. But conferring the right of vote in itself does not mean Swaraj. Swaraj will come into being when all are valued equally, all are honoured equally and all are socially held equal. But Swaraj of this kind does not exist in any country of the world. (ibid)

The Political Ideal of Sarvodaya

626. As the ultimate ideal of Sarvodaya, we conceive of a *society free from government.* We do not use the words *devoid of government.* Governments are also absent in societies where chaos reigns. A situation where there is no order and the evil-minded are free to do what they like, will be termed as one *devoid of government.* What we want is that lack of government should be replaced by good government in society and later on it should evolve into a government-free society. It is not that there would be no order. There would be order and govern-ment, but its authority would be distributed among villages. Punishment would not be required under it. Some moral ideas would be so much ingrained in the minds of the people that they would be acted upon in society. Even small children would have been trained in them. People living in such a social order would obey moral laws of their own accord. Such a society would really be a self-governing one.

(BG, III, 203)

627. The prime idea is that the whole world should be free of governments. ...If the world is afflicted with any malady, it is that of government. Actually the people do not need government at all. It is something which has simply come about in society. (L, 81-82)

The Immediate Objective

628. We shall have to understand that we are to prepare the people not only for good government but also for self-government. This self-government has two aspects. One is of the decentralized power, i. e., the whole power be distributed among the villages and the affairs of a village should be conducted by the villagers themselves. The second is of giving such education, inculcating such psychology and teaching such philosophy as are in consonance with a belief in the power of love and nonviolence as against that in the power of violence. (BG. III, 287)

629. We must devote ourselves to building up an independent people's power (Lok-shakti), and that in itself will be our true service both to the government and to the nation.

By 'an independent people's power' I mean a power inhering in the people, which is totally opposed to the power of violence, but is other than the power of the law and which it must be our task to call into being. We have handed over the power of the law to our government, and although it contains an element of coercion, we regard it as being in a different class from out-and-out violence because society as a whole has conferred these legal powers on the government. It is our task to create a situation in the country in which there will be no need to use even these sanctions of the law. If we can do that we shall have fulfilled our own true *dharma.* (TP, 21-22)

630. Let there be marriage between nonviolence and science and let the authority of nonviolence and compassion prevail in society. Meanwhile, though the penal power of the law will be needed, it is compassion which will rule and the power of law will only be used if it is unavoidable. The situation today is that it is the penal power which is ruling while compassion and nonviolence serve as maids. They may even disappear and with them perhaps mankind too. My dream is that as against it let there be rule of compassion and let it alone endure in the world, while the penal power of the law withers away. (VP. 12.2.1959)

631. Taking the persent conditions into consideration, one has to admit that there is a place for the penal power of the law. Yet, one feature of a nonviolent society will be that in it the biggest institution will be that of service. There will be some place in it for punishment and authority, there will be occasions for them, but they will be very minor.

(S, April-June, 1955, 602)

Purpose of the State

632. The State exists merely to apply to the whole of society the economic principle which is found everywhere to a greater or less extent in the family. This is the task beyond the powers of the family. If the state does not do this service, there is no need for its existence. If instead of performing this service it produces economic inequality, it will be right to destroy it and to establish anarchy. Administrators have spread fear of anarchy everywhere in order to make people submit meekly to their rule, however bad it may be. (SS, 39)

The Criteria for a Polity

633. By way of a brief summing up, we may lay down some principles in the light of which forms of government may be tested, (a) International brotherhood; (b) Cooperation of all the elements of a nation, a cooperation given with full knowledge, to the best of one's ability, spontaneous and springing from one's heart; (c) Unity of interests as between the capable few and the masses in general; (d) Regard for all-sided and equal development of every member of society; (e) The most extensive distribution of governmental power; (f) The least amount of governing; (g) The simplest governmental machinery;(h) The lowest administrative expenditure; (i) The smallest organization for defence; (j) Spread of knowledge everywhere, uninterrupted and unbiased, or free in the sense of not being forced into teaching only on approved lines.

(SS, 26)

Three Theories of Government

634. We have before us three different theories of government.

The first is that the state will ultimately wither away and be transformed into a stateless system; but, in order to bring it about, we must in the present exercise the maximum of power.

The second theory is that some form of government has always existed in the past, exists now, and will continue to exist in the future; a society without a government is a sheer impossibility. Therefore society must be so ordered as to ensure the welfare of all. There may be certain amount of decentralization, but all important matters must be under the Centre.

The third is our own theory. We too believe in a stateless society as our ultimate goal. We recognize that in the preliminary stages a certain measure of government is necessary, but we do not agree that it will continue to be necessary at a later stage. Neither do we agree that totalitarian dictatorship is necessary to ensure progress towards a stateless society. On the contrary we propose to proceed by decentralizing administration and authority. In the final stage there would be no coercion but a purely moral authority. (DV, 29)

State and its Future

635. In the early stages it was unrestrained violence that held the field. Gradually man learnt to curb and limit his violence and the institution called the state came into existence. The formation of the state did limit violence up to a degree. The advent of the apparatus of government created a new kind of law and order. Even the Vedas have said that the coercive power of the state is the personification of Dharma. But gradually the state grew stronger, became more and more powerful till it become all-powerful with the power of destroying the whole world with its military might based on nuclear weapons.

Never in human history had man been so overpowered by fear as he is today. The hydrogen bomb is the symbol of scientific progress and human servitude. Man is wondering how he could limit and tame the power of violence based on nuclear weapons. They are talking of putting a stop to the production of atomic missiles and weapons, destroying those that are already in existence.

It is an illusion to hope to limit or restrict or regulate the power of violence of the modern state. The only rational and sensible alternative is to understand that humanity can exist only when it discards violent weapons and accepts the ideal of building up a society in which there is no coercive state. Years back, I felt that it was an utopian ideal and would be realized only after a few thousand years, but now I see that the world conditions have brought it so near. (BTG, 50-51)

Government, A Man-Made Institution

636. Government is not something natural, it is man-made. But the condition today is such that the moment one is born, he comes under the control of a government. (BG, IV, 79)

The Managerial Class

637. The chief cause of all the turmoil and unrest found in the world is the managerial class. Some managers are rulers, some are officers, some are policemen and soldiers, and some are lawyers and judges. Thus they are of different types. There are some religious managers known as priests. The world is in disorder because of these managers.

(BY, 28.10.1955)

Government Servants

638. Our Government has at present fifty lakh servants. I consider it totally useless. It is not proper to have such a big servant class. In the society of today, they only serve themselves.

(VP, 12.12.1959)

People More Powerful than Government

639. The people are like a well, while the government is like a bucket. In other words, the power of the people is greater.

(BYB, 5.2.1954)

The Source of Strength

640. When the country is in foreign hands, and the urgent question is how to attain freedom, the source of strength lies in politics. At such times even saintly persons consider it their duty to take part in political activity. The fact is that even those who have no love for politics must take part in political activity while their country is in bondage; for in such times politics gives them the opportunity of renunciation, and in renunciation lies the source of strength.

But when a country gains its freedom the source of strength changes; it no longer resides in politics, but in social service; for, then the task is to cast society into a new mould, and to end economic disparities. These are social tasks, and they call for sacrifice, hard labour, strict self-discipline and complete dedication. Hence, it is in this sphere that strength lies.

(DV, 199-200)

Power Politics and Strength Politics

641. 'Power politics' is one thing and 'strength politics' another. Some people run after power politics, but power results in the erosion of strength. Strength is increased by selfless service.

(RLO, 67)

Power, Service and Social Change

642. There are some who think that real service can be done only by getting power. They serve in order to succeed in getting at places of power. Then they hope to use the power to serve. Organization and administration then become all important. They form committees, beginning from the village and rising up from the district and province to the all India level. Then they are logically forced to strive to keep power in all these committees in their own hands. A worker does not see how he is carried further and further away by events from immediate service. (H, 16.1.1957, 6)

643. Some changes can be brought about in society through power, some service can be rendered, but if the structure of the community is to be changed and if some basic transformation is to be brought about in society, it cannot be done through power. (PP, 29.7.1957)

644. Political power does not confer the strength needed to increase our social welfare. That strength and that spirit can only be found in those who serve society with single-minded devotion, untrammelled by bonds or by the duties of any office.

Therefore there should be within a society a large group continually engaged in service and continually on the alert. It should have experience in public affairs, but it should hold no position of authority and it should express itself fearlessly and dispassionately on public issues, so as to exert a moral influence both on the government and on the people. Such a group can be effective only if it keeps clear of office, not contemptuously but with an understanding of the limitation of power and with the realization that the source of strength lies not in power but in the service of the community.

(DV, 201-202)

Politics, Not Unimportant

645. We are not denying the importance of politics, nor do we want to run away from it. This is not escapism. On the contrary, our policy is based on stark realism. We want to change the spirit of politics. A government which is in power because it has succeeded in getting fifty-one per cent of votes against forty-nine per cent is not a representative government in the real sense of the word. Where are the people in whose name they govern? Where is the people's voice? They do not represent the life of the people. We want to end this system.

(B. 12.12.1956, 3)

Emphasis on Power-Politics in India Harmful

646. For hundreds of years there had been foreign rule. The people were made inactive. Everything is now being done by government servants. A mentality has developed that we have to do nothing. We want the same thing to continue after independence. It is termed 'freedom' when we are completely slaves.

There is inactivity in the nature of India. We have to remove it and then work. Only then India will progress.

(PP, 2.6.1957)

647. At present entering politics only means lack of involvement in the service of the people. Involvement in politics implies involvement in jealousy, hatred, quarrels and in attempts to serve one's own interests. Nothing is being done for the good of others. (PP, 11.1.1957)

648. In a country like India where there are innumerable differences like those of language, religion, caste, etc., politics will only create further differences. Hence, there can be no progress in India without ending politics and establishing *lokniti,* politics of the people. (A conversation on 27.1.1957)

Divisive Politics is Outdated

649. I want to say that this is an age of science. In this age politics has been left with no strength now. Man has acquired new types of weapons. Hence if divisive politics will prosper, man is sure to be annihilated. (PP, 5.9.1959)

Rule by All

650. It is obvious that 'rule by all' does not exist anywhere. Gandhiji is striving towards it and has evolved a method for it which he desires to experiment in India.

There is of course a form of government which, assuming the name of rule by the people and the outward appearance of such rule, masquerades in Europe and America. But a government which is based on violence, even though it may pretend to work on the principle of 'one man one vote', is really not rule by all.

As against this, if the people join together and of their free will, after deliberation, invest with power one or more of themselves, whom they know to be free from attachment and hatred, devoted to the welfare of all, and wise and capable, even though that government in form be 'rule by one' or 'rule by more than one', still if it is based on nonviolence it should in reality be regarded as 'rule by all'. (SS, 18)

Democracy, The Best Polity So Far

651. Of all the polities established so far, this democracy is the best. But in this democracy as well there is the same dependence on the army for state defence as in other polities. (VP, 6.2.1959)

Real Democracy

652. A real democracy means that every citizen is responsible for the welfare of society, and that every citizen's talents are being developed and used. (DV, 196)

653. Real democracy must rest itself not on force of arms but on the power of Ahimsa and the organized goodwill of the people. That is the democracy we are striving for. (H, 29.3.1952, 38)

654. As I understand, the difference between democracy and other polities is that democrats do not believe in army. In their philosophy army has a secondary place. However, the recognition given to the army in practice though not wishing it in theory, converts democracy into military rule. Hence, it should only be based on nonviolence. (VP, 6.2.1959)

The Origin of Present Democracy and its Consequences

655. Our modern democracy came into being as a protest against the power of kings, and for that reason it suffers from the same faults as the monarchy it displaced—the real power remains in the hands of a central government. (DV, 72)

Democracy and Monarchy Compared

656. Democracy is like a dairy milk, while monarchy is like a single cow's milk. A democratic government is representative of the sum total of its people's development. (H, 25.12.1949, 374)

Present-Day Democracies, Their Drawbacks

657. I am not opposed to the principle of democracy, but I think that the parliamentary form based on political parties is not the proper vehicle of the ideal form of democracy. I do not demand liquidation of democracy but I want to draw attention to its imperfection and artificiality. Mere counting of heads and elections are not the essence of democracy. The Congress got less than fifty per cent of votes polled in the last general election while the opposition parties combined to get more than fifty per cent and yet the Congress is ruling. In Kerala, the Communist got only twenty-six per cent of the total votes and yet could form their Government. Inside the ruling parties also the majority decides the policy. So in the final analysis it is a small minority that governs the country in the name of democracy. At the most it is a party rule and not a democratic rule. (B,18.2.1959, 351)

658. It is difficult to foresee where the present democracy would lead to. I am not discussing only the type of democracy found in India, but in other countries as well. Look at the condition of France, whose literature popularized the ideas of liberty, equality and fraternity. Even there, democracy has turned to be sham. Its cause is that there is something wrong at the very basis of Representative Government and it is that powers are concentrated in the hands of a select few. Where the power is centralized, democracy in the true sense cannot function properly. During a crisis, even a country like Britain delegated all powers to men like Mr. Churchil and the people became almost non entities. This proves that during a crisis democracy proves helpless whereas, in a critical hour, it should prove itself all the more effective. If the administration of the country is to be delivered over to dictators and military during a crisis period, it proves that democracy is an imperfect form of government. (B, 27.5.1959, 35)

659. At present we are talking about democracy and at the same time keeping capitalist economy and a military regime. We give lip-service to democracy but our actions are anti-democratic. That is why our democracy bears so little fruit and may soon bear none at all. (DV. 176)

660. The present democracy is a slave of bureaucracy. (BY, 12.11.1958)

661. It is no use saying that in a democracy people have the right and the opportunity to change the government every five years. A little serious thought will show how hollow is this contention. Four or five years are not a small period in these days when scientific advance has changed all the old values of time and space. What one government does today in the five years of its tenure very often binds the successive governments also, and cannot be undone or left unfinished by them. (B. 3.12.1958, 260)

662. Today there is military regime in Russia. In some other countries it is not so apparent. That is the only difference. Steam, water and ice are not three different things. They are the three forms of the same thing..... Democracy, communism and socialism, they are the three different names of the same thing. (L, 201-202)

663. Democracy and military rule are very close. For democracy claims to work for the welfare of society through representatives. Society is not asked to work for its own welfare... .Everyone assures that you elect our party and we would set everything right, make society happy and abolish disparities. But when they are unable to fulfil their promises, people get dissatisfied. At the same time, they also feel oppressed by the laws. Under such conditions it becomes easy for the army to assume power, assuring the people of comforts and ease. (VP, 10.12.1959)

The Indian Democracy

664. The democracy adopted in our country is a senseless imitation of the West. Here conditions are not like those prevalent there. Hence a lot of problems, troubles and obstacles have arisen. So long as we do not evolve and adopt a democracy that suits the conditions of our country, our troubles will not end. We shall have to seek measures that avoid conflicts and differences within the country.

In other countries of Europe, where democracy has been established, due importance has been given to local circumstances. In India too a democratic set-up has to be built up, consistent with the peculiar conditions and circumstances of the country. We have fourteen major languages and an equal number of States. The country is a vast one, about five times in area and six to seven times in population compared to England. In our country we have a number of religions with rich and philosophical backgrounds. The difference is easily perceptible, and yet we try to fully imitate England.....As such, how can a democracy alien to our soil be successful in India ? Besides, the general public of England is well-educated and cannot be misled. The poverty is far less in England and the votes cannot be bought over. People here are not so literate. The political parties pull them to one side or the other. The appalling poverty makes people easy victims to all kinds of bribery.

I, therefore, want to lay emphasis on two points. First, in elections the individual rather than the party should be given preference. Elections to Gram Panchayats, Municipal Boards etc. should be free of party lines. Members of the Lok Sabha should be regarded not as representatives of parties but of the whole country. Secondly, I want the formation of an association or society which would be absolutely immune to party bickerings and affiliations. Such an association would have equal consideration for all parties and serve them equally. It will work as a lubricant to prevent clashes between them. If these two conditions are fulfilled, I believe we shall achieve some success in democracy in India. (B, 17.12.1958, 276)

A Warning

665. The public is never keen on any particular polity. All that it is keen about is that its life should be an easy one.

(BY, 23.10.1959)

The Meaning of Lokniti, the Politics of the People

666. These days we have given currency to a new word, *lokniti,* (the politics of the people). It replaces the word *rajniti* (politics). Though the word is new, the idea is an old one. It means that the authority should be that of love and it should be exercised from within. There should be no external authority.

(VP, 29.3.1958)

667. 'Lokniti' means that power must actually pass into the hands of the people at all levels. Government must continuously either recede into background or wither away, and its place must be taken up by the people themselves. Initiative must pass to the people. (B, 30.4.1958, 9)

Why Lokniti Needed ?

668. I am greatly pained by what I see going on both in our social life and in our politics nowadays. If the kind of politics that have been going on in India since Bapu's death is to continue, I wonder whether Bapu has accomplished anything, and whether we have learned anything from his life or not. Bapu himself adopted from Gokhaleji (Gopal Krishna Gokhale) the phrase 'purification of politics', and I do not know of any other man who laboured as he did to achieve it. He did his work without ever allowing himself to swerve for a moment from his vision of truth. Has he had any influence upon the country and its politics? Not much, it would seem. It does not appear that our present political standards differ very much from those that held the field before.

I can see no other way to purify politics in this age of science except by establishing *lokniti.* The concentration of power means that we have democracy only in name, and not in reality. Democracy is committing suicide everywhere, and the only remedy is to bring *lokniti* into being. (DV, 54-55)

669. After independence, the people have become less independent, less self-reliant. We have to rely on the government for everything. Things have come to such a pass that we expect the government to do everything while we do nothing, not only in social and religious matter like untouchability, but even in our domestic affairs. How can the people become stronger so long as they depend so much on the government? A law may solve our problem but it will not make us stronger. What people really need is to become aware of their own inner strength, and that they can only do if they solve some of their problems for themselves. (DV, 56)

670. In India today there are 55 lakhs of government 'servants' and the number is likely to increase. It is said to be a method of curing unemployment. But it really means that the rest of the population has got to support those 55 lakhs of officials; it works out that every thirteen families have to support one family, for not only the official, but his family also, becomes dependent on others. We thus create a middle class which takes no part in productive work, and at the same time has a high standard of living. Not only are these peoples excused from any productive or physical labour, they also possess, if they are so minded, the power to oppress others. Moreover, people are clamouring for still more jobs to be provided for the educated unemployed, so that 55 lakhs become a crore, and then every seven working families will have to support one such unproductive family. There can be no more fearful danger to the country than the creation of such an unproductive middle class. How is this enormous financial burden to be of benefit to our poor country ?

There is only one way out, and that is what I call *lokniti.* (DV, 47-48)

Gandhiji and Lokniti

671. I would like my friends to understand that the work that Gandhiji did for nearly three decades for India's freedom comes under the category of Lokniti. It was not politics as we understand it today. When freedom came, he was trekking in

Noakhali. Not that he was opposed to political freedom or considered it as something impure or corrupt, but his place was, he knew, not in Delhi but in Noakhali. He was made that way. The political freedom which appeared in Delhi was only a by-product of his great work ...His mission was to awaken love and kindliness in the human heart and inspire man to his sense of duty. If he had been a politician, could he have advised the Congress to dissolve itself and become an institution of social service? He preached and practised Lokniti all his life. (B, 5.6.1957, 5)

Dangers of a Welfare State

672. I repeat that where a great deal of power is concentrated in the name of the welfare of the people and an army is maintained for its protection, democracy digs its own grave. (B, 3.12.1958, 260)

673. Today, in the name of the 'welfare state', we are concentrating all power at the centre. Even if the people do get a .certain amount of benefit out of it, I would still call it not 'well-fare' but 'ill-fare,' because it keeps power in the hands of a few. The idea of nonviolence will spread only when power is shared among the villagers. (DV, 76)

Political Decentralization

674. But decentralization is not to be confined merely to industries. The process of decentralization applies equally fruitfully to the authority of the State. Even thinkers who are avowedly intent on building up a nonviolent social order at times lose sight of this fact. They support the demand for industrial decentralization, but at the same time they often plead for a strong central authority (at least for some period) for the preservation of the former!.....Gandhiji, however, conceives of the decentralization of political authority as being equally necessary at every stage and period, and for all time. It is necessary in the beginning, during the middle, and till the very end. (KGM, 23)

675. I submit that real freedom and peace can come only when people have established Swaraj or self-rule in small areas.

Government will then be like a thread that keeps such self-sufficient and autonomous *taluka* units together. This is the only way of establishing peace in the world.

(B, 20.3.1957,5)

676. We want every village to have Swaraj—to manage its own affairs. We want to see all powers vested in the village, so that the job of the State Government will not be to give orders to the village but instead to keep the villages in touch with one another. In the same way the Government in Delhi would have no authority over the States, but would maintain contact between them. The higher the level of Government, the more extensive would the liaison work become, and the more limited would be its direct authority. The direct authority, the material power, will be exercised by the villages. The centre will be manned by persons of character and integrity who will thus exercise a moral authority. (DV, 105)

677. God practices this decentralization. He has given all His creatures a share of intelligence—from the scorpion and the snake to the tiger and the man. It is true that the shares are unequal, but each one has some and God has decreed that each one should direct its life by its own intelligence. As a result the world has got on so well that God has been able to take a holiday, and men have even begun to doubt His existence. (DV, 108)

The Need of Re-thinking on Political Parties

678. A re-thinking and reassessment of many of our democratic forms and techniques have become urgently necessary. We have fought against casteism and the practice of untouchability. Our fight against these evils is still going on. But a new division and casteism is becoming respectable. There are so many political parties. They grow like mushrooms and continue to sow seeds of division. Their function is to emphasize differences. A division of society among political warring groups is considered necessary for the growth of democracy. This artificial division in watertight separate parties has the sanction of political science. We have borrowed the apparatus, forms and institutions of democratic practice from the West. We have never cared to find out if they suited our ethos. The time has come when we have to re-examine and reassess the actual utility or value of some of the forms which we have adopted and are practising as a democratic ritual. (B, 20.6.1956, 4)

Political Parties, Their Drawbacks

679. The country is not growing stronger, Why ? Because there are mutual confrontation, envy and hatred. To them has been added a new difference, that of the parties which is the most terrible of all. They are under the impression that by creating a party, they dissolve all other differences. But it is mere imagination, a delusion. What have the last ten years proved? This new difference does not do away with the old differences. It has only intensified them. (PP, 2.9.1957)

680. Where party politics is in vogue, one party holds all the power and other has none. The second is always contending with the first to get the power for itself. The party in power boasts to the people about its own great qualities and achievements; the opposition points out its shortcomings and mistakes. Every party speaks ill of the other parties; this absorption in fault-finding is the result of their worship of power. They all dance attendance on power, and worship at its altar, and there is a continual tug-of-war between them. Each party claims that if you return it to power, it will lead you to heaven, but that if yon return the other fellows to power, they will lead you into hell. No one tells you the real truth—that your destiny, heaven or hell, is in your hands, and that no one but yourself can take you there.

As long as this sort of thing goes on, there will be no contentment, no peace and no freedom in the world.

(DV, 84-85)

681. Fidelity to truth requires that we should be able to look at a thing as the other person looks at it. I believe that it was not truthfulness for those who believed in the need of instituting a legal inquiry (in police actions) to remain silent and meekly submit to the leaders in the Goverment. But Congressmen would call it party loyalty. They think that party loyalty consists in supporting the decision of the party, right or wrong. They may criticize the action privately inside the party, but they must never say a word publicly against a majority decision of the party. I am opposed to this kind of party spirit. Loyalty to the party takes the place of loyalty to truth. That means, in simple words, one can never be loyal to truth if one is loyal to a party. Even good men unconsciously lose their sensitivity and respect for truth when they give themselves over to a party. (B, 5.12.1956,4)

682. There are three tenses in grammar—past, present and future. Likewise there are three periods in the grammar of these parties—pre-election, election and post-election. There is no fourth and they are supremely unaware of thc great Ghost of time. (H, 25.12.1954, 348)

683. People are fed up with parties which lead to the wasting of strength. One party weakens another party, and then this weakens the first one too. They both together weaken the country. (PP, 19.7.1957)

Parties Are Outdated

684. Political parties, whether in our country or elsewhere, which subscribe to narrow ideals and loyalties, are out-of-date in this Age of Science. They are the remnants of an age which is fast disappearing. (B, 3.12.1958, 260)

685. We have to understand that party politics is so narrow and useless that it makes no sense today. The ill-will and jealousies that were confined in old times to a few feudal chiefs or kings, have now been made countrywide by party politics. (B, 19.8.1959, 133)

Political Parties, A Refutation

686. These days it is the parties which dominate society. But even those who believe in them hold that it is not proper for them to remain in the parties. Take the example of the Assembly Speaker. What is his moral duty ? It is that he should be impartial. Then there is a judge. It is also expected of him that he would not be favourably disposed towards any party. There are government officials. It is also obligatory on them to serve all impartially. The President too is expected to provide equal protection to all.....What does all this mean ? It means that all those who discharge important functions, have to be non-party men. (PP, 23.7.1957)

Differences of Views and Political Parties

687. It is true that there will always be differences in views. But it is not correct that there will always be parties. A party can come into existence only when there be an absence of right thinking. (VP, 27.1.1959)

Not Totally Opposed to Political Parties

688. Many times people think after hearing me that I am given to attacking all the parties of today. But this attack of mine is from a long-term point of view, not for today. These parties may well exist for the present, but there should be good relations between them. The differences should only pertain to ideas. If so, they may be discussed in the presence of the people at the same platform, and the people, after consideration, may support any of them they approve of. Thus several political parties can exist without ill-will and in good relationship with each other. (VP, 24.1.1959)

How to Correct the Government ?

689. Nowadays people tend to talk about the need for an organized opposition to the majority party since without it democracy may be transformed into fascism. This is Western terminology, and because we have borrowed our ideas from the West, that terminology will continue to be current. There is nothing wrong about it, but it follows that not only the majority but also the minority ought to be respected; they should live and work together in friendliness even if they are political opponents, and their political disagreement should not be allowed to come in the way of their friendship. This will act as a sort of check, help those who hold office to keep straight, and save them from making mistakes.

But this alone is not enough. The moral and material welfare of the country will only be ensured by the establishment of a band of workers who will keep clear of the whirligig of office, who will be alert and watchful, conscientious in their study of facts and ready for sacrifice. (DV, 202)

690. It is the duty of Sarvodaya workers to stand between the rulers and the ruled, to point out mistakes on both sides, to foster mutual trust and understanding, and to increase the people's strength. They should identify themselves neither with the government nor with the people. They should be independent of both and render true service to both, by pointing out the virtues and faults of both sides. They should be friends of all but be members of no party. (DV, 207)

691. Some times people say to me: "Why do you stay outside? Why do you not take some responsibility for the country yourself ?" I reply that there are already two bullocks harnessed to the cart; should I be of any assistance if 1 were to become third? Suppose, instead, I were just to do a little road-making so that the cart can go in the right direction, I should be of much more use. (DV, 207-208)

The Need of a Common Programme

692. Another consideration which is fundamental to public welfare is that with so many different parties in the country, the only way to make any progress is to evolve a programme of work upon which all parties can agree. There may be divergence of thought, but let there be unity in action. If all can agree on the programme, progress will be assured. (DV, 115-116)

693. Some say that there will be a coalition government in the country when there will be an emergency. But I ask what need is there of an emergency to make people work together. Is there any less emergency these days? What is the need of an emergency in a country where there is so much poverty and so many problems ? Let us at least work together in matters on which we agree. Even if it slows down the pace of progress, it will be true progress. (VP no. 254 of 1958)

The Majority Method of Decision-Making

694. Perceiving truth has nothing to do with numerical majority. (BY, 2.11.1956)

695. The majority method (of taking decisions) has come from the West and the Westerners consider it to be a progressive political idea. To us it appears to be a totally crude one. (PP, 22.8.1957)

696. Formerly decisions were enforced on the point of sword; nowadays they are enforced by a majority instead. We claim that we have given up the use of sword because it is an unintelligent way of doing things. But majority rule is not an intelligent way either. Matters cannot be rightly settled by counting heads; the only result is discontent and strife, and every one is geared to the effort to overthrow one's opponent. (DV, 83-84)

697. At one time the minority ruled over the majority.....It did not result in any good. As a reaction to it, emerged the rule of the majority over the minority.... It has led to tensions in the world and given rise to the new problem of majority and minority everywhere. (BY, 10.1.1958)

Decision by Consensus

698. Things will go rightly only when we accept the idea of unanimity. (DV, 113)*

699. The Indian idea of a village Panchayat holds a special place among the political ideas of the world. It included the principle of 'God speaks through the five', which was accepted throughout India. This means that five members of the Panchayat must reach a common mind, and then only the decision was made. But now we 'pass' a decision by a majority of four to one or three to two, as though God speaks in the three! I contend that such proposals are not really passed, so long as they fail to convince even one person. Only that proposal deserves to 'pass' which commends itself to all. We

---

* Here and elsewhere also when Vinoba speaks of 'unanimity,' he means 'consensus' which implies lack of any active opposition, i.e., common consent.

must revive this ancient Indian tradition, for a people's democracy can only be built on mutual trust and cooperation. Truth and cooperation are essential to the prospering of its affairs. Without them, neither in India nor in the world can nonviolence ever be maintained. (DV, 112-113)

700. People object to this method (of consensus) on the ground that a single stubborn individual could prevent any decision being reached. But if a Gram Panchayat were unable to take any decision for this reason, it would cease to function and a new one would be chosen. It would thus be in the interests of the members to consider one another's point of view and to come to a common decision. This was the way in which people formerly managed their affairs; it is the way the Quakers do business today. (DV, 113-114)

701. Some may object that this would be all right for the villages but that at the provincial level their representatives would have to decide by majority. This would be so for the interim period (only). But these representatives would have been so chosen that they would cultivate the habit of taking all important decisions unanimously. The main things in life, such as food, clothing and education, would in any case be controlled by the village. In matters of secondary importance majority decisions would not hurt anyone. They would not be the kind of subjects about which a minority would care very much. But where difference of opinion arises on matters of primary importance like food and education, a majority decision leaves the minority with a feeling of grievance, and serious conflict may arise. It does no harm to decide by majority vote at state level, so long as the state controls only secondary matters. Even here it would be possible to rule that certain decisions need seventy or eighty per cent vote. Ultimately society must form the habit of coming to unanimous decisions.

Decisions at the centre will of course be unanimous. Even today they are so. In important matters the cabinet aims at unanimity, and if there is difference of opinion, decision is postponed and discussions are continued. So there is no need to give much thought to the centre. (DV, 114-115)

The Present System of Direct Elections, Its Defects

702. The increase of communal differences is the first evil consequence of (direct) elections. A second is that in the present set-up it is not possible for a man to stand for election unless he has wealth or property. How then is the voice of the dumb and poverty-stricken people to be heard?

There is another thing. We hold elections, but we do not even know our candidates by face. Hundreds of thousands of people cast their votes, but so far from knowing the character of the man they vote for, they do not even know his face. For the sake of elections we spend our money, we allow the poison of communalism to spread, and in the end we have no guarantee that those elected will be worthy of our trust.

(DV, 82-83)

703. If the candidates are asked to truly render the accounts of the special expenditures incurred by them in their elections, many of them would be found to be such as have not submitted their accounts correctly......My soul rebels at this lie committed on a national scale, this untruth practised by the representatives of the nation. (VP no. 269 of 1958)

704. The election has its own ethics. Its three principles are self-praise, speaking ill of others, and telling lies. (SKA, 20)

The Changes Advocated in the Election System

705. At least the present system of direct elections should be changed into that of indirect elections. For it, the party differences must be eliminated from the villages. There should be a general body consisting of all over twenty-one, and it should elect an executive by unanimity. Unanimity and non-party village organisation are essential conditions for it. The higher bodies should be elected by Gram Sabhas, the village assemblies. Thus the elections should be indirect.

(BY, 12.10.1958)

706. Our present system of democracy is unjust because it does not give the right to vote to young people under twenty-one.

There are many examples of young people, barely in their twenties, who did remarkable things. William Pitt became Prime Minister of England; Napoleon Bonaparte showed himself a brilliant general; in India one could name Madhavarao Peshwa, Shankaracharya, Jnaneshwar. Eisenhower commented that when a youth of eighteen is considered fit to fight for the country, why should he not be fit to vote for his government ? (TP, 130)

If Vinoba Were a Candidate ?

707. If I ever thought of contesting an election, my electoral programme will have three points : Disbanding of armed forces, abolishing the special class of men who are forced to take to scavenging, and banning textile mills. I am aware that no one will vote for me. We have to create a strong public opinion for our programme and then we may exert influence on the Government (for it). (B, 8.10.1958, 194)

Gandhians and Elections

708. It is true that we have our differences on some points with the Government. But the differences are not regarding external policy, but internal policy. It does not look proper that we should not participate in the elections because we call ourselves Gandhians. Non-participation in the elections may be proper only for him, who does not take the help of the Government machinery of law, order and justice, even if all his property is looted. He may keep himself aloof from the elections because it only means that he does not wish to use the rights and privileges conferred upon him by law.

(H, 21.7.1951, 182)*

709. We should not advise people to non-participate in the elections. It may be open to give personal opinion to an individual. But the elections are a public programme, and a person who takes Government shelter and avails of the rights and privileges conferred by it for his personal and institutional work, is not qualified to preach the boycott of elections. (ibid, 183)

---

* Also see 1206 f below.

Advice to the People and Organizations

710. The Congress should nominate good candidates and the voters too should vote for good candidates.

Question : But what is the definition of a good person ?

Vinoba : He must know his job, be impartial, be able to make his contribution to the work assigned to him and, last but not the least, there should be absolutely no doubt about his integrity. (S, June 1951, pp. 766-767)

711. By good persons is meant those who are sincere and honest. If those given to violence sincerely believe in it, it is also honesty. If communists believe in it sincerely, that is also honesty. I shall elect out of such persons. (L, 188)

712. Whenever there are elections, no candidate of any party should be elected blindly. It is not right to elect an undeserving person simply because he belongs to one's own party.

(VP, 17.12.1959)

Elections, Not Very Important

713. Elections do have some significance in the history of the country. But I want to say that we have attached too much importance to politics. I do not say this about India only. I say it about the whole world. There would be no peace in the world as long as it gives that much importance to politics as it has given so far. (PP, 15.2.1957)

Politics and Problems

714. If we look at our problems with a narrow vision, we shall never be able to solve them. Nay, they shall get complicated and more problems will follow. The issues of Korea, Iraq, Egypt etc. are hanging on since long. Now has cropped up a new one of Tibet, and some more will appear. I am convinced that politics cannot solve problems. Gone are those days. Politics bereft of mutual trust is bound to prove barren. I, therefore, feel that the problems of this world will not be solved by politics but by ethics and morals or spirituality.

(Cited by Suresh Ram in B, 7.10.1959, 186)

The Defects of Centralized Administration

715. Today Eisenhower, Bulganin, Eden, Chou and Mao have acquired the power of setting the world ablaze. If it comes into the mind of any of them to do so, he can do it. (L, 163)

716. The picture today is that the programme of work in every village is drawn up in Delhi and it is carried out by persons who do not even feel the need of visiting the villages.

(ibid, 164)

The Political Implications of Sarvodaya

717. Sarvodaya does not mean good government or majority rule, it means freedom from government, it means decentralization of power. We want to do away with government by politicians and replace it by a government of the people, based on love, compassion and equality. Decisions should be taken, not by majority, but by unanimous consent; and they should be carried out by the united strength of the ordinary people of the village.

(DV, 3)

Gram Panchayat, India's Unique Contribution

718. Gram Panchayat is India's unique contribution to social thinking. In remote past when Europe had hardly awakened to social consciousness, we in India had made considerable progress in political and social thinking.

The Panchayat system was evolved for dealing justice to all and providing protection and education to all. ...All had to submit to the unanimously agreed decisions of these councils. It can be regarded as a decentralized social order.

(B, 22.7.1959, 97)*

Chief Features of Gram Swaraj

719. (1) Disputes of the village will not be decided outside,

(2) The village will defend itself by its own strength.

(3) It will control its imports and exports.

(4) It will produce its own food. (PP, 30.12.1957)

---

* See also 519 and 699, above.

The Village Government

720. Village affairs would be managed by common consent, and not on any party basis. There would be a General Assembly of all villagers above the age of twenty-one. They would chose an executive committee of five, or seven, or ten members, which would run the administration of the village. But its decision would have to be unanimous. (DV, 119)

721. We have to make every village a complete and a thorough State in miniature. Thus, in every village there would be all the various departments as they are now in a State, such as Health, Industries, Agriculture, Education, Justice etc. As there is a Foreign Affairs Department with respect to the relations with other countries, there will be in every village a special department which would handle the affairs pertaining to other villages. (H, 24.9.1955, 240)

722. Some tell us that what you are suggesting is dangerous. If the village comes to acquire such powers, there would be a state within a state. We reply that such is a nonviolent structure. There should be a state within a big state and a third one within it. The main state would be of the village, which will have all powers. At the higher levels, the powers would be of coordination, of conducting external relations, etc. At present the whole of it is concentrated in the hands of one authority. We cannot conceive of a slavery greater than this.

(PP, 6.4.1957)

The Role of the Centre in a Gram Swaraj Polity

723. (1) The central government then will be a link to keep the village republic together. (2) It will manage the railway, postal and such other services. (3) It will look after big industries and mines. (4) It will be in charge of defence and external relations of the country. (5) It will be an overall advisory body. Powers will remain with the constituent republics. The central authority will gradually assume the shape of an advisory council. (B, 27.3.1957, 1)

The Existing Village Panchayats, Their Defects

724. Gram Swaraj, however, must be distinguished from the present Gram Panchayats or the Village Executives. These Panchayats have been created from above, i.e. by government legislation, and they function in the existing set-up of the villages. This means that those who own more land, who are more educated and have greater influence in the administration, also dominate in the Panchayats. The whole power at the village level is thus concentrated in their hands. I, therefore, call them a decentralized scheme of exploitation. Still the Government appears to be in a hurry to encourage the formation of these Gram Panchayats. It is a common experience that their formation encourages today village feuds and disputes. After a Panchayat has been established in a village, it becomes almost impossible to do any constructive work there peacefully. The clash of interests that we notice in political parties is also extended to the village.

(B, 28.1.1959. 324)

What to do in the Present Context ?

725. Four things need to be done :

(i) There should be a resolve on the part of the Government and the people that they would not resort to violence.

(ii) We should solve our main problems by the power of the people which is independent of the Government.

(iii) There should be freedom in the field of education.

(iv) The present system of elections should be changed. At the village level they should be direct, and indirect at the higher levels. (BY, 11.5.1956)

A Programme for Gram Panchayats

726. (i) Every Panchayat should organize a study circle which will acquaint the people of the village with new ideas and important developments taking place in the national and international fields. The centre will specially provide for the study of Gandhian and Sarvodaya literature. Selected writings from such literature should be read out and explained to the people.

(ii) The Panchayats should undertake to bring about an increase in production as one of their primary responsibilities. As long as the produce does not increase and the vast unemployment found in the villages is not liquidated, villagers are not likely to feel the urge for offering their cooperation to any developmental authority.

(iii) The Panchayat should consider it their duty to see that no person within their area remains unemployed and goes hungry. Just as the boycott of foreign goods helped the attainment of Swaraj, so would the boycott of mill cloth help bring about Gramraj.

(iv) Since land is the basic factor of all production, the land must be distributed to all. The ownership of land should belong to the village and there should be no one without land.

(v) The real power of the Panchayats lies in the people's support. The Panchayats should therefore follow their will and act under their control. They should not care whether the Government recognizes them or not. The people must always rely on their own strength and go forward.

The Panchayats should carry out these five functions. Then only will it be possible to establish Ramrajya in our villages. (H, 11.9.1954, 228)

Patriotism

727. Love for one's country is decidedly more inclusive but taking into consideration the whole humanity, it is petty and narrow, (BD, 17)

Nationalism

728. The good of India is included in the good of the world. Hence let us now think of the good of the whole world. The principle of nationalism has become outdated. We have now to establish the principle of universalism. (VP, 27.1.1959)

Imperialism

729. Imperialism means excessive attachment to wealth, political power and to imposing a civilization on others. (RR, 114)

The Need of a World Outlook

730. Isolation and separation, in the world today, means annihilation and death. Co-existence has become a condition for survival. Nonviolence and brotherhood are no mere altruistic and idealistic concepts. They have the sanction of stark realism. Because of the phenomenal growth of science, brotherhood and love have acquired a new relevance. Society cannot last without them. If hate and rivalry continue as before, human society will be destroyed by modern science. If brotherhood and love become the cementing force in society, modern science will create a new world of freedom, peace and plenty. (B, 1.5.1957, 7)

731. A seer used the term 'universal man' in the Rigveda ten thousand years back. We have to be like that. This is the demand of the time, and it has the assurance of self-knowledge. We think that both science and self-knowledge are equally assailing narrowness. Let us have that broad outlook, no matter whether we are engaged in household work or in cleaning our lane, or even in conducting the government. (VP, 23.3.1958)

The World Outlook of Sarvodaya

732. The objective of Sarvodaya is to demolish the walls standing between various countries. Just as we are today free to move within India from one State to another, are welcome to live anywhere, can go for sight-seeing, education or business (to any part of the country), similarly a man should be free to come and go to any place in the world. This is what we have to do. (JJ, 74)

733. According to the nonviolent way of thinking, human society is one and in it separate nations are conceived of merely for the sake of convenience. If a particular nation has the good sense to adopt nonviolence, it will not regard itself as separate from and as opposed to the others. It will be as anxious to safeguard the legitimate interests of neighbouring nations as those of its own. (SS, 65)

The Concept of the World Government

734. If a World Federation is formed, what would its nature be? All power of service would vest in the lower institutions. The higher institutions would only tender moral advice. But it would command such moral sanction that all people would act upon it as if it were binding on them.

(A conversation dated 22.7.1957)

735. I have not the least doubt that there would be an effective World Panchayat. On one side there would come into existence such a World Panchayat and World Committee, and, on the other, Gram Panchayat and Village Committee. Such would be the two ends and the intermediate regions like provinces and nation states would lose their significance by and by.

The Village Panchayats would be functioning well, and the need of coordination at the higher levels would go on being reduced. Then there would be no districts or collectors. The Village Panchayat would have direct link with the national government. All the intervening authorities would disappear and in times to come there would be a World Panchayat. The National Panchayat might continue to exist as a link between the Village Panchayat and the World Panchayat, but the State Panchayat would not be there.

(JJ, 46-47)

736. Such people of the world as have very high morality and character and are free from attachment and hatred, would be elected to the Centre and they would only advise, not rule. In other words, the Centre would have more of moral authority and less of physical power. World peace would only be established if we have such political structures in India and the world. Otherwise it is totally futile to hope for world peace.

(VP no.292 of 1958)

The United Nations Organization

737. The UNO is a sort of World Panchayat, but none there is interested in it. There are several matters pending before it and it itself is in the dock. ...All groups in it are increasing their military capacity and are openly working against each other. Some are in one bloc, some in the other. Thus, the world has come to be divided into two blocs. (JJ. 45)

738. I am a man of faith and I trust every good-intentioned organisation. I believe the UNO to be based on good intentions. But I feel that although they sit round one table, they do not trust each other. If they develop mutual faith, they will get better results. (S, Aug. 1955, 48)

739. It is very enouraging that India and Pakistan have stopped war at the instance of the United Nations Organization. The time has come when countries of the world should surrender some part of their sovereignty and power to the UNO and make it strong. (BY, 1.10.1965)

The UNO Needs a Peace Army

740. The UNO army is much smaller than the armies of the USA and the USSR. The UNO should either raise an army bigger than the armies of those two countries or form a peace army. I once suggested that the UNO should have a peace army of seven lakh volunteers. I also promised to supply one lakh volunteers from India, because India's population is one-seventh of the world's population. (SE, Aug. 1973, 64)

How would the UNO Peace Army Act ?

741. When there is a war between two countries, the UNO Peace Army would go and stand unarmed between the fighting units. In this manner they would establish peace.

(M, April 1977, 338)

What is Meant by Peace ?

742. These days absence of war is regarded as peace. But peace really connotes absence of fear. There would be peace only when no part of the world is afraid of or exploited by any other part. (H, 1.1.1955, 330)

743. Merely an absence of war is not peace. What is needed for peace is a constructive approach. (KKO, 50)

744. By peace I mean something dynamic, something which will develop the power of the individual and the dynamic strength of the people to a degree that will enable them to meet any situation.

Shanti or peace, therefore, cannot be negative. It has to be something positive. (SE, June 1956, 414)

745. Peace as wrongly understood in India is not peace but lack of sensitivity. ...What peace is there in lying calmly on a cushion bed. Peace has value when there are problems and efforts are being made to solve them. If peace means maintenance of *status quo,* that peace is worthless.

(BY, 23.12.1955)

746. Peace is something mental and spiritual. If there be peace in our (personal) life, it will affect the whole world.

(KKR, 108)

Peace and Armaments

747. It is a delusion that only when all nations are well armed and strong, will there be peace among them.

Efforts to establish nonviolence through violence have failed innumerable times, and they shall not only fail in future too but shall also make the whole humanity unsuccessful.

(BG, III, 33)

The World Peace Movement

748. Some advocates of peace point out that many nations of the world require peace today for they cannot develop themselves without it. Hence they desire peace in the world. Their movement is known as the World Peace Movement. There are several European countries which desire peace in spite of the communists being very strong there. ... Even China wants peace, and so do Pakistan and India. They say that "we need peace greatly for we have to raise the standard of living of our country and we have to abolish poverty". But this alone cannot lead to peace because it has no independent value for them. Its value lies only in that they require it for other purposes.

As long as mankind has no independent thirst for peace, there can be no peace in the world. (BG, III, 35, 36)

The Moral Rearmament

749. Another endeavour is also going on for the establishment of peace in the world. It is of the Moral Rearmament for which some people are collectively working. They try to go to other countries and to do something noble so that there be greater mutual love and friendliness. One of them had come to meet me. I had a discussion with him. I asked him, "It is good to go on performing small services to promote mutual love, but does your organisation hold that one should not take up arms in case of a war ?" He said, "No, there has been no such decision. However, it has been decided that there would be no participation in a war of aggression." At this I said, "These days there is no difference between aggression and defence. The two wars are indistinguishable."

The sum and substance is that they are good men, but they are undecided. There is lack of thinking in those who believe in establishing peace by increasing armaments while persons believing in negotiations lack trust and those who believe in establishing peace through service, lack resolution.

(BG, III, 34)

Pacifists

750. Nonviolent resistance to war is the final result of a nonviolent attitude and not the first as many Western pacifists seem to think. (SE, Nov. 1954, 139)

Birth Pangs of a New Order

751. There is conflict all over the world between India and China, between Indonesia and Malaysia, between North Vietnam and South Vietnam, etc. I regard this as the birth-pangs of a new order in which nations will be transformed into provinces of a world state. (TTR, 21)

Future of the Army

752. As society evolves, the concept of heroism and the duty of the warrior will also go on evolving. The duty of a warrior can only be that he should be prepared to dedicate himself to the protection of all. Hence, the best men should be classed as warriors.

Their method of fighting will be that of satyagraha. Hence while the importance of the army will be no less (in future) than what it is today, its form will go on changing.

(BG, IV, 255)

Army and Cowardice

753. In fact, arms bear no relation to bravery. Hence do not be under any delusion that if we maintain an army, our cowardice will go away. When we keep an army, our cowardice does not leave us but we do make fools of ourselves. We are fools in that while we cannot maintain an army on the levels of Russia and America, we squander away billions of rupees of a poor country on steel by purchasing arms.

(BY, 26.11.1958)

Military Power and Strength

754. It is wrong to think that a country's strength lies in its military power. ... A nation will become really strong only if it is free from internal conflicts, if it becomes self-sufficient and the people within are united by bonds of love. If we make our country strong like this, whatever be the threats or dangers that may confront us, none of them will cast any shadow on us. On the other hand, our greatness will certainly have a good influence on outside world. (BTG, 16)

755. This country will have to be defended not by arms but by fearlessness, ethical conduct and unity. (BG, IV, 256)

A Plea for General Disarmament

756. Nuclear weapons should, of course, be abolished. But the conventional weapons appear to be no less frightening. The nuclear arms tend to bring us nearer to nonviolence because they impel man to think and ponder. But pistols and daggers put nonviolence far away. These weapons appear to be small, but they are the parents of nuclear arms.

(Message to New Delhi 1962 World Anti-Nuclear Convention)

Disarmament When ?

757. Renunciation of arms can take place only when there will be a plan for decentralized production. It cannot happen earlier.

(BY, 9.12.1955)

Sarvodaya and Disarmament

758. Sarvodaya thought is worthless if the Sarvodayites feel that army is indispensable. (VP, 17.12.1955)

India and the Disbandment of Army

759. **Question:** Is there not sufficient public opinion for nonviolence in India to prevail upon the Government to disband the army ? Let India be the first country of the world to do it.

Vinoba: Unfortunately India is not today morally strong enough to take this step. I agree with you that India should be the first country to do so. On account of the special type of our struggle for freedom, the world does expect this leadership from her.

I am trying to build up the nation like that. There is not yet the required public opinion for it. But the Indian Government under the leadership of Pandit Jawaharlal Nehru is trying to follow what Gandhiji taught us and which Panditji calls 'co-existence'. If this idea spreads, it may be possible to disband the army. (SE, March 1955, 284)

760. Some courage, imagination and faith are needed for disarmament, and I will say, India can certainly come forward in unilateral disarmament because of its great tradition. So also other countries of the world because of their own particular situations. As regards unilateral disarmament, I have as much hope from England as from India. (SE, April 1959, 402)

761. It will be an act of wisdom as well as courage if India reduces her armament. This act will enhance her reputation and prestige in the world. It will make her powerful in the real sense. (SE, June 1956,427)

762. I do not mean that the army should be disbanded this very day. What I say is that its strength can well be reduced to half at present without any risk. I simply want to ask if it is not desirable to disband it later, though it may well remain at present. Keep in mind that if at present it has been allowed to exist, it is to be reduced in future. This would never be possible unless you give up your reliance on arms. (L, 204)

763. The other day a person asked me if I approved of the advance of the Indian army in view of the Chinese aggression. I replied to him, "The army is not meant to be fed on bananas, mangoes and biscuits, and to be kept in the barracks. It would be a different matter if it is disbanded." Then he said that if we had no army, the Chinese would have walked in straightway. I rejoined, "Just think over it. If a big country like India disbands her army, it would raise her moral strength tremendously. In that case an attack by China would amount to a world war."

(B, 20.1.1962, 317)

The First Step to International Nonviolence

764. As a first step we should create such conditions in the country that the police or the army becomes unnecessary for internal peace. If we can achieve this, the next step of the extension of nonviolence to external defence, would become apparent.

(B, 21.1.1959, 316)

Not Afraid of Big Wars

765. The whole world is today thinking of a Third World War and if we continue to think about it constantly, it may as well come about. But I am not afraid of world wars. I am afraid of small wars and quarrels. To me a world war appears to come very close to nonviolence. I always say to friends who believe in violence, "If by reason of your faith, you cannot take the vow of nonviolence, do not bother about it. But at least take this vow that if you fight at all, yon will fight world wars, and that you will on no account fight small wars or busy yourselves with petty quarrels." I have even said that world wars are divine. When we do not understand what is right straightway, the all-merciful God sends world wars to stimulate our thinking, and to draw us speedily towards Ahimsa. A world war frees man's mind from limitations which make him think in narrow grooves and impels him to think in terms of humanity as a whole. This is a big step towards Ahimsa. But this is not true of small wars. They are the sworn enemies of Ahimsa, and all the time put Ahimsa further and further away.

(H, 8.1.1950, 388)

The Nature of Modern Wars

766. The wars of these days are ideological wars. If the ideology is mistaken, there can be no victory, no matter how powerful the weapons be. In the last World War, Russia was not stronger than Germany but it could successfully face Germany because the battle of Stalingrad was not merely a battle of soldiers. All the workers there, agricultural and industrial, considered it to be their war. Hence their must be clarity of ideas.

(VP, 16.11.1962)

767. It is a mistake to believe that wars are fought only on the battle-fields. Modern wars are fought on three fronts, the ideological front, the home front and the battle front. The ideological front is assuming greater importance these days. Otherwise, how do you account for the sudden decision by the Chinese for unilateral cease-fire?

They did it because they felt that though they were winning on the battle-fields, they were losing heavily on the ideological front. They had banked on the disunity that was so much in evidence in our country till the other day. They had hoped that India would simply disintegrate under the impact of their attack. But the exact opposite happened. The whole country rallied to its defence, even the communists.

The Chinese Government had also hoped that India being a non-aligned country would not be able to get help from any quarter, but their hopes were belied and she is getting help from many countries. The biggest thing is that the sympathy of a greater part of the world was with India.

(B, 15.12.1962, 262)

768. There is no place for emotions in the techniques of the present-day wars. They are fought after much deliberations on all the aspects of every move. Commands for march or retreat are given on the basis of decisions taken after full thought. Thus, there is no place either for fear or any emotion...When something is done after deliberation, it does not have much of the feelings of enmity. What are required at the time of war are lack of animosity, fearlessness and composure of mind.

(VP, 20.12.1962)

Attitude towards War

769. **Kaka Kalelkar:** The Central Government is solving the problem of Kashmir by military force. It is not at fault. Should they have sat down and given up resistance ? They had no preparation for nonviolent resistance. There is neither the inclination for it nor the organisation and nor even any ready technique for it. Under such conditions what method of resistance could a government adopt except that of the use of arms. We too do not have the qualification to advise it. We have not the capacity for it. In such circumstances if our Government resorts to violent resistance without committing aggression, we should support it. There is no alternative so long as we are unable to develop (the method and/or the capacity for) nonviolent resistance. Resistance is a primary duty; non-resistance is a sign of cowardice.

Vinoba: What we have to ponder over is how intense is our faith today. There is a method of nonviolence. What does our faith say if the people and the government do not favour it? Should we also descend and adopt the usual method of violence ? Or should we live up to our faith and get ourselves annihilated? Some may perhaps feel that it would be better to come down than let a few persons sacrifice themselves. Let them dilute their faith a bit. My own faith ordains that we sacrifice ourselves. That would result in good. It would also be the fulfilment of our duty. But if there is not that much strength, then should we behave like cowards ? Should we sit down and take to non-resistance ? Should we remain inactive? My answer is that there is even penance, *tapasya,* in sitting silently. Inactivity, while the process of thinking is going on within us, is a constructive activity. We must not adopt either of two attitudes in any case—to descend to the level of society and to resort to violent resistance, or to be a coward. We should either get annihilated by acting according to our convic-tion or to ponder over the matter, keeping ourselves aloof. A penance which combines reflection with inactivity is also a mode of service. If we cannot do what is correct, let us at least not do what is non-correct. If we cannot take a correct path, then refusal to take a wrong path is not inactivity. Let us keep aloof and wait. They also serve who wait purposely. During this period, let us ponder over how to develop nonviolent strength. At present I do not find any other way out except that of penance which, though inactive, goes on acquiring nonviolent strength. (Proceedings of 1948 Sevagram Constructive Workers Conference, 5-6)

770. I do not contradict those who take up the position that war is an unmitigated evil. I even respect them. But I also plead this much that alongwith it, discernment too should be appreciated. ...I neither want to be dogmatic nor can I become one. . ..My whole inclination is towards the outlawing of war, towards opposing it. I do not take up any middle position. I am with those who are opposed to war, but in spite of being with them, I hold that there should be some discernment.

(BY, 17.5.1963)

771. If we look only to the outward form of nonviolence, it will not be found to be potent enough. Hence I do not want to waste my energy in resistance to outward symbols of violence.

I find great solace and much strength in the phrase of the scripture, 'Resist not Evil'. It does not say resist evil in a nonviolent way. The attempt to resist violence outwardly will only prolong its evil. When light shines, it dispels darkness. There is no resistance between light and darkness. Darkness merely vanishes. Those who believe in the power of love, nonviolence and compassion should reiterate their full faith and try to persuade people for right thinking.

As regards helping war-efforts, I said humorously that by walking I am doing both—supporting and opposing war-efforts. If you like, I am helping war-effort in that I am freeing the railway and other transports for military movement. I place no impediment. Thus I am helping war-effort. Or, if you like, by not buying a ticket and refusing to use the railway, I am not giving a single penny for war and thus I am opposing the war-efforts.

The main thing is that people should not go mad, lose perspective and their sense of proportion. ...Sometimes cold war is far worse than war itself. There is a 'cold war' and also a 'hot peace'. One thing we must appreciate about India is that the whole nation was forcibly disarmed under the British regime. Hence, there is a sort of inferiority complex among the educated people. (B, 19.1.1963, 305)

772. When I was asked about my reaction (to Chinese attack in 1962), I firmly said that we should fight China because it was the aggressor. The Sarvodaya leaders were confused and asked me to explain the propriety of my advice. I said that before we could practise nonviolence in perfection, our Shanti Sena (Peace Army) must do a lot of groundwork in creating a peaceful atmosphere within the country so that the police and the military become redundant. When we have not done our duty, how could we clamour for the abolition of the army? What was the army for ? Not for eating bananas! At that time I found it relevant that our army should fight the Chinese army and I advised our soldiers to fight to their heart's content, but without any rancour against the Chinese.

In the Bangladesh War also our army behaved in an exemplary manner.... .This war was fought quite in accordance with the message of the Gita. When we were victorious on one front, we stopped the war and announced unilateral cease-fire. We did not occupy Bangladesh but handed it over to the people of that country.

When the world government comes into existence, when an international judge will decide on the problems between one country and another, then only wars will cease. Even then a thief may attack us. Then we shall first receive his blows without retaliation and later, if necessary, we shall fight him with all our strength and even kill him, but without any enmity towards him.

If I remember correctly, Gandhiji held the same opinion. When Kashmir was invaded in 1947, the same question arose whether to fight the invaders or not. Gandhiji approved of the army action and said that though nonviolence should be adhered to in individual life, the government of a country would have to compromise with violence.

(Sarvodaya, Sept. 1974,74)

773. We should find out ways of abolishing war, but even then if they continue and we have to go to render aid to the wounded soldiers, we should do it. We should not refuse it on the ground that it is a part of war, but we must keep in mind that it is not our real work. (S, March-April 1953, 567)

774. I have no hesitation in admitting that I am not at the highest level of nonviolence.

(Proceedings of 1963 Arambagh Sarva Seva Sangh Session, 76)

1962 Chinese Aggression

775. My basic view as a Shanti Sainik (peace soldier) remains unchanged that in this world no good can come out of arms or weapons of war. I can never give up my opposition to armed conflict or war in any form; yet, at the same time I also feel that India was not intending war, and was always prepared for peaceful negotiations. This is, therefore, an aggression against India by China and is absolutely wrong. It is not even befitting from the point of view of communism. I would therefore call it expansionism. China may be using the language of communism with the hope of winning the sympathies of certain nations but ideologically it is expansionism.

Such expansionism in the present age can only lead to utter destruction. It is to the credit of India that she does not believe in expansionism. She has not done so throughout her history, nor have I seen any trace of it among her people in my twelve years' trek throughout the country. Therefore my sympathies are with India. I have thought over the problem not as an Indian but in its world context.

I appeal to China that she should retrace her wrong steps for the good of the world. She will then discover that India desires her friendship.

I also express my hope that the Indian Government, though engaged in fighting because war has been forced upon her, will do so without enmity and hatred, only because it has become necessary to fight....There should be no change, no lowering of standards in the policy India has been following since independence—a policy of friendship to all and enmity towards none. (SE, Dec. 1962, 201)

776. You are aware that lately China has been in conflict with India. The Chinese later affected a retreat of their army and expressed some readiness for settlement. But the two parties are claiming to be cent per cent right. It was due to this difficult situation that the non-aligned powers came forward to evolve a settlement. They have conferred with Chou En-lai in Peking and with Pandit Nehru in New Delhi, and have placed their proposals before both of them. The proposals, however, have not been disclosed. They are being studied by them....I would, therefore, appeal that even if the non-aligned powers' proposals are not acceptable in full to either of the parties, they should generally be accepted. (B, 2. 2. 1963, 309)

The Way to Meet Aggression

777. If we want to repel the invaders successfully, we must forge unity among all sections of the people. This real unity cannot be achieved so long as large sections of the people remain hungry and naked. A hungry man cannot feel the national urge to defend the country's freedom. The well-off section of society must, therefore, donate a part of their possessions, specially land, to the landless people. This is necessary both to increase production as well as to put up united defence against the Chinese aggression.

(B, 27. 10. 1962, 201)

778. Indians residing in the areas taken possession of by the Chinese Government, should not cooperate with it at all.

(BY, 16.11.1962)

779. We will not find any incident in Gandhiji's life which can indicate to us what we are to do in case of international quarrels and conflicts. We shall have to think about it ourselves, and no superficial thinking will do. We shall have to think in a new way. I cannot go here into details since it is a matter for discussion. However, if invaders come, I would tell them that they may come out of love and for talks. Our children would go to meet them. They would not be afraid of them. Our girls would go to meet them; they would not be afraid of them. We would lovingly invite them, but if they want us to do something wrong, we would tell them that we cannot do it even if they kill us. (BY, 4.6.1965)

Aggression and Shanti Sena

780. Our fellow-workers feel that the experiment of (Delhi-Peking) Friendship March is something better than what Baba (Vinoba) is doing, and to go and take up positions between the two forces on the front would still be better. It appears to them that it would be the best programme......To me the idea seems to be crude with nothing scientific about it. What should predominate in satyagraha—spiritual power or physical power? A physically strong man is recruited for the army. Is it also necessary for satyagraha ? Can one with good physical health only participate in it? If one has to go to the Himalayas, will Jayaprakashji, Baba or Dhirendrabhai be able to go there ?

Hence it must be realized that because of physical strength playing a predominant role in it, it would be an extremely crude experiment of satyagraha. If you want to practise satyagraha in the international field, you must search for a spiritual method, and if you have not discovered it so far, it should be admitted. But this satyagraha cannot be one in which physical strength predominates. (SSH, 125, 126)

781. Many of us naturally feel that it would have been better if some of us had gone on the front and done something. It is a matter of some weakness that we could neither do anything nor are we in a position to do anything. However, if we reflect over the question as to where strength or weakness lies in such international matters, we will find it in thought and love. If our thought is pure and along with it there is love to strengthen it, there will be strength. Suppose we go on the front and do some demonstration work, it would result in nothing except removing our mental dissatisfaction and providing us some solace. But that sort of solace would not be desirable. It would be better if there is some dissatisfaction and it results in the clarification of ideas and the purification of our mind and heart.

Ram Manohar Lohia tried to do so. He wanted to enter NEFA, but he was stopped. If we also go and refuse to turn back and the Government puts us in jail, we may get the satisfaction of having done our duty, but will it be proper ? Today the Government does not prevent you from putting your ideas before the people. The whole field of work is open to you. If instead of doing it, you go, sit in jail and derive satisfaction, that satisfaction would not be as potent and stimulating as the dissatisfaction can be. I am reminded here of a sentence of a moral philosopher, that "a dissatisfied Socrates is better than a satisfied pig." (SSH, 126, 127)

How to Solve International Disputes ?

782. What to do when this (Sino-Indian) conflict begins afresh? Let there be negotiations. If the dispute is not being solved by negotiations, then let there be arbitration. (VP, 23.1.1962)

783. **Vinoba:** There will be an International Tribunal to settle all disputes of the world.

Question: How will it be constituted ?

Vinoba: The people of every country will send to it their men of learning and high character. These shall only have moral sanction. They will not only settle disputes but will also have advisory functions. (VKS, 59-60)

Indo-Pakistan War of 1965

784. A war is going on between India and Pakistan. After giving careful thought to it, I have come to the conclusion that this war has been imposed upon India and I, therefore, support the stand taken by the Government. But this does not mean that I am happy over it. I am sure that the Government also does not feel happy about it. (TTR, 10)

Military Action in Goa

785. As far as I am aware, it does not appear that either the people of India or their leaders have any desire to extend their territory, and I say so in spite of India's action in Goa which, though not pronounced wrong by anybody, did belie the world's expectations of this country. The people of this country considered Goa to be a part of India and they were not wrong about it. (BY, 28.5.1964)

Essential Conditions for Internal Peace

786. Let me tell you that if status quo continues, if the poor in the villages are neglected and if disparities go on aggravating, no force will be able to check internal disorder and external aggression. (TTR, 12)

787. For peace and security within the country, we must cast off mutual differences and share our weal and woe together. Sharing decreases misery and increases joy. (ibid, 16)

Police in a Nonviolent State

788. People ask whether in a nonviolent state if there is no army, there will at least be a police force. Those who reply say that there will be police but of a somewhat different kind. But why not say in other words that there will be no police, but only an alert band of public spirited workers, as well as citizens, who are conscious of their own duties ? Such a reply is not given because these questions and answers do not relate to the ideal state but to the stage which we have reached at present on the way to nonviolence, and to the utmost we are able to imagine on the basis of conditions now prevailing.

(SS, 68)

All Are Criminals or None

789. I do not believe in dividing men as criminals and non-criminals. To me, no man is a criminal. Some men are branded as such and are put in jails. But some criminals are to be found outside—only they are not so in the eyes of law.

(B, 17.9.1958, 176)

790. It is held that the pleader, the judge and the police etc. work to eradicate crimes and robberies. But they are all of the same fraternity as thieves and robbers. They punish the innocent and feed the culprit. (H, 5.2.1955, 390)

791. It is true that there has lately been an alarming increase in crime which is bound to cause concern to all those who have the well-being of the people at heart. But there is nothing surprising in it. The surprise rather is why it is so little, looking to the appalling conditions—the ignorance, the poverty and the injustice—in which our people live. The conditions indeed are so exasperating that it should have been far more than it is.

The real difficulty in this regard lies not with thieves and dacoits who can easily be managed but with us—the respectable and educated city-dwellers. We are committing far more crimes than the former, but nobody takes an account of it. All exploitation and hoarding of wealth are a form of stealing. (H, 31.7.1954,180)

792. "It is the rich who perpetrate crimes, not the poor," some one from the audience intervened.

"I agree," said Vinoba, "the real offenders are we, the white-collared gentry, the makers of criminals."

(H, 28.6.1952, 150)

Punishment

793. The punishment of a thief in olden days was to chop off his hands. ... That makes them a burden on society. Who wants that today ? Nowadays a thief gets only some months' imprisonment. But this also needs to be changed. Who is the real sufferer of the punishment ? It is his wife and children. If the earning member of the family goes to jail, it is they who suffer. .. .Where is justice in sending the thief to jail and in starving them to death ? My head and heart revolt against it.

(B, 7.10.1959, 189)

794. People are afraid that crime will increase if a deterrent like capital punishment is abolished. Those who know something of the psychology of a criminal will understand that a deterrent like capital punishment hardly enters his mind when he is seized by some insane passion. Our civilization and culture have looked upon public opinion as the final sanction of right social behaviour. It is not the penal code that keeps men and women on the right path. The existence of proper values and public opinion is an effective guide to good conduct. In an ideal Sarvodaya society law will not need a penal code. It will express itself as the conscience of the people.

(B, 17.4.1957, 2)

How to Deal with Crimes ?

795. There are always in society a few noble individuals who do not require public opinion to hold them within the limits of morality. Similarly there are also wayward and indiscriminate individuals who, unmindful of public opinion, go against the laws of morality. But the general public or the great majority of people observe what is ordained and avoid what is prohibited by public opinion. Such public opinion naturally constitutes the basis of law or restraint, and the vast majority of people always respect it. The few wayward individuals who remain outside this number should be put in the company of the few who are high-souled, instead of being submitted to forcible restraint. (SS, 35)

796. It is obvious that if we are really anxious to eradicate crime, then we must find out its root cause which lies in the faulty organisation of society. We must purify and where necessary rebuild the social organisation.

Simultaneously with the purification of the social organisation, there must also be purification of thought. Efforts should be made to introduce and establish in our social consciousness the idea that it is a sin to hoard wealth and avoid physical labour. (H, 31.7.1954, 180)

797. If there is a wicked man in the village and he refuses to listen to others, then instead of punishing him, the members of the Gram Sabha will undertake fast. This will make his heart melt. However, it will prove effective only if they have faith in it. If they believe in chastising him and still undertake fast, there is no faith. (AG, 33)

798. I tell you, love, compassion, generosity and forgiveness have a higher place in life as moral attributes than hard-hearted punishment. Let us therefore adhere to love, compassion and nonviolence while dealing with problems arising out of crime and punishment. (CN, 133)

The Need of a Shanti Sena (Peace Army)

799. The basic problem of the world today is the establishment of peace. Perhaps in no other age has there been such a world-hunger for peace. There are countries whose whole way of thought, up to yesterday, was deeply dyed in violence; today even those countries long to find release from violence. True, they go on increasing their armaments, but nevertheless they are wondering how to get rid of them. The sheer inertia of habit makes for the stockpiling of arms. But intellectually people have come to understand that arms will achieve nothing —nothing, that is, except losses for the poor and the blocking of all progress in real welfare, consequent on the immense expenditure of resources on the army. Even those countries where revolutions have taken place through bloodshed desire peace today. Why ? Because whereas in the former days the weapons were in the hands of men, it is so no longer; men are now in the hands of their weapons. If the spark of war should now set the world on fire, no man will be able to control it. Mankind has, therefore, lost faith in the possibility of solving its problems through war or violence. That in itself is a great thing to have happened and the way forward is now open. If arms can no longer settle our disputes, then some other way of settling them must be found. That is what the Shanti Sena is designed to do. (SSE, 1-2)

800. Today there is an explosive situation in the country. There can be a sudden explosion for any reason whatsoever. I am realizing every day how great a need there is of Shanti Sena today. (NA, 83)

The Birth of Shanti Sena

801. The Shanti Sena is not a new proposal. We owe both the word and the idea behind it to Bapu*, who himself endeavoured to give it a practical shape. He was both its commander and its first soldier. As commander he issued the order 'Do or die', and as a soldier he obeyed it. That is, his life and actions give us a complete picture of what the Shanti Sena is. No doubt, he also expounded his ideas freely in words, but it was through action, through life, that his thought was most fully expressed.

(SSE, 2)

The Functions of Shanti Sena

802. The Shanti Sena is an army which offers its services in perpetuity to all men without distinction. ...A sick man is given the same care, no matter what his caste, his religion or his politics, and no matter whether he lives nobly or wickedly. All that matters is that he is a man in need.

We have therefore to set up this sort of army which will serve the needs impartially, disinterestedly, without asking for any reward. Its whole vocation will be to confront hatred with love. (SSE, 64-65)

803. To be a Shanti Sainik (peace soldier) means to be prepared to leave everything, home, public work etc., and go wherever he may be called. This is one point in which he differs from other Lok Sevaks; his other pledges are the same. The work of the Shanti Sainik has therefore two aspects: his regular, day-to-day duties are of a 'Seva Sainik' (one who serves) while his occasional duties are those of the Shanti Sainik. Other workers also may devote themselves to regular constructive work in their own locality, and together with this they will, as occasion arises, take the responsibility for keeping the peace in their own locality. .. .But the Shanti Sainik is not only a permanent servant of the community, he is also ready at any time to go wherever he is called upon to go.

(SSE, 52-53)

---

* 'Bapu', which stands for 'father' was a term used for Gandhiji by those who felt nearness to him,

804. I would wish, at any rate, that we should avoid entangling ourselves in social and political questions. It is not the duty of the Shanti Sainik to find solutions for all problems of society. His job is to help people in their physical troubles and do his best to help them also in their mental worries. In addition, he will be taking every chance of helping them to understand the ideas of Bhoodan, Gramdan etc., and bringing Sarvodaya literature to their notice. .. .If he aspires to do more than this, and to put an end to their differences, he will get into difficulties. He should not take up such matters without consulting his leader in the Peace Army; otherwise it may result in the work of the Shanti Sena being hindered. (SSE, 132)

Qualifications of a Shanti Sainik

805. Those who enlist in the Shanti Sena will consider it their duty to serve the whole community, to help all the needy, without regard for caste, religion, sect, party or any other distinction. The Shanti Sainik must treat everyone, high or low, in the same way; like water he must be humble, gentle, clean, pure and cool. Jnaneshwar has a lovely passage about water : 'so gentle is water that it can touch even the eye and cause no pain, yet so strong that it can crack open the very rocks. Its special virtue is that it does not attack the obstacle in its path; if it cracks the rock, the rock is responsible....' Like water, the Shanti Sainik must be very humble, for is he not the healer of all *ashanti*, lack of peace?

The first requirement for a Shanti Sainik is that no one should be afraid of him. The various political parties also must have no fear of him; if they are afraid, he must show by his conduct that he has no partisan spirit, that he is out to serve without looking for any reward, and that he has no inclination to join any party but is working only for Sarvodaya, the welfare of all, and is ready to give his life, if need should arise, for that cause. (SSE, 46-47)

806. A member of Shanti Sena, whether a man or woman, must have a living faith in nonviolence. This is only possible if one has a living faith in God. ...Without that, one would not have the courage to lay down one's life without anger, fear and desire for vengeance.

This messenger of peace should have equal respect for all the prominent religions of the world. If he is a Hindu, he would have equal reverence for other religions found in India. He should have the knowledge of the principles common to various religions.

It need not be mentioned that one who works for peace should have a blameless character. He should be reputed for his impartiality. (SSH, 119-120)

807. The Shanti Sainik accepts the principle of *aparigraha,* non-possession, and does not accumulate unnecessary possessions. But this does not mean that he must give up all he has. If a man has land, let him give away one-sixth of it, and let him be prepared to give it all up if Gramdan comes about. Let him hold the rest of his possessions as a trust, and let him simplify his personal wants. I do not expect anything more than that. (SSE, 140-141)

The Pledge of a Shanti Sainik

808. The main principle of Shanti Sena is that they should be free from partisanship, free from hatred, free from fear. They will trust one another, will fear none, and will frighten none. They will consider no man their enemy; their hearts will be filled with love. This is the pledge of the Shanti Sainik. (SSE, 45)

The Training of Shanti Sainiks

809. It is necessary that Shanti Sainiks are trained for their work. The Sarva Seva Sangh should take it into consideration and plan for it, and the method of training need to be fully thought out. I have a few suggestions to make.

One is that there are some sources of power of which we have as yet little or no knowledge. For example, we know something about the power of words, but we know very little of the power of silence. It too has great power, and it can sometimes exercise a very great influence for good upon the mind.

The second is that music linked with devotion is a great peace-maker. This is another thing which must claim our attention.... In the training of a Shanti Sainik there should be a place for music full of devotion and of devotion full of music.

Let us remember that no matter how much service we render we still remain debtors for the services we ourselves have received from society in our childhood. Even if we labour continuously to repay society, something would still remain, and in the end it is we who must ask society to kindly write off the balance and free us from the debt. In short, our workers should be taught what service means, and the spirit in which it should be rendered. They must learn the attitude that 'keeps on serving', not that which 'gets it done with'.

Another need of ours is training in the science of orderliness. ...Our huge armies were (sometimes) defeated by small armies of only five thousand strong, because they lacked an orderly plan of action. The enemy forces were disciplined and ours were not. We have to acquire the habit of discipline, and it must be included in the training of our workers.

Then take the matter of thought. We must not allow our minds to get excited or flurried. We must be able to meet any attack on us with a peaceful mind and in full possession of our power of thinking. For in this age of science, a man whose mind is disturbed by anxiety is sure to be defeated.

(SSE, 67-68)

810. Some portion of the primary training of the army is also essential for Shanti Sena. It is about discipline, drill, chorus singing, etc.

A volunteer should know how to carry the wounded. He should have such articles with him as are needed for First Aid. ...He should know how to extinguish fire, how to enter safely a place on fire, how to climb up with or without a load and to descend safely. (SSH, 118)

811. They must be familiar with Indian thought, with the idea of *samanvaya,* synthesis. They must also be trained in the techniques of various kinds of useful work. (SSE, 47)

812. There can be two opinions regarding the training of Shanti Sainiks. Some talk of short duration camps, while others of a course running for two or three months. Both are needed. There should be a training school as well as camps.

(SSH, 114-115)

813. For increase of knowledge, refresher courses should also be arranged. They should teach the worker how he can serve best. (SSH, 31)

Discipline in Shanti Sena

814. A man joins the Shanti Sena...of his own free will. But once he has joined, he must accept the whole of its discipline..... He must use not only his intelligence in carrying out the work which is entrusted to him, but he must also be ready to give complete obedience to whatever command is given.

(SSE, 40)

Special Dress for Shanti Sainiks

815. The members of this Sena should have a special dress so that they may be identified without any difficulty.(SSH, 120)

Women and Shanti Sena

816. If women will take up the work of Shanti Sena, the face of the world will change, and we shall be able to achieve freedom from the problems which we are facing today in the country and abroad. Men cannot do all this. They are not in their proper senses. They cannot think it out. The only solution they can find is to increase armaments. Thus in this age of science, when men's brains have become paralysed, if our women come forward with their divine qualities of restraint and modesty, and use their mother-power, they can establish the rule of compassion. (WP, 53)

817. In the path of violence, men will always lead. But in the path of nonviolence, women can go ahead of them. So it is essential that women should lead, and that too in their own way. The way of women is the way of compassion. (WP, 52)

The Strength of Shanti Sena

818. Higher the trituration of a homeopathic medicine and minuter its quantity, the more powerful it becomes. The process of nonviolence is exactly similar....In other words, the purer are our feelings, the stronger will be our Shanti Sena. (SSH, 49)

Maintenance of Shanti Sena

819. The conclusion is that we should not assume responsibility for our own maintenance, but commit ourselves to God.

Nevertheless, for the present, I do not want to surround the Shanti Sainik with more difficulties and hence if Sainiks get their support from particular persons in the existing conditions, I shall not object to it. But they should accept it only if those persons are wholly upright and honourable. It would, however, be better if we depended entirely on the common people. Suppose that at present my brother is meeting my expenses, then at a later stage I should be able to ask him not to continue giving me my maintenance but to give Sampattidan (donation of money) instead. As our movement develops, we should aim at being supported by Sarvodaya Patra alone. (SSE, 143-144)

Shanti Sena and War

820. **Question:** What will the Shanti Sena do when confronted by an armed force in times of war ?

Vinoba: What is the work of the Shanti Sena ? Wars are not a daily occurrence; even quarrels do not occur everyday. But the Shanti Sena must be at work everyday and twenty-four hours of the day.... It will be the Shanti Sena's task to remove the root causes of unrest—the gulf between the haves and the have-nots, the pride of ownership, the insistence on 'mine' and 'thine', on high and low, on caste distractions, on religious differences and disputes. These are all causes of unrest, some economic, some social, some religious.... The Shanti Sena will, therefore, be a full-time service army, working to remove these causes of dissensions and to find peaceful solutions to national problems. The result will be a cleansing of the national mind and the growth of mutual goodwill. When that takes place, the government will not have to spend much on the army; the moral strength of the nation will be increased and it will be able to make its influence felt in the international field.

The full-time friendly service which it renders will make it respected both at home and abroad. (SSE, 134-135, 136)

The Limitation of Laws

821. The very idea that law can reform society is wrong. Law stands for superficial treatment. In case of an abscess, we treat it externally when the disease is internal. Consequently, though the external treatment cures that abscess, a second one erupts. For a real cure, there should be internal purification. (VP, 5.3.1958)

822. Legislation and coercion will not create a happy and free man. We can see in recent history how idealistic and well-meant social efforts end in futility. ... It is obvious that legislation can only bring about a superficial change. If we want a radical change, we have to bring about a change in the heart and mind of man. We have to appeal to every individual and open his eyes to the new truth. (B, 20.2.1957, 4)

A Shortcoming of Law

823. If we leave everything to the government, we cripple ourselves. The government enacts laws, but the laws cannot discriminate. It applies to all equally, without differentiating when it should. (VP, 1.3.1958)

When Will Legislation be Effective ?

824. There is a place for legislation in nonviolence, but it will not serve its purpose unless there is a congenial climate for it. (VP, 28.5.1959)

Linguistic States

825. Though the idea of linguistic division is good, it should not be based on pride and hatred but goodwill and love. ... We must consider the whole of India as one and all languages as sisters and, therefore, mutually helpful and not hostile. So there must be mutual love and not hatred. The importance of linguistic division is simply for the convenience of service and administration. If it does not foster goodwill and love, there will be no good left in it. (H, 30.8.1949, 203)

The Problem of Kashmir

826. The people are now realizing the mistake of partitioning the country. It gave recognition to a state based on religion, something which was not compatible with our thinking. It also did not suit the times.

We agreed to the partition out of the compulsion of circumstances. We do not want to undo history. But if we now look upon Kashmir as a Muslim-majority area and hence entitled to secede thinking that it is not proper for it to remain in India, we would be repeating the mistake after fifteen years or so.

There is not the least doubt that the problem would only be solved when there would be a confederation of India and Pakistan. It cannot be brought about by force, but by love.

(BY, 28.2.1964)

827. Political problems cannot be solved through politics; they can be solved only through spiritual approach. The essence of spirituality lies in unanimity and mutual goodwill.

Kashmir is directly connected with six countries—India, Pakistan, Afghanistan, China, Russia and America. ... It is, therefore, necessary for the people of Kashmir to raise their mind to the supramental level and evolve a world approach to their problems. They must liberate their minds from the events of the past and develop an objective and scientific outlook.

(RV, 287)

IX
CONSTRUCTIVE WORK

The Essence of the Constructive Programme

828. The whole of the constructive progrmme is a programme of love. (KD, 54)

The Importance of Constructive Work

829. It is by constructive work that the power of nonviolence is generated. Just as destruction is reckoned as a powerful means of violence, similarly reconstruction is a basic source of nonviolence. (VP, 11.6.1958)

The Type of Constructive Work Needed Today

830. The times have changed now; it is a new age. The work to be done now requires greater depth and it is a difficult task. The work of getting independence, of the removal of a foreign power, was not so difficult as is the work that lies ahead.... Now we have to take up in hand a new work of social and economic revolution. I feel that the old methods will not do. (S, May 1951, 575)

831. Shri Patil* asked today if the same constructive programme which had been chalked out before independence, would continue even after it ? Or it would have a scope and need for some change ? I had also been thinking on it. The main changes we should think of are to give up reliance on money and to depend on bodily labour. We should do as much as we can by bodily labour. If we need donations, let them be of bodily labour. If we thus run our activities in future, our whole life will acquire a lustre. (ibid)

---

* It is Sri R.K. Patil, a formar I.C.S., who has been very close to Vinobaji.

832. Khadi, village industries and other such activities constitute branches of the Sarvodaya tree, while Bhoodan, Gramdan and other similar activities are its roots. If attempts will be made to make the branches grow by cutting them off from the tree, they would not succeed.

(A talk with workers on 30.4.1957)

833. We should do two things first—bring about unity between men of different religions and languages, and remove the chasm between the rich and the poor. (PP, 8.9.1959)

A Criticism of the Present Constructive Work

834. These days I feel very uneasy. I find that Sarvodaya work is acquiring the form of a system and losing its essence. Bapu did not want that our workers should get entangled in the externals of Khadi, tannery, village industries, etc. He hoped that they would lead to the development of the inner qualities. But this aspect has been greatly weakened now.

I am greatly perturbed over it. In the absence of the development of inner qualities, the whole Sarvodaya ideology would lose its vigour. Khadi and village industries are not Sarvodaya, which can only be realized through self-knowledge and *brahma-vidya,* the knowledge of the Brahma. In order to expand our activities, we are getting more and more tempted towards government help everyday. However, it is apparent to me that as the government aid will increase, we shall be losing more and more. Presently we lack the ability to accept the government help without losing ourselves. This lack can be removed by acquiring inner qualities and *brahma-vidya*, the knowledge of the Supreme.

I frequently hear about constructive activities, but I do not notice any strong base for them anywhere. The whole work seems to be devoid of life. Should I regard such activities conducted on the aid of the government as constructive work ? If these activities are not based on ideology, if they do not develop inner qualities, how can I call them constructive work ? If we examine ourselves, we shall find that our ideas are far ahead of us. We do talk of superficial equality. It is said that difference in salaries in our institutions is only one and a half or two times. Thus there is a talk of superficial equality, but it is only an artificial equality. Unless there is an inner feeling of equality, external equality will not achieve anything.

Bapu gave a new direction to knowledge, action, austerity and devotion. India has been familiar with these since olden days, but Bapu applied them in a new way. He linked them with social change and revolution. Similarly he joined Khadi, Nai Talim, nursing the sick and other activities with social change. His approach was that all these should help in the development of inner qualities without going against the good of the world. But what has happened is that while the grosser aspects of these activities are with us and we have got tied up with them, the basic purpose has been lost.

(BY, 26.6.1959)

The need of an Integrated Outlook

835. I am definitely not satisfied with the present constructive work, its institutions and its direction. Hence I want to repeat once more before you all that in order to complete the work Bapu left to us, there is now the need of making some basic changes. The mode of carrying on these activities will have to be thoroughly changed. They all will have to be thought out in the context of Gram Swaraj. (ibid)

Real Village Reconstruction

836. What we generally term 'village reconstruction' is in fact a development activity. Village reconstruction is a different thing altogether. We have nothing like a village today. The Government in Delhi has our consent and we provide it with money. That is why a Central Government exists. The same is true of the State Governments. The household exists as an institution because it commands both our consent and money. But it is not so with the village. Hence I say that a real village will come into existence only when people agree to Gramdan, implement it and provide it with money. Later on, what will have to be done further will be the work of development.

(Cited by Dattoba Dastane in BY, 16.2.1962, 7)

A Programme for Sarvodaya Centres

837. The workers must first find out what are the felt needs of the people amongst whom they are living. They must study carefully the conditions of the people and find out the basic deficiencies of their life. They must ponder over the basic social problems and begin experiments in solving them. They must find out how the implements used by the people can be improved. They should find out if their diet is wholesome, balanced and healthy. They must pay special attention towards village sanitation. ... They (the people) must be taught how to turn human waste into manure. Village industries have almost declined everywhere. They must be revived. There is an urgent need to change the whole structure of the social life in the village.

The people of the village have some shortcomings, some defects. But at the same time they have some good qualities. We should develop those good qualities. They do physical labour daily, a habit which educated persons lack, and it is generally they who work in such institutions. Hence let all of them lead a life of physical labour.

Workers in a centre like this should undertake a detailed study of the social and economic life, of the basic causes of poverty and suffering.... Sarvodaya centres should start some ameliorative activities and provide partial employment to the needy. But they rarely face the challenge of village unemployment. They have a feeling that it is too big a problem for them.

An individual, they think, may work for small reforms, but he cannot bring about any radical transformation. Sarvodaya centres must become laboratories of social change. They must find out how to create a will in the people for an immediate radical change, and give them an instrument with which they can bring it about. In short, our centres must carry on experiments for (1) improving the quality of social life in the village, (2) making some bodily labour an essential part of their daily life, and (3) finding out a method of bringing about a radical change with the consent of all.

There is one more point I would like to stress. Our Sarvodaya centres have not been paying enough attention to study and intellectual equipment. Some of the workers have looked upon it as a luxury. This attitude is harmful....We serve the people because we are out to change the social order. They must therefore study deeply the religious, cultural, social, economic and political trends of our social life. They should try to understand the significance of our spiritual tradition.

Sarvodaya is a comprehensive philosophy of life. It has great depth. It should be studied and reflected upon in all its aspects.

Workers in a centre like this must be humble. They must develop the capacity to befriend everyone around them. They should have no likes and dislikes. They must be generous and appreciative.

It is only then that these centres will become power houses of Sarvodaya thought and spread light, learning and right efforts around them. (B, 19.6.1957 and BY, 28.6.1957)

A Programme for Cities

838. There should be town or Nagar Swaraj in cities like Gram Swaraj in villages. I mean that the urban municipality or city corporation should be free from the influence of political parties and its members should serve the city people without any bias of party, sect or creed. ... Further, there should be Shanti Sena in the city with one Shanti Sainik for every hundred, who will serve the people in normal times and in times of disturbances throw himself into the fire of conflict like Ganesh Shankar Vidyarthi. (TTR, 69)

Constructive Work and the Masses

839. A building without strong foundation is apt to collapse by a blast of strong wind. Similarly, no work can be accomplished without creating in the masses an interest for it.

(B, 20.5.1959, 28)

Constructive Work and Government Aid

840. We are not boycotting the government. It realizes taxes from us. What harm is there if we get it back? Hence, it is not that we shall not take any help from it. We are not to non-cooperate with it, we have to abolish it. But as long as it is there, we can take its help. Only it will be on our terms.

(BG, VI, 167)

841. We should not accept any such help as makes us decrepit or lame. True, that the Government is ours and it is duty bound to help constructive work. Thereby it does not lay us under any obligation either. But we should be careful and see to it that it does not hurt us in anyway. The nature of the government help should be like the brick prop set up while building arch in a house, which is removed after its erection. The government help should decrease year after year and by the time it comes to an end in four or five years, the project in question should be complete. (SE, March 1962, 279)

842. Our workers should be strictly maintained on popular support. We may take help from the government for our work, but not for the workers. If they depend upon government money, they will lose their identity. (ibid, 280)

843. After his return from South Africa, Gandhiji adopted a policy of cooperation with the government. He said he would cooperate as long as he believed in their bonafides.

If we object to the acceptance of government help on the ground of our belief in a stateless society, we would be committing a double mistake. First, it would mean that we have lost all faith in human goodness, and, secondly, it would postpone the day when stateless society can come into existence. I had once mooted the idea that deliverance and acquisition are two separate categories. I am afraid that some friends have been carried away by it without understanding its deeper implication.

The ideal of stateless society may become feasible when men who are working for deliverance, i.e. for a radical solution, and men who are working for reform join hands in putting down things that are evil, When the evil is removed and goodness remains, then the parting of ways would naturally come.

We must not forget that our lives do not express nonviolence. We have a faith in and a devotion for the ideal. This is all that we can claim for ourselves.

(B, 2.7.1958, 84-85)

Sarvodaya Activities and Trust Funds

844. The Bhoodan movement took whatever help it could from the Gandhi Memorial Fund. It was natural and legitimate for it to take that help in the initial stage of the experiment. But if we depend on such support after the initial stage is over, it becomes a hindrance to further development.

(B, 28.11.1956, 4)

What Bhoodan Really is ?

845. Land-gifts have significance only so far as they are an index of a change in the outlook of the donors. A land-gift is not a religious act of charity. It is a conscious act of a person who desires to bring about a change in the social order. The old idea of charity assumes a revolutionary importance if its social context is understood properly. (B, 22.8.1956, 4)

846. The Bhoodan movement is not one-sided affair confined to just one sector of our economic life. It includes all efforts aimed at building up a strong and noble life throughout our land. It certainly includes moral regeneration of our people. The redistribution of land and promotion of village industries will help in eradicating poverty and clear the way for moral uplift. (H, 10.4.1954, 43)

Objectives of the Bhoodan Movement

847. My mission is not to stave off a revolution. I want to prevent a violent revolution and create a nonviolent one. The future peace and prosperity of the country depend upon a peaceful solution of the land problem. (H, 8.12.1951, 349)

848. Bhoodan wants peace and love to become the dominant values in society. All problems ought to be solved by negotiations in a spirit of friendliness. (B, 6.2.1957, 5)

849. We seek to reconstruct society on a new basis. That is the purpose behind the Bhoodan work. It is not merely to collect land... What we want is to establish new values—to make morality the guiding principle of social life and to make economics, which enjoys undue importance at present, subservient to the former. ... The Bhoodan movement is for us an instrument for achieving a nonviolent and peaceful change of values. (H, 12.6.1954, 122)

The Basis of Bhoodan

850. The basic idea of Bhoodan Yajna is that wealth, intelligence and all such things which a man has, belong to society and they should go to it. ... If something remains with somebody, he is its trustee. (BAC, 43)

851. Just as air, water and the sun are freely available to all, even so all must be allowed to have a claim on land, which is equally a gift of God. (H, 26.12.1953, 341)

Wider Implications of Bhoodan

852. Some persons think that there are some who have only to ask and not to give anything. But I say that there is none who has not got something to give. There is wealth, there is land, there is intelligence, there is labour, and, if nothing, then love at least is there. All have to give. (PP, 7.3.1959)

853. The present national boundaries are bound to be demolished, and it is already happening. The whole world is sure to become one, and this cannot be prevented. ... The people of a country with less land are entitled to go to another which has more. This is the implication of Bhoodan and its message in the world context of today. (VP, 23.2.1958)

Replies to Objections against Bhoodan

854. We should not feel uneasy at the word *dana,* gift, in the term *bhoomidan yajna* since Shankaracharya has explained the word *dana* as equitable division. I use the word with that connotation. (H, 17.5.1952, 102)

855. Some say that Baba is distributing poverty. They do not realize that if there is poverty in the country, it should be shared, and if there is wealth, that too must be shared. In fact, it is not a movement of distributing poverty, but of joining the hearts. (KKR, 74-75)

856. Your contention is that very small plots of land hamper production. You will have to substantiate this axiomatic proposition of yours. No doubt, you can carry on cooperative farming in future by imparting its training to all. But there is no ground to observe that small plots of land tend to reduce production, specially when you know that our people are inclined towards individual farming. (KW, Vol. I, 99)

857. The movement (Bhoodan) I am carrying on is not, as some seem to imagine, a counter-action against the communists. It is based on a positive ideology, which stands on its own right. The rays of the sun are not a counter-action against darkness. (H, 27.12.1952, 374)

Bhoodan and Gandhiji

858. **Question:** In what sense do you feel you are carrying on Gandhiji's work ?

Vinoba : I do not think I am carrying on anybody's work, but I think that after Swaraj, this work of Bhoodan comes in the natural course. And I believe that Gandhiji also would have turned his attention to this problem. The solution of the land problem is not so important as the method of solving it, and so far as the method is concerned, I feel I am trying to put into practice the essence of Gandhiji's teachings. (SE, Aug. 1955, 51)

The Achievements of the Bhoodan Movement

859. The little achievement we have had so far is not at all negligible. It is, in fact, inspiring. Till today no political party or organisation in the country has been able to distribute one million acres; nay, not even half as much land to the poor. The Congress swears by the landless labourers and the P.S.P., the Communist Party, and the Jana Sangh all are for giving land to the tillers. The government also promises to provide the landless with land. But the combined contribution of all these agencies is not to the extent of one million acres.

So, we see that the Bhoodan movement has surpassed the combined efforts of the government and the political parties. Never do I entertain pessimism in my heart. For, I have seen that His blessings are more in comparison to the quantum of labour put in the Bhoodan movement.

(B, 13.5.1961, 25)

Sutanjali, Yarn-Offering*

860. It is a thing pregnant with tremendous power. Only we have not yet recognized it. We want the people to offer *sutanjali* as a sign of the realization on one's part of one's responsibility to add to the wealth of this country by agreeing to do physical labour. I look upon it as a vote for Sarvodaya. The *sutanjali* work will be of great help in inculcating the dignity of labour among our people.... I envisage another important use for *sutanjali.* Until now we have been conducting our institutions with the help of money from our friends and sympathisers among the rich. There was nothing wrong in it. But now times have changed; we are now in the age of the supremacy of labour. It is a welcome change and we should help it. One of the ways in which we can do so is to run our institutions on the basis of labour. (H, 16.5.1953, 87)

Sampattidan, Wealth-Gift

861. From Bhoodan to Sampattidan was a natural step, and the idea that along with Bhoodan I should also ask for Sampattidan, did occur to me and held my mind. But the land problem was a basic one and I saw that unless something was done to meet it, it might develop into a big

---

* It meant offering of one hank of self-spun yarn from every person on the 12th of February, the day Gandhiji's ashes were immersed in the holy river Ganga.

danger deterimental to the security of the nation. I, therefore, thought it fit first to concentrate my energy only on that question.

But as the work of Bhoodan progressed, it became increasingly clear that the idea behind the movement could not be fulfilled unless we went further and asked for a portion of wealth and property. Hence I made up my mind that I must also ask for a share of wealth and property from the people. I have now done it and placed my demand at one-sixth of it; but it is for the people to decide what they can and will give me. The idea behind the demand is that all wealth, even though we may acquire it with our individual effort and skill, is not for us alone, but has been granted to us by God for all of us. The energy and initiative which went into the making of this wealth are themselves a gift of God. (H, 29.11.1952, 340)

What is Gramdan ?

862. Gramdan is an expression of the spirit of the age. It asks people not only to break the narrow domestic walls and consider the whole village as one family, but goes further and asks all villagers to meet together to consider their common problems and to solve them with one mind.

(B, 20.2.1957, 1)

863. Gramdan symbolizes human compassion. It is an essay in collective living. It presupposes mutual sympathy. It is the beginning of culture....When we have learnt to experience the joy of forgetting ourselves and serving others around us, we may be said to have acquired some culture.

(B, 26.12.1956, 6)

Merits of Gramdan

864. In Gramdan you have a synthesis of individual freedom and surrender to society. You have to bring about a total revolution with the consent of the people. It proposes to convert every village into a family unit which takes care of the basic needs of food, clothing, housing, education, sanitation, etc. and does not depend on the State or the Centre.

Every village will thus become a model of village republic with people governing themselves, and thus India would become a Union of Sarvodaya Republics. (TTR, 65)

865. I submit that defence on the border in this age of nuclear warfare is a minor affair and that the real defence has to be offered in villages and towns. If they are torn by dissensions and dissatisfaction, they can be anybody's prey. Gramdan seeks to unite the people and convert every village into a strong fortress. (TTR, 96)

866. Without overall village planning no village can be self-sufficient, and without Gramdan no village can have over-all village planning. Therefore Gramdans are essential.

(SE, Aug. 1957,64)

867. People think that it is a great sacrifice to give Gramdan. It is not a sacrifice but a sound investment in good living.

(B, 6.3.1957, 5)

The Dual Objective of Gramdan

868. Gramdan has a dual objective before it, namely, to wipe out social disparities and to reduce economic inequalities.

(TTR, 48)

The Advantage of Block-Dan

869. If all the villages in a block join Gramdan, you can ask the Government to change its plan in the light of Gramdan, and thus the people's power as *jana-shakti* and the Government can combine together to set up Gram Swaraj. (ibid, 45)

Relationship between Bhoodan and Gramdan

870. The first step of Bhoodan was that "let there be no landless in the village" and its last step is "let there be no owner of land in the village". (SG, 14)

871. Had I talked of Gramdan from the very beginning, it would not have proved effective. Gramdan could have only come into existence as a consequence of Bhoodan. There was compassion in Bhoodan, while Gramdan visualizes cooperation and equality. (G, 28)

Gramdan and the Sino-Soviet Pattern

872. Now in Gramdan the ownership of land is transferred to the village community. Some people are afraid that it resembles the Sino-Soviet pattern where the individual does not own land and the desired increase in production does not materialize. Russia and China have also come to realize this truth. But there is a distinct difference between Gramdan and the Sino- Soviet model. There the ownership of land is appropriated by the State, while in Gramdan I want you to surrender it to your own village community or Gram Sabha, which will be entrusted with all rights and privileges. Surely, there is a world of difference between the State and Gram Sabha. While the State is external, Gram Sabha belongs to the village itself.

These days land ownership involves the three rights of inheritance, of cultivation, and of sale or purchase. In Gramdan, while the first two are safe and secure, you have to forego the third one. You are at your liberty to pass on your land to your descendants and to cultivate it as you like. But you can no more sell or mortgage it. (GG, 3)

Post-Gramdan Work

873. These scraps of paper, these votes for Gramdan lend strength to all our work. They contain a tremendous peace potential.

What next then ? First, form the village council. Next, give the landless some land, so that they have practical evidence that something is being done for them. Then start a village fund by pooling one-fortieth of all produce for village development. After that, get the government to recognize it as a Gramdan village.

The next step is freedom from drunkenness, police and law courts. That means a Shanti Sena to keep the peace in the village. Disputes should not go to the courts but be settled on the spot. Then there should be a weekly meeting for prayer and for reading Sarvodaya news to the people. If ten or a dozen leading villagers give small contributions, the necessary journals can be bought and the village can also give a small donation to the Sarva Seva Sangh. This is the way to generate real power, much more than the voting system.

(TP, 130-131)

Development Work in Gramdan Villages

874. Gramdan of a block will facilitate the reconstruction work. Block Development, Panchayat and Gramdan will then operate in harmony. But if you ask me to take up some villages in order to make them model villages, I will refuse to be caught in your parlance. It is sheer illusion to imagine that you can have ideal or air-conditioned villages surrounded by hot air. Mine is only to bless the wedding and not to run the household. The responsibility of reconstruction work in the villages is of the people themselves who offer Gramdans and of the Government which charges all sorts of taxes. (TTR, 108)

Bhoodan-Gramdan, A Revolutionary Movement

875. Our work is so much of a fundamental revolution that it involves revolution both in the end and the means. Communists think that their aim is revolutionary, but it is not so. For, their God is the same as that of the capitalists. But Gramdan, Bhoodan, Sampattidan etc. are all completely revolutionary. (BY, 23.11.1956)

Sarvodaya-Patra

876. We need a Shanti Sena in every village and every town. ...Its needs can be met very simply if Sarvodaya-patras are kept everywhere; if the Shanti Sainiks are supported by the people's 'vote for peace' of which the Sarvodaya-patra is the symbol, they will truly have nonviolent strength behind them, and their work will be successful. (TP, 82)

877. In Sarvodaya-patra my rule is that only children should put in it a handful of grain. Had I allowed the elders to do it, I would have got double quantity of grain. It is worth thinking why I myself reduced the amount I was to get. It is not that I have no use for it at all. It will be used for workers. But its main aim is to give a training to children and to obtain a pledge from every family that they would not take part in anything which disturbs peace. (SP, 23)

The Triple Programme

878. Gramdan, Khadi (Village-oriented Khadi), Shanti Sena— this is our triple programme. To this trinity, these three seen as one, we must offer our service. If the three aspects are separated, they will all wither away. (TP, 82)

The Village-Oriented Khadi

879. Only village Khadi is real Khadi. We cannot claim that the cloth we have produced so far is really a symbol of nonviolence. There is very little nonviolence about it; a bit of what the English call 'charity', but no compassion. (TP, 80-81)

880. We have been working for Khadi for nearly thirty years now, but so far we have produced Khadi in the village and sold it in the town. We do not want to remain selling agencies any more; we want to produce Khadi in the village primarily for the consumption of the villagers. (B, 18.7.1956, 5)

The Qualities Needed in the Workers

881. Feelings of brotherhood and fraternity should be manifest in us to a greater extent than in communists or those who do not believe in nonviolence. Even communities having faith in violence live with mutual love and affection. We claim to win over even our opponents with love. There should, therefore, be a constant growth of affection amongst us. Let us realize that we are one and indivisible. (H, 8.9.1951, 235)

882. He must be firm in his faith that every man is good at heart and what he has to do is to bring out this goodness in the open. (H, 26.12.1953, 344)

883. It is not men of limited vision and narrow minds who can undertake this task of transforming society. It needs workers of high character who can rise above petty egotism and attachment to fruits. (H, 11.7.1953, 150)

884. Compassion and freedom from acquisitiveness are the basic attributes of a Bhoodan worker. He must have the compassion of a mother in him. A mother desires nothing from a child.

One has to be very vigilant and see that one does not develop any attachment to home, name or position. One has to be very humble if one really wants to serve.

(B, 7.11.1956, 3)

885. He would not be in any political party or in any other institution wherein elections are held or some such things are practised. Our worker would love all, and yet keep himself aloof.

(BY, 14.12.1956)

886. Even if the workers are small in number, they should be completely dedicated. They will then be able to function as yeast to convert the milk of society into curd.

(In a talk on 21.1.1957)

The Two Types of Work and Workers

887. After experimenting at Wardha I saw that merely moving about for propaganda did not serve the purpose. Some steady work should also be carried on along with it. But when steady work went on, Ashrams were established and organizations were set up, life in them was circumscribed within certain limits. They did not feel the need of keeping contact with the people living around them, nor had they the time and capacity for it. So propaganda also ceased. From both the experiences I came to the conclusion that work should be carried on both ways—some work should be steady and some should be by moving about. We should establish a proper ratio between steady work and propaganda work. (H, 3.9.1955, 209-210)

Advice to Workers

888. The work of ours is not of a sectarian nature. We should not even call ourselves 'the Sarvodaya group' because that also gives a wrong impression. Let us think ourselves as human beings and nothing else. Otherwise even this Sarvodaya Samaj, with all its freedom from institutionalism, will, little by little, become a sect, a narrow group in which we shall be separated from others. (TP, 34)

889. It would not do to simply take the ideas to the people, for by nature the people are inactive. On being explained, they would understand the idea, will like it, but will not act on it because they have not done so till now. ...The Indian society is an old society. The old understand an idea, accept it, but do not act according to it. (BY, 5.7.1957)

890. Mine is the way of less activity (*kriya)* and more action *(karma).* A pure-hearted and gentle action produces greatest effect.

Let our workers understand that their work needs nothing else except purification of the mind and heart. (VP, 3.13. 1959)

891. I would like you to remember a few things, which are very important. They are:

1. There must be friendliness among workers. Team work is possible only when we are not too critical of each other.
2. There must be no break in the work. Like a flowing river we must be ever at work.
3. We must keep some time for study. Workers must meet regularly and discuss the various problems before them. They must be well informed about important world problems. (B, 29.5.1957, 5)

892. We are willing to excuse our own faults however glaring they may be, but we are intolerant of and hard with others.We have a tendency to impute motives to others. If workers do not have real tolerance and goodwill for each other, how can they ever create nonviolent strength ? So I would ask you to be vigilant and cultivate three qualities: (1) to work in cooperation even when you differ, (2) to be tolerant of the short comings of others, and (3) never to impute motives to your colleagues. No constructive work can succeed if workers do not possess these qualities. (B, 20.3.1957, 4)

The Training of Workers

893. Proper arrangements will have to made for the training of workers. This should be of dual nature. First, they are to be imparted theoretical knowledge along with practical training in industries, music, religious songs, and medicine to be able to treat simple ailments. Secondly, they should be provided spiritual education after the manner of Sankaracharya,

(VP no. 349 of 1958)

Workers' Organization

894. A Sarvodaya worker does not insist on a rigid system or form. He does not believe in fixed frames and moulds. He does not mistake mere organisation for strength. He pins his faith in the power of truth. He is not deceived into thinking that if weakness is organized it becomes strength.

(H,17.1.1950,139)

895. We are not against setting up an organisation as such. You can form local organizations. But setting up an organisation on an all-India scale involves enforcement of discipline and then, as we know from experience, everything becomes bogus. We want to keep clear of this pitfall. A big organisation, while it becomes useless so far as work is concerned, engenders a feeling of vanity in its members. It then serves as a label which people use for selfish ends. (H, 1.8.1953, 170)

896. Ours (Sarvodaya Samaj) is spoken of as a loose organisation. Words often fail to express the exact meanings. If the word 'organization' has at all to be applied to this body, I would say that this is an unartificial organisation. It is not a manipulation but just a natural mutual contact. (H, 3.4.1949, 40)

Constructive Work and Power Politics

897. A friend says : "I am fully in sympathy with the Sarvodaya Samaj. But I do not join it because it eschews politics, and in the modern world there can be no social revolution without an institution being organized for political purposes also." I say to this : "You have made three assertions, each of which is erroneous. First, you seem to think that one is required to join the Sarvodaya Samaj. It is not so. Whoever believes in the Sarvodaya ideal, is in it whether or not he gets his name registered in it. ... Secondly, you assume that there is no politics in the Sarvodaya ideal. Of course, it does not contain the shortsighted politics of the power-seeking variety, because that does not make for Sarvodaya, the 'well-being of all'. ... Tulsidas has expressed it in a very telling manner : 'Generally people desire their personal good. A few desire the good of their own people. But only the servants of God desire the good of everyone.' The servants of God cannot subscribe to the politics of this or that party. Certainly theirs is not the politics which makes for disunity and dissipation of energy. They have their own kind of politics which is meant for uniting and strengthening all. Thirdly, to think that in modern times, a social revolution can be achieved through political power betrays an incapacity to read the future. One man rule is gone; gone is the rule of a minority; the rule of majority is in the process of liquidation; the stage is now set for the rule of all by all. And the rule by all does not mean voting rights for all, but a sincere cooperation emanating from the unity of hearts. The age is approaching when the truth, 'one in all and all in one', will rule the world. ... An ideological revolution is what we aim at. And an ideological revolution can never become the handmaid of politics in any age. People often think that they could rapidly bring about great changes if they were in power, they could educate as they liked and convert the people to their way of thinking. But this is an illusion. A tower of cards is easily built, but it topples down also with equal ease." (H, 17.6.1950, 138)

898. You should take a lesson from Gandhiji in this respect. Constructive workers had to resign their posts in constructive organizations when they wanted to join any satyagraha movement. So, too, even now constructive workers wanting to join politics have to leave their positions in the constructive organizations. The reason for this is that not only we ourselves but even others should not entertain any doubt about our intentions. They should be satisfied that our work is not of a doubtful or mixed character. (H, 1.9.1951, 229)

899. People often ask me why I am out of politics and why I do not accept responsibility in the government of the nation. I answer : "Two bullocks have already been yoked to the cart; of what use it would be to take me as a third ? The best way for me to help the cart along is to repair the road so that it can travel in the right direction." We must devote ourselves to build up an independent "people's power", and that in itself will be true service both to the government and to the nation. (TP, 21)

900. Today it (politics) has become so extensive that it has begun to encroach and engulf all aspects of human life in society. In such large field where rivalry exists, not merely in different ideological approaches but also in the conflicting attitudes, practices and procedures, the evolution and progress of human mind will get arrested and hampered.

Hence my attempt to create a band of workers who will not have any party labels. It will be above all sects, parties, isms, conventions and practices. It will be an assembly of pure, impartial, free-thinking individuals who will serve people as man to man.

But I shall not be satisfied with mere humanitarian service. The band of workers I have in view will engage themselves not only in humanitarian service, but will also think of all aspects of human life and serve mankind in all walks of life. They will yearn and work to transform the politics of the state into the politics of the people. They will endeavour to remove all the bitterness that is there in society and establish people's justice. They will place before the people the defects and vices that they notice in different parties and among the officials of the State. They will welcome and respect what is good in them. All their efforts will be directed to obliterate party differences and to establish a society transcending party affiliations and labels. (SE, Dec. 1954, 164-165)

X

EDUCATIONAL IDEAS

Defects of the Present Educational System

901. Thirty-seven years ago I left college and set out to look for knowledge. In college they had taught me many things, but knowledge was not one of them. After I had left the college behind, the infinite gateways of knowledge were opened to me. (TE, xiii)

902. At present mistakes are being made in the field of education in two ways. First, millions of people do not get education, and, secondly, those who get it, do not receive the right type of education. Thus the condition is that on one side there is lack of education and, on the other, miseducation.

The present education is concerned only with two faculties —power of memory and capacity for arguments.... There are several other faculties more important than these, but the present education pays no attention towards their development.

Considering the needs of the country, this education is of no use. ...The state of affairs is that a boy starting from the age of six, continues to study till the age of twenty or twenty-one, and for these fifteen years he does no work or labour. He is incapable of standing inclemencies of weather and of doing anything, be it agriculture, carpentry, weaving or cooking. He has no knowledge of dietetics. Thus he comes out of the school without any preparation for practical living.

(S, Feb. 1950, 17-18)

903. One great misfortune that befell this country on account of the British rule was that while some got English education, ...

others did not get it, creating two classes, one of the learned and the other of the unlearned. This further led to an increase of differences and conflicts.

The second misfortune was that the standard of living of those who were given education was raised, which was against the cultural traditions of this country. Here a spirit of sacrifice has been deemed to be a concomitant of learning and knowledge, and it has been held that while there is not much harm if those who are uneducated indulge in the enjoyment of sense pleasures for they are ignorant, it is not proper for men of knowledge to indulge in them.

The third misfortune was that work was not linked with education. The result is the tendency in the educated to enjoy pleasures without doing work and to look down upon physical labour.

These three defects of education are as dangerous as the derangement of the three humours of the body under the Indian system of medicine, which proves fatal to a patient.

(BY, 11.6.1957)

904. Students are not imparted such education which will inspire them to help increase production and to make physical labour entertaining. Rather, they are imparted education which makes them good for nothing. Hence, I detect seeds of danger and ill omen in the prevailing system of education. If it persists for some more time, it will destroy villages and drag the whole country into the ditch of urbanization. (B, 13.5.1958,21)

The Teachers of Today

905. A conversation with teachers in general is quite enough to enable us to understand the psychology and characteristic of far too many of our 'teachers'. To be 'only a teacher' means to be : (1) completely ignorant of any kind of practical skill which might be useful in real life; (2) incapable of learning anything new and indifferent towards any kind of craftsmanship; (3) conceited; (4) buried in books; and (5) lazy. 'Only teaching' means being a corpse cut off from life; it means dead-alive teaching from a dead-alive man ! (TE, 168-169)

906. A complaint is made these days that students lack discipline, but it is so because they have no respect for teachers, and this respect is absent because there are no real teachers these days. They are simply employees imparting education. (BY, 4.10.1957)

907. What is the place of a teacher in our life today? Many difficult occasions arise when we consult parents, friends, and some times even political leaders. But do we ever consult our teachers ? In fact, it is a *guru,** who can give the best advice. However, there is no place for a *guru,* left now in our life. There is no faith in a *guru.* There are professors and teachers, but no *gurus.* (VP, 28.8.1957)

The Students of Today

908. It cannot be said from the life of students these days that they aspire for learning. They are candidates for examinations. They do not have any inquisitiveness for knowledge. It is told of much talked of hostels these days that they provide all sorts of comforts. On the other hand Vyas has said, "If a student wants comforts, how can he acquire learning, and how can an aspirant for learning get comforts ?" But today there is a desire for learning and comforts together. (PP, 25.8.1957)

The Educational System Needs Change

909. On the day India attained independence I had said that as a new flag necessarily followed in the wake of the establishment of a new State, new education or Nai Talim should also follow in its wake in the same manner. I do not see anything but want of sense in now maintaining here the same system of education which suited those who kept the country under bondage. (H, 28.1.1956, 379)

910. Everybody knew that the system of education introduced by the British was aimed at strengthening the bonds of our slavery. How could it be expected to help promote the advancement of the country ? Gandhiji, we know, had advocated the

* A Guru is much more than a teacher. He is also a preceptor, a spiritual guide.

scrapping up of the old system. He had placed before us a new system of education which he thought could serve all our needs better and more satisfactorily. If those whose business it was to bring about the required change in education did not like Gandhiji's scheme, then the least they should have done, knowing as they did that the old system was quite unserviceable, was to close the schools and colleges for some time during which they should have taken counsel with one another and worked out a new scheme after their own liking.

The point is that with the attainment of freedom we should have made a fresh start in the right directions in every field of national life. Instead, we find that either old things are being continued or the changes which have been introduced are only superficial. (H, 13.2.1954, 397)

What is Education ?

911. Education does not call anything new into being, but it is the means by which the sleeping essence is awakened.

(TE, 7)

912. Education implies making oneself fit for society. By it is meant the development of the powers of the intellect, the sense organs and the physical body, and this can be had by association with noble souls. (PMV, 82)

The Task before Education

913. There is no true joy for the man whose life is cut off from the heavens above and the world of Nature around. This means that the task before education is to change the whole system of values and the way of life that is current in our cities. How this is to be done is not a question for you and me alone, but for the whole humanity. (TE, 39)

Tests of Education

914. Self-control, fearlessness and independence of thinking, these are three tests of education. Only that country is educated wherein these three qualities find expression. (SHV, 349).

915. Education should be looked at from two viewpoints—that of spiritual life and that of the situation around. The two tests of education are that it should lead to spiritual development and should correspond to the situation. (S, Feb.1950, 17)

916. Whether the children have been educated or not should be decided by the criterion if they have developed such qualities as loyalty to truth, spirit of service and fearlessness. What is to be looked into is how far they have developed practical knowledge and qualities useful for social service. (S, March 1950, 83)

The Fundamental Principles of Education

917. Learning for the pupil must be an unconscious, natural process. (TE, 9)

918. Education is a by-product of practical work. A man who follows any useful occupation is being educated by it, whether he knows it or not. Children ought to be educated in the same way. Adults learn the hard way by their mistakes. Little children are not strong enough for that, so provision ought to be made for them to learn without too many mistakes in an atmosphere in which they gradually grow to be self-reliant. (TE, 17)

919. There are two things which ought to be looked for from education.

The first is that education, which is given at the national expense, ought to be of use in practical affairs. A child should be so educated that he is competent to come forward and serve the world around him, and return tenfold whatever he has received.

The second thing which we expect from education is that all the student's faculties should develop as a harmonious, integrated whole. (TE, 20)

920. There is no knowledge without deep, concentrated study. Study that is merely extensive has a number of short comings. Strength is frittered away in pecking at too many subjects at the same time; nothing is properly grasped and fully mastered. Study ought to develop steadfastness of mind, reason, independence and power of thought, new concepts, new enthusiasm, new zeal in the search for truth. These are all signs of a lively mind, and this liveliness of mind is suffocated by excessive quantities of study. (TE, 19)

Government and Education

921. Patanjali thinks of God as the *Guru,* the Teacher. ... In all my reading I have not found any other book of religion or psychology which refers to him as *Guru.* ... We, on our part, should imitate him in our methods of learning and teaching. This *Guru* teaches us with the purest detachment of spirit; He is in the highest sense disinterested. He imposes nothing on his pupils.

But nowadays what is happening is that governments, both in our country and elsewhere, are doing their utmost to keep students under their thumb and impose upon them the ideas upon which the governments themselves are based. If the government is communist, communistic ideas are instilled. ... If Fascists were to take over, they would all be taught Fascism. Each and every government tries to mould the minds of students according to its own brand of thought.

This, in sober truth, is a great danger to democracy.

(TP, 86-87)

922. I am personally of the view that just as judiciary is independent and the government has no authority over it, similarly the education department should be free and independent.

(VC no. 4, 7)

923. If the education is in the hands of the government, it is open to two objections: (1) It acquires a rigid form and is coloured by the complexion of the government, (2) All teachers become employees.

What should really be is that education should be in the hands of public men of knowledge and if the government so desires it may somewhat help it. (VP no. 346 of 1957)

924. The education of each village should be in the hands of that village itself. Of course, the government may run such colleges and schools of technology and science as are free of any ideology, but with regard to the education involving development of mind and heart, the whole of it should be in the hands of the people themselves. (VC no. 4, 37)

The Type of Education India Needs

925. As most of our people live in villages, the education of the nation as a whole should be village-centred, so that the villages may benefit by it. The people of the towns must be given the kind of education which will direct their interest towards the villages, so that there may be healthy cooperation between the town and the village. The country will greatly suffer if the towns get one kind of education and the villages get of another kind, incompatible with it. (TE, 225)

926. Today when we want to rebuild our country, we ought to see that the education of our boys and girls consists of both *vidya* (learning) and *vrat* (self-control). The *vrat* would include control over the senses and proficiency in *karmayoga* (the performance of action). A student must be proficient in agriculture, cow-keeping, spinning and weaving, and a few other useful crafts. He should be good at all things which are helpful and necessary for village life. He must have acquired the capacity to earn his living in an independent way so that there never will be any occasion for him to feel driven to seek employment and thus suffer loss of freedom. If he has learnt to control his senses, serve his teacher and do his work efficiently and devotedly, he may be regarded as having mastered the *vrat.* Then he must also acquire *vidya* or knowledge : knowledge of the body for health, knowledge of the self for spiritual development and knowledge of the language for social intercourse. The knowledge of these things will enable him to do his *dharma,* that is, to do his duty towards himself and towards the society of which he is a part.

(H, 10.7.1954, 153)

What is Nai Talim (New Education) ?

927. That education which destroys old values and establishes new values, will be called Nai Talim. (KKO, 46)

928. Nai Talim is not a system; it is a far-reaching educational idea. It is a seed-thought like the Brahma-vichar (the idea of the Supreme) which was so widespread in India and to which so many different systems of thought—Advaita (Monism), Dvaita (Dualism), Vishisthadvaita (Qualified Monism) and so on—were all rooted. (TE, 62)

929. Nai Talim is a philosophy of living, it is an attitude towards life that we have to bring to all our work. (TE, 63)

Education Must Never Grow Old

930. The education which is being given at Sevagram is called Nai Talim, but I would like to call it Nitya Nai Talim, Ever-New Education. I mean that education ought to be like the water in a river. The river goes on flowing, but the water is never the same. In the same way education should go on changing continually with the experience of every passing day.

Everyday brings us ever-new experience, and we must have the strength to adapt our lives to ever-new experience. (TE, 83)

The Newness of Nai Talim

931. People ask me, "What is the newness in your system of education ?" I reply, "There is no newness. In ancient times knowledge was acquired through physical labour, and it is the same with our method. An educated man looks down upon physical work. He will take bread, but will not grind flour for it. He needs cereals and vegetables produced in the fields, but he will not himself produce them. He will like to put on clothes, but he will not spin for it. He dislikes going to the village for work. We have to eradicate this abhorrence for bodily labour. (DK, 8)

A Purpose of Nai Talim

932. There are several purposes of imparting education through crafts. The greatest of them is to remove the vanity of the educated and to link action to knowledge. (ibid)

Nai Talim and Social Order

933. Nai Talim is in complete opposition to the prevailing socio-economic system. If it is said that Basic Education is but one method of teaching whereby children are taught various subjects through the medium of handwork, it is entirely a mistake. Nai Talim or New Education cannot but create a new social order. It cannot live unless it did so.

(H. 18.6.1955, 123)

Nai Talim, Some Misconceptions

934. Many believe that if boys are taught a smattering of craft, and if they are made to do a little spinning on the wheel, you have Basic Education. Some others believe that if less attention is paid to learning and knowledge, you have Nai Talim. And there are still others who feel that once the process of learning is somehow associated with handwork, you have complete Basic Education. They do not bother themselves whether the association is natural or not; they do not feel that this aspect of the question deserves much attention.

All these three views are faulty. The purpose of Nai Talim will not be served by teaching students a little of some craft. Boys and girls receiving their education through Nai Talim will be so proficient in their crafts that they will perform their work as easily and naturally as fish swim in water. (ibid, 121)

935. We have named this education as 'Basic Education', but we do not understand the meaning of the word 'basic'. We imagine that it merely means the *first* stage of children's education. It means far more than that. It means that this is the foundation, the base, upon which the whole of our education, from the beginning to the end, has to be built, whether you call it primary, or middle, or higher. It will not do to have one kind of education for the villages and another kind for the towns. It will not do to have one kind of education for the first four years of school life, and afterwards some other kind that is quite unrelated to it. We have the right to use the word 'basic' only if we are agreed that the whole education of the country should be built up on the foundation of Nai Talim. (TE, 61)

936. Some people think that Nai Talim means that less attention is given to knowledge than to work. But this is a misunderstanding. They do not realize that the big difference between Nai Talim and ordinary schools is that their (latter's) knowledge is superficial while ours (former's) is solid and firmly grounded. This is because their instruction tends to be theoretical while ours springs from experience, so that ours has an assurance which theirs lacks. The assumption that Nai Talim will turn out students less well-informed than the old system, is quite unfounded. (TE, 163)

937. Nai Talim does not come into existence by simply joining knowledge and work. It should be related to life and our life should be pure and beautiful. (S, June 1951, 740)

Principles of Nai Talim

938. The principle of Nai Talim is that knowledge and work are both forms of the same thing and therefore it is impossible to distinguish between knowledge-process and work-process. Educational activities are those which from one point of view appear to be learning, while from another angle they appear to be labour. There is no real educational activity when the knowledge-process is isolated, nor is there any education in the labour-process alone. A real educational activity is one where we cannot tell which of the two predominates. Moreover, this integration must be natural and unimposed. (TE, 58)

939. The philosophy of Nai Talim does not accept the unequal values assigned by our present society to physical and mental work. It takes the position that every kind of service rendered by a man, whether it is physical or mental, is ethical in its nature; the salary which is given to him is economic in its nature. The value of an ethical act cannot be calculated in economic terms.

The spiritual principle of Nai Talim is that knowledge and work are not two things but one. It is a mistake to say that knowledge is higher than work or work higher than knowledge. Nai Talim is education based on the unity of knowledge and work. ... Knowledge is gained in the most natural way, for whatever we do becomes a channel of learning.

The social principle of Nai Talim is that all human lives are equally to be respected. All the various social and class divisions are therefore forms of falsehood. (TE, 71-73)

940. Education prior to that of the university will be for self-reliance, and the education of the university will be through self-reliance.

(Proceedings of Ninth Nai Talim Conference, 1)

941. The idea is that the recurring expenditure should be met from the earnings of the pupils. But income is not the main thing. We have to avoid the ill effects of the craft. If we make the children labour like a machine, it would be their exploitation, and that we do not want. (DK, 157-158)

Expectations from Nai Talim Centres

942. What we expect from centres of Nai Talim is that ideas will be thoroughly studied and canvassed, and also tried out in practice. The teachers and students will plan together, discuss and conduct experiments to test their theories, and as a result of their work the world will be enriched with knowledge united with experience. Where a vigorous churning of ideas is integrated with practical experimental work, there we have Nai Talim. Where there is mere discussion of ideas without a practical basis, we have the old type of education which is so common everywhere. Where there is practical work and experience, but no thinking or discussion, we have the bodily labour (of a type) which is being carried on by innumerable peasants. The Nai Talim teacher and student must unite in their own persons the peasant with the philosopher.

(TE, 161)

Meaning of Self-Sufficiency in Nai Talim

943. Self-sufficiency, then, has three meanings. The first is that one should not depend upon others for one's daily bread. The second is that one should have developed the power to acquire knowledge by oneself. The third is that a man should be able to rule over oneself, to control his senses and his thoughts.

(TE, 28)

Choice of the Craft

944. We should choose such a craft as touches every aspect of life. (DK, 162)

945. The earlier Nai Talim has become old now. At that time the only basic craft was that of spinning. I was present when that scheme was being formulated, and it was my own scheme. But now I feel that either agriculture or cow-keeping should be its main basis. All other crafts should have a secondary place. Among them, however, spinning should have the chief place. Even small children can spin, and hence there is enough scope for it. Along with it, there should also be other crafts like smithy, cooking, etc. (VP, 17.2.1959)

946. Nai Talim need not have the same form everywhere. There may be several of them. (S, June 1951, 722)

Craft Implements

947. The new teachers will have new means to convey knowledge. It is to be understood that the vehicles of knowledge used thirty years earlier will not do now....Hence in this age the old teaching tools will not do. It is true that even small tools are useful for teaching children, but they will have new implements after a year or two, and they will be taught through them. (VC no. 4, 19)

Fishery and Poultry-keeping as Basic Crafts

948. Kakasaheb believes in nonviolence as fully as I do; it is as unthinkable for him to take flesh as it is for me. He has written an article about fishery, in which he says, "Fishery is an occupation of great educational value and one which may well be followed as a basic craft." I agree that it satisfies our criteria of what a basic craft should be, and that it may be made the basis of general knowledge in the same way as other crafts.

However, when I think of this occupation, I find myself unable to think of using it as a means of education for children. I would have to teach them first how to make a hook, and then how to bait it with some kind of flesh, so that the fish may be attracted to eat it—in fact, I have to show them how to deceive the fish. ...There is a lot of untruth in this, as well as violence. I cannot do it, and I cannot think of using it for education.

I am not opposed to poultry-keeping in the same way. The objections which I have against fishery do not apply to poultry-keeping. Other considerations of a different nature arise with regard to poultry, which I shall not enter into here. (TE, 111-112)

Crafts, A Warning

949. It seems to be considered as a 'must' that all social studies be taught only through crafts. But this rigidity of outlook is mistaken. (TE, 133)

Meaning of Correlation

950. A friend asked me what was *correlation.* I said that the meaning of correlation was to coordinate knowledge and action. Then he said, "If it were so, we could engage students in atom bomb factories ; this would be action and through this medium they will be given knowledge also, and since the distinction between knowledge and action will disappear, it will be a correlation method. Do you agree ?" I said that I did not agree. I further said that in correlation there is unity of knowledge and action, but I would not engage students in a bomb factory because it violated the principle of Sarvodaya. Such an industry would not do in Nai Talim. At this he said, "Then you should interpret correlation as something wherein the difference between knowledge and action disappears and where both the ends and means are pure." I felt happy on hearing it and accepted it. (SHV, 60)

A Triple Programme of Education

951. There is no need to go on teaching from cradle to the grave. Give the knowledge that is needed today ; see that your student becomes capable of learning for himself whatever he may need in future; call into play his own latent powers. That is our threefold programme. We may call its three aspects

(1) direct knowledge, (2) power to gain knowledge and (3) self-knowledge. (TE, 88)

Subjects in Nai Talim

952. There are no rules and regulations about what items of knowledge should be included in a Nai Talim syllabus, and what should not be included. All kinds of knowledge may come in, but on one condition—a condition that challenges us. We eat today to satisfy today's hunger ; we do not eat for ten days ahead; similarly, the child should be given the knowledge that is needed to satisfy the demands of his life today. This is the principle which should regulate the acquiring of knowledge; otherwise it becomes a form of greed.

If we reckon our syllabus by subjects—geography, history, arithmetic, geometry, and so forth—there will be no end to it, and (it is of) no value. Instead, let us think in terms of the development of speech and of reason, the development of the body, the mind, and the senses. (TE, 87)

953. Nai Talim must provide complete knowledge of all that is basic in life. There is no need to memorise great chunks of history or meaningless lists of kings—that would be to put a useless burden on the children's minds. But they must know the fundamental ideas by which man lives and grows. Some knowledge of philosophy, religion and ethics is essential. The children must also know something of the distinguishing features of our own and other societies. They must know the basic concepts of science. They must be throughly familiar with the laws of health, nutrition, hygiene, cookery, etc. Nai Talim must demand thoroughness in these fields of knowledge, and also a thorough mastery of language, the ability to express one's ideas in the proper way. Handwriting must be beautiful; the children must have a knowledge of literature. Thus, in Nai Talim, knowledge must never be imperfect; but it must never be irrelevant also. (TE, 97)

Teaching of History

954. Do any of you imagine that what is taught in the name of history is the truth ? There have been two world wars in this century; one version of their 'history' is written in Germany, and quite other versions in Russia, America and England. (TE, 137)

955. If we really want to make progress, we must select the essential in history and leave out the rest. I am not saying that history is completely useless. ...But society will never make progress if its past history haunts it like an evil spirit. It is true that it is an inspiring experience to read the glorious deeds of old; but the men of old days did evil as well as good, and why should we load our memories with *all* their doings ? We should take the good and leave the evil. (TE, 140)

956. Man never writes the history of his humaneness, but only of its denials. Hence one cannot get any knowledge of human nature from history. What are recorded in it are the incidents that go against human nature, and then the history that is constructed from them, consists of nothing but violence all around. (SHV. 289)

Geography Teaching

957. Wherever we happen to live is the centre of the world for us, simply because we do live there and the world lies all around us. This is the basis on which our teaching of geography should be built upon. (TE, 85)

958. It will not do for the teacher simply to get up and talk about Lapland. Let a natural opportunity arise. It is the teacher's task to seize a natural opportunity to widen the children's knowledge and it is not at all difficult to create such opportunities. (TE, 136)

Teaching of Science

959. If any subject can be singled out as more important for us than others, it seems to me that it is science. (TE, 126)

960. The kitchen must be looked upon as our laboratory. The person who works there ought to know how many calories, and how much protein and fat are obtainable from various kinds of food. He ought to be able to work out the kind of diet needed at various ages and for various kinds of work.

In the morning everyone goes to answer the call of nature. Hence in the school there must be a special study of the science of sanitation. In what ways can the excreta be used? What is the effect of the sun's rays upon it? What harm is there in leaving it uncovered, and what diseases does it spread ?

Some boy falls ill. Why did he fall ill? Did the disease visit him for nothing, or did he have to spend some money to persuade it to come ? In any case you must treat it like a guest, and find out why it came, how it came and so on. Now that it has come, you must learn as much as you can from it.

If every piece of work is tackled in this way, the teaching of science will have begun. (TE, 136, 137, 138)

The Knowledge of Languages

961. The mother tongue and the national language constitute our two eyes. One who knows only one of them, will be considered 'one-eyed'. The Sanskrit language is the third eye. We require the knowledge of the mother tongue to serve the people, the knowledge of Hindi for fostering nationalism and that of Sanskrit for religion and philosophy. (KKO. 123)

The Teaching of English Language

962. The English language is highly developed. There are priceless treasures in it, and therefore if someone wants to learn it, he must. But there is a scientific way of learning a language. First of all, the mother tongue should be fully learnt with its grammar, and then one can learn any other language also easily. (Report of 13th Nai Talim Sammelan, 16)

963. Many people consider education to be incomplete without English, because it is a window on the world. 1 agree that it is so, but if the house has only one window, opening in one direction only, the people inside the house get a very one-sided view of the world. If you want all-round view, you need at least seven windows—English, French, German, and Russian for the Western world, Chinese and Japanese for the East, and Arabic for the region west of Iran. With only one language window your view will be incomplete and misleading. If we depend on that language only, we shall not be able to think independently. (TP, 117)

Two Important Points Regarding Subject-matter

964. No irrelevant knowledge be given; only that knowledge be imparted which has a bearing on life. (SHV, 180)

965. The second thing to be kept in mind is that we should not think about the various subjects in isolation. The child should not feel at the time of learning that it is being taught arithmetic or history or literature. Knowledge is one whole, it cannot be divided. (DK, 163)

The Medium of Education

966. The medium of education should be the regional language of the State. Roughly speaking, I would say that it should be the mother tongue. The national language should be a compulsory subject for all from the beginning to the end. In order that the services of university teachers be available throughout India, no matter to what particular regions they belong to, they should have the option of lecturing in the national language, if they are unable to do so in the regional language.

(S, Sept. 1950, 127)

967. It is good if some of our children learn English as a language. But why should we allow it to continue as a medium ?.. .We must begin to think in our own language, otherwise we cannot give full expression to our personality. (H, 24.3.1951, 29)

Religious Education

968. There is no doubt that religious teaching is a subject of great interest and importance. But the word 'Dharma' has unfortunately acquired a very narrow, communal meaning, and for this reason many thinking people are opposed to any teaching of Dharma in schools at all. My own point of view is that true religious teaching is not a matter of literature. The essence of religion is a sound character, faith in God, and the conviction that the soul is other than the body. This essential religion can only be learnt from the company of good men.

My only plan for religious teaching, therefore, is to choose good persons as teachers.

To learn by heart the words of the saints is certainly a very profitable exercise, but I would not call it religious teaching; I would rather call it the teaching of the purest literature.

As a foundation for reverence towards all religious traditions, one may certainly teach the lives of their saints and tell children about their rules of life, their festivals and disciplines for purifying the mind. But this should be regarded as history or social studies rather than religious teaching.

There is a belief current in all religions that merit can be obtained directly from certain ceremonial forms and outward actions, without paying any attention whatever to the purity of heart. This superstition has to be destroyed. The children must get into the habit of testing everything by the challenge of experience. If that attitude were firmly established, I should consider their religious education to be complete.

(TE, 117-118)

The Place of Art in Education

969. Art has a place in our school syllabus from the very first class, for without it we cannot realize our ideal of education through craft. But there is a difference between the *technique* of art and the *vision,* or the spirit, of art. A man who possesses a true vision of art will not behave in any ugly manner in his own life. This is the vision which the children should acquire....The beauty of orderly living is a part of the appreciation of beauty in art. (TE, 145)

Cultural Activities

970. Sometimes it also happens that in a school, work is kept up, but side by side there is recreation also. I do not grudge it; it is all right. There should be some recreation as well. There are dramas, there are dances, and music is played. These three I accept. But we should bear in mind that the pupils of our country are hungry. We should never forget it, and remembering it, if you like, you may dance; if you want to sing, do so, and if you like to play an instrument, you may do it. But keep this before your mind's eye that a corpse has fallen in front of you, a hungry man is dying, another hungry man is preparing for death, and one is already dead.

(Report of 7th A. I. Basic Education Conference, 30)

971. It is supposed that dancing, music and dramas are for recreation, for joy. But if joy is a thing apart from the activities of our daily life and if it is necessary to set apart a special time for it, we should realize that there is something fundamentally wrong with our scheme of life. The truth is that our life should be full of joy, for joy is the essence of the soul. Therefore our striving should be not towards the attainment but towards the purification of the joy that is in us.

(Report of 5th A. I. Basic Education Conference, 10)

The Place of Books in Nai Talim

972. Books do most certainly have a place in education as tools of knowledge, but it is a very minor place. The major need for the teacher and the student is to become work-partners, and this can happen only when the distinction between the teacher 'teaching' and the student 'learning' can be overcome. (TE, 58)

973. We never seem to have any doubt that by reading he (a boy) is obtaining knowledge, and that reading is in fact the direct road to knowledge. It is nothing of the sort; on the contrary, book learning is like a curtain that shuts off from the world of real things. (TE, 35)

Vacations

974. For thousands of years there had been in India the teachers and the taught, but it had not occurred to any one to arrange for a long holiday in the schools. Such holidays came into education only with the coming of the English system.

If we admit the need for a long holiday, we should reconsider the question of its timing. (TE, 209)

Punishments and Rewards

975. Today our education is robbing him (a child) of all initiative and inculcates fear in him. If he commits a mistake, he is beaten. So out of fear he becomes obedient. That is, instead of imparting fearlessness, you have taught him cowardice. First of all you beat him, which is an expression of anger. Secondly, you create fear in him. Thirdly, you mistakenly identify him with his body, and he accepts your authority out of fear; that is, he loses his independence of mind. You see how wrong the action is from the beginning to the end.

(B, 15.5.1957, 5)

976. It is not only beatings and threats which strengthen violence, but the offering of temptations also does the same.

(L, 142)

Why Indiscipline among Students ?

977. If there is indiscipline among students, the fault lies with the teachers, the educational system and the social order. Today discipline has been made a virtue to be acquired and observed in preference to all others. I say that in fact the teacher should feel remorse if his students accept his teachings without being really convinced. He should be happy if a student rejects his teachings and thinks independently for himself. (B, 28.11.1956, 6)

Adult Education

978. Adult education should be through craftsmanship, so as to enable the unemployed to do useful work and at the same time to develop their intelligence. (TE, 214)

One-hour Schools in Villages

979. There is a great deal of time wasted in the schools which are being run nowadays for our five-year olds. ...Moreover, really poor children cannot attend these schools and the education given in them is of no real value.

My suggestion, therefore, is that we should have one-hour schools. They would be held in the early morning about sunrise so that children might be free to work during the day and every child in the village, even the poorest, is able to attend. These morning classes would be for the 3 R's.

In the evenings there would be an hour's class for adults. One may call it a 'listening class', for it would not teach reading and writing....This class would deal with every type of knowledge needed in practical life. All children would go to the morning class to learn to read, but for general knowledge they would go to the evening class. No holiday would be necessary in either of them.

The teachers of these schools would be doing their own work during the day, and so they would not need large salaries. The villagers would give them a share of the yearly harvest in return for their services in one-hour schools.

(TE, 218, 219)

University in Every Village

980. My idea is that full provision for education ought to be made in every village. Each one of them should have its university or Vidyapeeth. For, every village, no matter how small, is a microcosm ; it contains the whole world in miniature. Therefore complete education must be available there. The village is in close touch with the natural world of creation, and therefore has ready at hand the materials for the study of physical and natural sciences. ...The human community is established in the villages from ancient times ; history and sociology can well be studied there. Moreover, the greater intimacy in which men live in villages is conducive to the development of ethics and religion. (TE, 226-227)

Rural University

981. The teachers and the students will be provided with a well-equipped library necessary for them. They will be supplied with the tools and instruments required by them. They will have the needed land and other things. Some buildings too will be constructed for them. The rest they will build for themselves. Having done all this for them, they would be told not to expect more. Thereafter let them live collectively and present before the country a model of the best type of life. There will be discussions, there will be experiments, and the results of these experiments will be placed before the country. But the main feature of this university will be that both the students and the teachers will stand on their own legs, work with their hands and earn their living. And that too not just anyhow, but in the very best manner. (SHV, 94-95)

Examinations

982. I have no real, sound knowledge of the subjects in which I had to take examinations, but I do know well things in which I was never examined. My own experience, therefore, does not lead me to attach any value to examinations. They are exactly like purgatives that people take to cleanse the stomach—one takes an examination and all of one's knowledge is cleared out! (TE, 25-26)

983. When we take an examination, a supervisor has to be appointed to watch us, to see that no student copies from another. It is to me a very saddening spectacle. For if it is possible to suspect us of being capable of copying from others, then, as students, we have already failed. (TE, 92)

984. This test of education is completely one-sided. What it does at the utmost is to examine the ability for argumentation and the power of memory. It cannot find out the progress made by the boy in what we term 'self-development'. (SHV, 349)

De-linking of Jobs with University Degrees

985. Government jobs should not be linked with the university degrees. Every department should conduct its own examinations in which anyone can appear. On being successful in them, one is to be considered qualified for the job. This would provide encouragement to private educational institutions and at many places educational experiments would be tried. (In a talk on 11.1.1957)

Importance of Women's Education

986. My test for teaching will be girls' education. I will test how much of devotion, knowledge, etc. they have acquired. (VP no. 174 of 1957)

Education for Men and Women to Be Mostly Similar

987. Men and women generally need the same qualities. Such qualities as love, parental affection, devotion etc. should equally develop in men and women. Some think that the knowledge of cookery is for women only. I consider it to be incorrect. Both should have it. However, there may be some difference. Women can learn a few things particularly. They can develop art to a greater extent, but in the early stages all the qualities will be almost the same. Later, there may be some difference. (PMV, 82-83)

Co-education

988. I am of the view that there should be at least co-education of boys and girls till the age of fourteen. (VP, no. 259 of 1958)

989. Artificial segregation of boys and girls will not lead to their development, but either to perversion or to an extremely one-sided education. (SSH, 96)

Role of Teachers in Society

990. A teacher is a bridge between the past and the future. He has to bring about a peaceful social transformation. (B, 3.8.1958, 134)

991. If anyone can reform society, it is the teacher, not the police or the military. (BY, 3.8.1956)

992. The Acharya's (teacher's) duty is to understand all trends of thought, to transform men's minds and hearts, and to point the way to a transformation of their lives. (TP, 95)

993. The teacher in our school should also be the servant of the whole village, and the village school should be the centre of village service. If the village needs medicine, it will be supplied through the school, and the children will help. If the village needs cleaning, the school will be the starting-point, and the teacher and the children will help the people to do the work. The people will turn to the teacher to help them settle their disputes. The school will make plans for the observance of festivals. In this way the school will become the centre of the village community; it will develop whatever is of value in the village and introduce the things that are lacking. (TE, 174)

What a Teacher Should Be ?

994. As a worker of national education, it is the duty of a teacher to make his own life a pattern of what the life of the nation ought to be. The discharge of this duty will lead to the emitting of the rays of education all around him, and they will influence the atmosphere of the whole neighbourhood. Such a teacher will be a school in himself and to associate with him will be to get educated. (VV, I, 60)

What a Teacher Should Do ?

995. Many people, including myself, were pained that a police force entered a university campus; and it is indeed a painful incident. But we must consider the whole of India as our campus.

1. Acharyas should make their influence felt throughout the country.
2. They should exercise their influence on political parties.
3. They should deliberately plan to make police action unnecessary in the future.

We should be thinking on these lines, rather than giving all our attention to minor incidents on the university campus. (TP, 96)

996. I call myself a teacher, and I am never so happy as when I can devote myself to study and teaching; it is such a peaceful and satisfying kind of life that I should probably live a hundred years if I could stick to it. But I had to leave it and come out, because India was in danger. I expect you also to take up some project in a district or comparable area. There is no need to go to every village. Select a rural area and make a complete survey of the villages in it so that you are familiar with the conditions there. Then consider what you can do to improve them, and draw up a plan of action. Survey the villages and plan to help them, survey the towns and take it upon yourselves to see that no riots occur there. If riots do break out, do everything you can to stop them. (TP, 106-107)

Qualities Needed in a Teacher

997. A teacher needs to possess at least three qualities. The first is that he must be an affectionate and loving friend to his students. This is of such importance that without it he can never be a teacher at all. The second is that he himself must be a tireless seeker after knowledge, always studying, continually adding new items to his store. He must become 'an ocean of learning', a votary of science.

The teacher needs a third quality also. Political activity has a powerful attraction for students today, and the students are under the care of teachers. ...Teachers are in a position of great authority and they should keep clear of all political involvement. ...If a teacher gets involved in politics, he is no longer his own master; he is a mere tool in the hands of another and loses his independence. (TP, 108-110)

Teachers and Salaries

998. I hold that the prestige of a teacher does not depend upon the salary he receives. But unfortunately the general belief is otherwise these days. It is something extremely foolish.

It is a blunder to make wealth decide the respect one should get. It is a wrong concept imported from the West. (BY, 22.8.1958)

999. These days teachers agitate for increase in their salaries like scavengers and labourers. I wish that the scavengers demanded the abolition of their occupation itself rather than increase in their emoluments. When I thus think about the scavengers, I would even say more strongly about the teachers that they ought not to agitate for any such thing.They are *guru* (teachers) and they should remember their *guruta* (eldership). Their complaint should pertain to their being deprived of their contact with the students instead of being about their salaries. (SHV, 346)

The Biggest Reform Needed

1000. The biggest reform that will have to be done in the eduational system is to re-establish the former relationship between the teacher and the pupil. (BY, 12.10.1956)

Duties of the Students

1001. The first duty of students is to preserve the full independence of their minds. If anyone has a right to full freedom, it is the student. Knowledge cannot be had without faith, but it is equally essential that along with faith he should have intellectual freedom.

The second duty of students is to exercise self-control. Only a man who can control himself has the right to freedom. A student must feel confident that he can carry out his own resolutions...This means that he must be able to control his body, his impulses and his mind.

The third duty of students is to devote themselves to service. Knowledge cannot be had without service.... The elders have experience, and they open their hearts to those who serve them, and give them all they have. Students then must devote themselves to the service of elders and parents, of the poor and the afflicted, and of society. They should not think that this service will leave them no time for study; they should have faith that knowledge is acquired by service.

The fourth duty of students is to be alert to what is going on around them. They should study all the movements of the modern world and the current ideologies with open minds. Their outlook must be broad and they must not allow themselves to think within narrow limits.

(TE, 185, 187, 189, 190)

Students and Politics

1002. People often ask whether students should or should not take part in politics. The thing we have to realize is that we are all now the citizens of the world. The whole world has become one neighbourhood. In thinking about politics we must therefore make a new approach and look at political problems from a universal standpoint. This universal, all- embracing political outlook I call 'lok-niti'; in it the whole world is one, and we are all its citizens; in it no one rules over another and everyone rules over himself. That is the kind of politics, and the kind of society, which we have to create. But the kind of politics which will make the world citizens, ought not to be called politics at all. It is 'lok-niti'. Students therefore ought to become experts in 'lok-niti'.

Why should students take any part at all in the kind of politics which splits up society ? They should study 'lok-niti' with its universal, unifying approach. They should also study and discuss the pros and cons of the current political ideologies— communism, socialism, welfarism, Sarvodaya— and train themselves to think broadly and comprehensively.

(DV, 58, 59)

Student Organizations

1003. People often form student federations. If such organizations are started, then rest assured that there would be no 'students'.

A student should be free. Let him think independently. He ought not to bind himself to any particular ideology.

(BG, VII, 40)

Education and Nationalism

1004. So far I had been saying that education should not be in the hands of the government, but now I wish to add that there should be no nationalism in education. (BY, 24.8.1956)

Why No Progress by Nai Talim ?

1005. In Bihar State an important and far-reaching experiment in Basic Education is being carried on for a number of years, and is being watched with interest by the whole country. But it does not seem to be doing so well as it should. Gandhiji said that Nai Talim ought to be self-supporting, but the complaint today is that it is expensive.

The reason for this is that although we talk about a change in our scale of values, no such change is visible in our practice. In Nai Talim institutions, just as elsewhere in the Education Department, there are different scales of pay and the same notions of salaries and increments are prevalent. The Government also appears to have no fully thought-out programme. (TE, 201)

1006. I am in the habit of going to see the work of basic schools that happen to lie on the route of my Bhoodan pilgrimage. I ask the teachers as to where their own children are studying.

The usual reply is that they are in Gaya or Patna or some such town. Why do they not keep their children with them, where father and teacher, and a good type of education, are all to be had together ? The reason, obviously, is that they have no faith in Nai Talim. (TE, 202)

1007. Today Nai Talim is being opposed because Nai Talim schools are being started only in villages and the villagers get the impression that it is somehow inferior, a kind of Government charity for them. (TE, 204)

Government Experiments in Nai Talim

1008. The way in which Nai Talim has been and is being accepted these days is so one-sided that it is not without danger. I have been observing it for years. They are mostly the State Governments which are conducting the various experiments of Nai Talim. The result is its caricature everywhere. Nai Talim is based on a philosophy of life, and when this philosophy is not accepted, all that is achieved is a poor, ugly imitation of some of its external features in isolation. Under these circumstances, nothing but a bad name can be expected for it, and it is what is happening today.

But the responsibility for this perversion lies on those who have put it under the care of the governments. What should have been done was to set up a few pure models of Nai Talim at different places.

The experiments conducted by the Government officers so far have been of two kinds. In one there has been a deliberate attempt to prove it to be expensive, lacking in knowledge and content and capable of creating dissatisfaction both in the guardians and the students. This has been clearly a dishonest approach. But let us not discuss it. The other is an honest approach. But even there the new values underlying it have not been accepted. While maintaining the old values it has only adopted some of its features. In spite of its being an honest approach, it does not exhibit the real nature of Nai Talim. Hence it is essential to conduct as many experiments as possible on the basis of the new values.

(SHV, 121-123)

The Family School

1009. Since man lives in a home and learns to think in a school, there is no harmony between his life and thought. The remedy for it, on the one hand, is that the school should enter the home, and, on the other hand, the home must penetrate the school.

The only kind of school that can be called 'a family school' is one in which the edifice of education has been erected on the recognition that the hostel or the teacher's home constitutes the foundation of education. (SHV, 52)

A Suggestion for the Interim Period

1010. It is not possible that the people may take over education into their hands all at once. Till that happens, it is bound to remain in the hands of the government, precluding any reform. Hence there should be such independent schools in the country as will be able to act as models for the government. By 'independent' is meant that the government will have no control at all over them, be it of any type. If, in spite of it, the government helps them, it does not matter. This is one definition of 'independent' schools. But there are also institutions which are totally independent in the sense that they neither accept government aid nor any control by it. As such there should be three kinds of schools in the country: (1) government schools, (2) schools of ever-Nai Talim accepting government aid but not controlled by it, and (3) fully independent schools, accepting neither government help nor its control in any form whatsoever. They would be looked upon as the best schools, and it is they which would be undertaking independent research and experiments to show the way for the progress of the nation. (VP, 17.2.1959)

XI
PLANNING

The Fundamental Principles of Planning

1011. It should be a postulate of national planning that at present all can and should be provided full employment. Let them do it with such tools and machineries as are capable of it. However, if only some can be provided work on the plea of efficiency, it would not be national but partial planning. (RKSM, 42)

1012. The government plans ought to give the first priority to the raising up of the lowest, the poorest and the most depressed. (DV, 128)

1013. While planning, the past, the present and the future have to be taken into consideration. (KKO, 54)

1014. We hold that the centralization of the whole, or of the greater part, of the government system makes its subsequent dissolution more difficult. We must therefore start at once to introduce decentralization, and this will be the basis of all our planning. ... In short, all our planning will be directed towards a progressive abolition of government control by means of regional self-reliance. (DV, 30)

1015. There are some spiritual ideas relating to life. Man does not develop by simply planning from above from the economic standpoint. The approach of the whole of planning should be that man becomes kind-hearted, evolves further his life and becomes whole. Otherwise, there will be three 'D's in the country as we see today—Defence, Development and Degeneration. (KSP, 32)

1016. Planning must primarily mean employment and food to everyone. They talk of raising the standard of living. No one would object to it if it could be done, but before we talk of increasing the standard of living, we have to assure ourselves that we would first remain alive. Let us first assure minimum livelihood to all. (B, 18.4. l956, 3)

1017. A society based on nonviolence cannot function through intermediate agencies. To bring about such a society, village industries should thrive. All should get food and all must work. The economy of the nation should be planned on the lines of a joint family. (H, 2.8.1952, 187)

What Types of Plans Needed ?

1018. It should be clear in a plan as to what part of it is directly concerned with the people at the lowest level, what part is for the middle class and what is meant for the city people. I know there are several things which are for the good of all. They should be dealt with separately. (BY, 6.4.1956)

1019. Our plan should be such that whether there be world war or any other world turmoil, it would not be interfering with the plan. (Ambar, 10)

1020. The very basis of the planning should be such that we may be able to implement it with our own internal resources without expecting help from outside. (BY, 31.5.1957)

1021. In the language of economics, a 'nonviolent planning' would mean that the need of management should dwindle gradually and gradually and ultimately it should disappear altogether. (S, May 1952, 1532)

Democracy and Planning

1022. If we correctly understand 'democracy', our planning from this very day should be such that the army would be least needed. Let the people take up the responsibility of defence upon themselves and not leave it to others. In other words, they should be so much free of fear and feelings of enmity that there would be no need of the army at all. (ibid, 1533)

Criticisms of the Indian Plans

1023. The Five-Year Plans are drawn up in Delhi. The people living there have no idea of the conditions prevailing in the forest and rural areas. (BY, 31.5.1957)

1024. Our main objection against this (First) Plan is that it is based on a different outlook, an outlook which is far removed from ours. This is the basic defect; all others are included in it. However, avoidance by me to dwell on the points of difference beyond what is necessary for clarity of thinking, creates the impression that, on the whole, I am for the Plan and that it has my approval. And this impression is not wrong. This attitude of approval to a thing based, on our own admission, on an outlook which is different from ours, springs from a desire to prevent confusion in the minds of the people. Today we may, if we decide to oppose the Plan, retard its progress, but it is not the same thing as the capacity for reconstruction. We have not yet enough hold over the people to place our own programme before them and to get it implemented by them. I therefore think it improper from the point of view of nonviolence to use our influence in creating confusion and preventing even the good points from being given effect to. (H, 23.5.1953, 93)

1025. Though we have attained independence, our basic problems still remain unsolved. The Government has drawn up a five-year Plan. After its working for two and a half years, they have now realized that in spite of the Plan unemployment is growing.

A little modification of the Plan will not help us much. For there is a fundamental error in the Plan. The planners have committed a serious mistake in their approach to the subject. They are all great patriots. They no doubt aim at serving the country. But if they do not go deep and reach the core of the problem, their efforts are foredoomed to failure. I told the Planning Commission in clear terms that it is a postulate of national planning to provide full employment to all, ...If the Charkha or Takli will give full employment to all, we should not hesitate to adopt them. (H, 5.9.1953, 209)

1026. The First Five-Year Plan laid greater stress on agriculture. But in this Second Five-Year Plan, it has been presumed that the old emphasis on agriculture is not needed. However, it is dangerous to base our Plan on this assumption. Hence, in my opinion, it is essential to lay a very great emphasis on agriculture in future as well. No matter whether we plan for Khadi or village industries or mechanized industries or any other thing, they must all be based on the foundation of every village maintaining a stock of grains needed for at least two years. This is a basic principle. (BY, 31. 5. 1957)

1027. The Five-Year Plan which has been drawn up has neither the perspective of equality, nor that of compassion. Its main approach is of the increase in affluence, wealth and production. (NA, 66)

1028. It is generally said that the First Five-Year Plan was completed. But what was completed was in fact the Plan-period and not the Plan targets. People's cooperation was lacking in the execution of the Plan.

I really wonder why the people are not cooperative if the Plan has been formulated for their well-being. What a paradox! I want to offer water to the thirsty but he does not want to drink ! What does it mean ? It only means that we are not offering water to one who is really thirsty but emptying the whole vessel on the hand of one who is not thirsty. This is what is happening in the present plans. The thirsty are not getting water. (B, 7.1.1959, 300)

1029. Why is the people's prosperity not increasing even after the plans ? Why is the standard of living not rising ?... When I think over the matter, I find that it is like pouring water in a big vessel with four or five holes in it. ... We are spending 300 crore rupees per year on the army, 200 crore rupees on 5.5 lakhs of Government servants and 100 crore rupees on importing foodgrains from abroad. Thus we are spending a total of 600 crore rupees per annum on these things. These are big holes in our development plans and we have made them deliberately. (ibid)

1030. When the people ask them (ministers) why the plans are not successful, they argue that the population is increasing.... Overpopulation is only a convenient reply that they have found out. The fact is that they have no work to provide for the eradication of unemployment. The only employment that they have to offer is that of service. It means that this plan has only created a new middle class of service employees.

(ibid)

Community Projects

1031. How can there be a Community Project when there is no community. (VP, 4.12.1957)

1032. Nowadays 1 am moving about among the villagers and I know very well the miseries of the poor. 1 meet those who are in charge of Community Projects, and they too tell me that the Projects help only those who have some pull. (DV, 186)

Decentralization of Planning

1033. The method of Baba's (Vinoba's) planning is different from that adopted in the present plans. Their method is that of nationalised planning, i.e., the plan for the whole of the country is drawn up in Delhi. Baba wants every village to prepare its own plan. (VP, 16.6.1957)

Small Schemes

1034. If we plan and work out small schemes with our own resources and capacity, the progress of the country would be greater than it would be if we burden ourselves with big schemes. ... We can perform big tasks, but they would not be done till we acquire skill in performing small ones. (L, 216)

Plans and External Aid

1035. I do not find anything particularly objectionable if the Government wants to take advantage of the foreign assistance available without strings. But such foreign help cannot sustain the nation.

Merely outside help cannot take the country much forward. There is also a danger in such aid, even if it be without strings.

Hence I would only say that caution must be exercised.
(VP, 17.12.1959)

Cooperation in Government Plans

1036. People ask me how far they should cooperate in the Government plans. I say to them, we should certainly cooperate in those plans which we approve of, but we must keep ourselves free. We cannot accept any of these plans and projects as our own and get entangled in them. We may give to Government our advice if and when sought and may also occasionally help it when there is need, but it will be a mistake to make its plan any of our responsibilities. .. .My own attitude is, as I told you, to go our own way, ...devoting all our energy and time chiefly to our chosen mission. When we take to criticising others, we waste a good deal of energy. I therefore think that both criticising others and getting involved in what is not our own work are undesirable and eventually detrimental to our cause. (H, 23.5.1953, 94)

1037. Even if we are basically opposed to the Government Plan, we must admit that its aim is the good of the people. Hence though we find fault with it, criticise it and feel that it is totally wrong, yet we have to acknowledge that its objective is good and that our own aim is the same. If, however, we do not think so, we should not cooperate with it in any way whatsoever.
(VP no. 188 of 1958)

XII
SATYAGRAHA

The Meaning of Satyagraha

1038. Gandhiji taught us several things, but the most important of them is 'Satyagraha'. It has a very wide connotation. Faith in truth in the whole conduct of life is Satyagraha. In this sense a prayer too is Satyagraha. Control of the body, speech and mind is also Satyagraha. A habit of early rising is also Satyagraha. However, in a restricted sense, it means 'a method of resisting injustice'. People are familiar only with this meaning. (HS, 17.10.1948, 284)

1039. People think that Satyagraha only means picketing, but it is not so. A Satyagraha appeals to the minds and hearts of the people through right conduct, right speech and right thought. One who lacks faith in the power of thought, is no Satyagrahi. (S, Aug. 1949, 37)

1040. Satyagraha means, in other words, insistence on truth through love. (BG, IV, 109)

1041. It is clear that the land problem can be solved either through killing, or through legislation, or through compassion. ... Some say that besides these three, the fourth is the method of Satyagraha. On this I maintain that Satyagraha comes under compassion and my trek for land-gifts is also a form of Satyagraha. It has truth, compassion and penance. If along with it some other form of penance has also to be undertaken, it too must have compassion. What involves truth, compassion and penance, is Satyagraha. (ibid, 243)

1042. Satyagraha is a way of life, a way of doing things and in special circumstances a method of remedying things. (VC no. 34-35, 507).

1043. These days a totally wrong meaning of Satyagraha has come to prevail among the people. It has become a threat. In case a Satyagraha is reported anywhere, it produces an adverse instead of a favourable reaction. Satyagraha is taken as a pressure tactics. In fact its purpose is to free the society of all kinds of pressures. There are various kinds of them which prevent men from thinking freely. The process of removing these pressures from the mind resulting from various circumstances, is known as Satyagraha. It is no Satyagraha to add one more pressure to the many already there. Satyagraha attempts to free the intellect. There are several methods for it, one being of continuous service and the second, of continuous self-purification. Wherever there will be such a Satyagraha, people will experience peace and their hearts will be touched. Satyagraha is used for the very purpose of removing the veil over the intellect. To explain the ideas and to do the necessary service for it, to establish the friendly feelings, and not to allow the slightest fear to enter the mind and heart of the opponent, is Satyagraha.

(VC no. 34-35, 496)

The Essence of Satyagraha

1044. To hold to truth, to work for it and to suffer for it so that the others may be converted to it, this is the essence of Satyagraha. (H, 16.8.1952, 203)

The Power and Mark of Satyagraha

1045. When the sun rises, the darkness is dispelled. True Satyagraha has a similar power, so that the very sight of it compels a man to think where he had been unwilling to think, and to purify his thinking when his thoughts had run on very different lines. The veils of illusion are removed and there is a new openness of mind. Where it takes place, it is a mark of Satyagraha. (DV, 156)

The True Character of Satyagraha

1046. The word (Satyagraha) plainly indicates aversion to what is bad or untrue and attraction to what is good. But in the effort to reject the bad and retain the good we should not forget to contemplate the cosmic aspect of God. You must not forget for an instance that the person who stands in front of you is an aspect of you yourself. You must set about correcting others as gently, with as much sympathy, as you pluck a thorn out of your hand. You must remember that it is you yourself who is being corrected though the act may be an outward one for somebody else. You must not be angry or impatient. You must understand that there is good where you see bad. If you can enter into the heart of the person with whom you are dealing through the door of this goodness, you will be able really to help correct the bad. (SW, 124)

Some Misconceptions about Satyagraha

1047. We have been thinking so far that Satyagraha is something negative. We have been under the impression that when we are incapable of resisting with the help of weapons or when we do not want to do so, we must resist without weapons and it will be Satyagraha. But this meaning of Satyagraha is partial and one-sided. We have had so far only a glimpse of Satyagraha. We have yet to develop much of its potentialities. Satyagraha is not anything negative, but something positive. It implies basing one's whole life on truth. (BAC, 67)

1048. People think that a Satyagraha is only conducted against an enemy. A person who feels animosity towards anybody cannot be a true Satyagrahi. (BYB, 21.8.1953)

An Excellence of Satyagraha

1049. In Satyagraha the saint and the brave become one. They are threaded together, not sewn. This is an excellence of Satyagraha. (VP, 26.9.1957)

The Four Principles of Satyagraha

1050. (a) Satyagraha is not negative but positive.

(b) It should proceed from the gentle to the gentler and then to the gentlest.

(c) On the very hearing of the word 'Satyagraha', one should feel happy.

(d) Let there be no insistence on your part. Let it be on the part of truth. (BY, 7.2.1958)

Satyagraha in a Democracy

1051. It is a fact that many people in this country are afraid of the word Satyagraha. This should produce in us great concern. Satyagraha for us is a sacred watchword and one which we believe has the power to save the world. We even claim that the accumulated experience of human history finds its fulfilment in this principle of corporate Satyagraha, and that it is from this that nonviolence will derive its strength. But nowadays people are afraid of the word *satyagraha* and go so far as to say that in a democracy, where the people are in power, there is no place for it. It is true that Satyagraha would have no place in an order where every decision is made unanimously. Wherever society is so organized that decisions have the consent of all, any independent corporate Satyagraha would be unnecessary. Nevertheless, even in such a society, a mother might use Satyagraha against her son, or a son against his mother, or neighbour against neighbour. The word 'against' in this context has not the same sense as in violence, but indicates helpfulness.

There is a reason why people are afraid of Satyagraha, and this also is a source of danger to nonviolence. Men have got it into their heads that Satyagraha is a negative thing, a method of forcing an issue or exercising pressure which is of very doubtful propriety. This is the only meaning of it in the minds of the general public and because of it some individuals are strongly attracted towards it. On the one hand there is fear and dislike, on the other hand there is this attraction. ... It seems to me that it would be a mistake for us to take now as our model the type of Satyagraha conducted in Gandhiji's days. The circumstances of those times demanded negative work. Nevertheless, side by side with this work, Gandhiji set going a lot of constructive and positive movements. That was his genius; and he saw that unless there was a positive approach even in the negative programme, the accomplishment of that programme would give rise to new dangers.

It follows that we cannot consider the Satyagraha of those days as the final model of Satyagraha. We must grasp the idea that any Satyagraha which takes place under a popular government must be different in form from what went before. It is not that there is no scope at all for Satyagraha under a 'democracy'; that is an entirely mistaken notion. But it is equally mistaken to imagine that the negative Satyagraha of pre-independence days will find much scope or exert much influence in a popular, democratic set-up. The Satyagraha that can influence a democracy must be much more powerful, that is to say, much more constructive. (DV, 152-155)

1052. Satyagraha is a force of love and if someone said that there was no room for that force in democracy, it would mean that there was room for hatred in democracy. But none would accept it and none would desire so.

But I must confess that nowadays Satyagraha has degenerated into a threat and it has produced its due reaction. A true Satyagraha would quickly touch the hearts of all; nay, it would hit the target as assuredly as the arrow of Rama. But it requires the purity of Rama to wield this precious weapon. If an impartial and devoted servant of man finds an injustice being perpetrated and, after trying all ways of peaceful persuasion with goodwill and love to open the heart of an evil-doer, is unable to do so, he is entitled to offer, and it becomes even his duty to offer, Satyagraha with feelings of anguish and compassion in his heart. No social order can deprive him of this right.

But it must be conceded that in a democracy which is responsive to public opinion and is based on elections there cannot be frequent occasions for resorting to Satyagraha, in the sense of an intensive and final weapon.

(H, 20.9.1952, 253-254)

1053. The question of Satyagraha can only arise at present in moral matters. When it is our government and the laws are ours,

questions should be settled with the help of the laws.
(S, May 1951, 609)

1054. If something is recognized by law and favoured by public opinion, but is not being implemented, it can provide an occasion for Satyagraha. (VC no. 34-35, 517)

The Form of Satyagraha in a Democracy

1055. In a democracy Satyagraha can never take the form of the exercise of pressure. Its correct form is that of the change of heart. As a form of pressure it can well go with other polities. In a democracy its form will be that of a change of heart or of an entry into it through constructive work. Otherwise, democracy will not thrive. (VP, 14.3.1958)

Satyagraha in the Present Age of Science

1056. Martin Luther King : Would you kindly throw some light on the possibilities of Satyagraha in this nuclear age ?

Vinoba : Nuclear age is an age in which we cannot afford to have conflict of mental attitudes. Otherwise, nuclear weapons are sure to solve out the whole problem of humanity by doing a clean shave ! So the necessity of this age is to rise, if I may use the word our philosophers have used, not only over the body but also over the mind, and think on a supramental plane. The mental creates conflicts of various types ; the supramental will save us from these. I think this supramental is also coming with this nuclear age.

Satyagraha is to let truth take care of itself. Let us not come between truth and ourselves. We ourselves often become an impediment and hinder truth from playing its role. If we allow truth to work its own way, that is, if we rise above our mental level, I think Satyagraha will proceed (make headway). While meditating about Satyagraha, that remarkable utterance of Jesus has helped me very much, "Agree with thine adversary quickly". If you ponder deeply over this sentence, you will get a clue for the type of Satyagraha which is needed for the nuclear age. (SE, April 1959, 401-402)

1057. One can easily understand how Satyagraha will operate in a simple situation. For instance, an armed man may lay down his weapon when confronted by a man of compassion. Saint Narada, thus converted Valmiki, who came to attack him with an axe. But the situation today is different. A man who drops a bomb from a plane or detonates it by just pushing a button from a safe hide-out is not confronted by his victims. And even if among them is a man whose eyes reflect infinite compassion and whose speech is sweet with million human kindness, will it be of any avail ?

Well, then, if we have reached these heights of scientific knowledge, let us also delve deep into the powers of the Spirit. There is now need to go deeper than the level reached by the ancients. If some individuals have come to possess the power to reduce the world to shambles by just pressing a switch, we must now acquire a power which will radiate from one place throughout the world. Satyagraha will cease to have any meaning if it cannot do this.

It is both necessary and possible to be in living union with a new power which will neutralize the power of the nuclear system. (B, 9.7.1958,92)

1058. In view of the phenomenal progress of science, we must rise from the plane of mind to the plane of intellect. As such, Satyagraha must not create agitation or tension in the minds of the opponent. Satyagraha must avoid collision of minds and seek harmony in thought. That is why I describe my Satyagraha in terms of gentle, more gentle and still more gentle. The mind of an opponent refuses to change and thinks of retaliating under compulsions and conflicts. Our nonviolence should rise on psychical plane in this atomic age. ... Recently science has put such weapons in the hands of men that if wrongly used by agitated minds they might destroy humanity. As such Gandhiji's nonviolence should now have more subtle and finer forms to enable it to neutralize the forces of violence in this atomic era and arouse world conscience. (B, 18.2.1959., 350)

Satyagraha for Internal Problems in Present-day India

1059. During the pre-independence era, everything we did had a negative aspect. It was then a question of 'end or mend'. The same slogan cannot hold good after the achievement of Swaraj. We cannot now ask our businessmen or the wealthy to 'Quit India'. We have, therefore, to understand fully the principle of Satyagraha and to develop a definition. Even Gandhiji did not prescribe any 'science of Satyagraha' because it is an evolving idea. (SE, June 1956, 419)

1060. There are three important developments. We live in freedom, democracy and atomic age. These three factors have basically changed our conception of Satyagraha. The new technological era has made the world smaller. Our nonviolence must, in this context, be potential enough to meet the challenges of atomic weapons and spread the message of peace. We cannot afford to waste the power of nonviolence over minor day-to-day internal struggles. Our nation must accumulate it for higher moral world progress. We must confine the solution of our internal problems to the following four courses :

(1) Constitutional means.

(2) Change through the ballot box.

(3) Persuasion.

(4) Social change through people's efforts.

(B, 18.2.1959, 350)

Satyagraha against Land-evictions

1061. I have always been impressing upon the tenants to refuse to get evicted and suffer all tortures cheerfully. If the landless labourers pick up a little courage and gather self-confidence, all the manoeuvrings of the rich landholders would come to naught. (H, 11.9.1954, 227)

Satyagraha, A Process of Nonviolent Assistance in Right Thinking

1062. I had said that Christ stopped after saying 'Resist not evil'. It was right. But we interpreted it as 'Resist not evil with evil'. Gandhiji also did the same. But in the context of today when ideas assail ideas and for spreading them arms are used, the sentence 'Resist not evil' should be taken literally and we should talk of 'nonviolent assistance in right thinking" instead of 'nonviolent resistance'. We should assist in right thinking.

If in assisting right thinking one is compelled to oppose at any time or to noncooperate, it may be done. But its form must be of rendering nonviolent assistance in right thinking. It should appear to oneself that he is really doing so and to the opponent, that he is being assisted.

(Report of 1963 Arambagh Sangh Session, 25-26)

Need of Education in Resistance and Noncooperation

1063. Just as one aspect of education, or awakening the consciousness of the people, is to teach them to cooperate with the state as far as possible, and that voluntarily and with full knowledge, the other aspect of education is to teach them to recognize the proper occasion for noncooperation and resistance, and when such an occasion arises, to offer nonviolent noncooperation and resistance.

For this purpose, early in life children should be taught exceptions to general rules. For instance, side by side with the teaching that children should humbly carry out the orders of their parents, the parents themselves should teach their children that if their orders do not appeal to the children's conscience, the children should respectfully break the orders.

(SS, 46, 47)

What Does 'Resistance of the Wicked' Mean ?

1064. 'Resistance of the wicked' connotes 'resistance to wickedness', and it implies search in one's own heart of the wickedness observed outside. (VC no. 34-35, 464)

Resistance to Injustices, A few Considerations

1065. It is said that the Gramdan movement is likely to become strong if the power of resisting injustice is awakened in the people. There is a double approach in this. Attempts can be made from both sides. If there is a possibility of the gift of a block, it may be proper to put up with other things for some time and to devote oneself to securing the gift. One should act like Bhima. He was taking his meal and a demon was beating him. Bhima said, "Let me eat, and while I am doing so, you may well beat me. I shall not fight you, giving up my meal. I would see to you after I have taken the food." Thus, even if some injustices are being perpetrated, it would be proper for us to remain engaged in our work when our strength is not much. We may, however, take them up if we have enough of strength.

Secondly, it may also be that resistance to injustice would awaken the power of the people. If such a possibility seems to be there, one may also take it up. It all depends on the circumstances.

What generally happens in the case of resistance to injustice is that when we go to help the people in small matters and do something against the officials involved, case is filed against us and we have to run to the court again and again and much of our energy comes to be wasted in pursuing the case. The main work remains undone.

Then this too has also got to be considered that injustices are inherent in the existing structure of society and the Gramdan movement is itself directed against it. As long as this structure does not change, its inherent defects will have to be put up with. (VC, 35-36)

1066. A friend from Rajasthan recently asked for my opinion regarding a problem in Satyagraha. He is agitating in a village on behalf of the Harijans for the right of drawing water from the village well. Someone has also started a fast in this connection. At this, the villagers have come forward with an offer to dig a separate well for the use of the Harijans. Now the friend has asked if he should accept that suggestion.

If I were to follow the line of thought current till now, I should have said, "Let the fast go on; by agreeing to the new well, the right will be lost." But I am not going to give any such advice. I intend writing to him to accept the proposal of their digging a new well. What sense is there in going on knocking one's head presuming that there is an obstruction. Whatever be done presuming the existence of caste differences will only serve to strengthen those differences. At the new well the Harijans will draw water, and others as well. This will lead to unification, obliterate the differences and by and by feelings, of love will develop between them.

Mine would be considered a weak advice in terms of the mentality of today. But it is no weak advice. It is rather a strong advice since it does away with the mind itself. Instead of allowing the minds to collide with each other, we must think of rising over it. (BY, 4.7.1958)

Fasting as a Method of Satyagraha

1067. Bapu (Gandhiji) taught us several methods of resisting injustice from time to time, and experimented with them in his life. One of these methods is that of fasting. It is not a new thing. All religions have recognized its importance in one way or another, and have prescribed it for the purification of mind and heart, self-control, atonement and for finding God. Naturopaths use it for the restoration of health. But Gandhiji employed it for a totally different purpose. He awakened the conscience of the nation through it. These fasts were of two kinds—fasts for limited, specified periods and fasts unto death, terminable only on the achievement of the purpose of the fast. Of these two, the fasts unto death are being frequently resorted to these days.

Of the many fasts undertaken in the country in recent years, hardly any of them has been such as I could defend from the spiritual and moral points of view.

Fast has a special place among the spiritual weapons of nonviolence. But it is being used today either as a pressure tactics or to draw the attention of the people towards certain things. It is not proper to use this mighty weapon for petty purposes. On the contrary, such misuse only discredits it.

Fast requires not only proper justification but also a qualified person to undertake it. ..... Fast requires purity of mind and heart, discernment, impartiality and complete absence of ego. ... Only he is qualified to undertake it who has rendered mother-like service to the world for long.

However, it should not be resorted to if the situation in the country or neighbourhood is unfavourable, even though the person may be entitled to it and there be justification for it. It can be undertaken only when all these three factors are favourable.

The inner voice can only manifest itself in a pure being. Under any other condition, it may not be the voice of God but that of Satan. (HS, 17.10.1948, 284)

1068. I hold that fast is a valuable weapon available to a Satyagrahi (one who undertakes a Satyagraha), and I do not want to deprive him of it. But its effectiveness depends on its proper use. If the government is on the wrong track, if the public does not listen and has gone astray, a great soul, feeling greatly distressed, may undertake fast as a prayer to God. But when the government is considering a matter and there is scope for arguments, when there is an opportunity to prepare public opinion for a people's movement, it should not be undertaken.

Recently there have been fasts for linguistic provinces and along with them violence too was used. Thus both fasts and violence were tried together to solve a problem. Hence these fasts were no indications of the abundance of love. They were a method of exercising pressure, and hence can only be reckoned as a variety of violence. (BYB, 14.8.1953)

1069. If fasts are undertaken, they should simply be either for the purification of the mind and heart, self-introspection, self-meditation, or for strengthening the power of our resolve. If we try to dominate people on the strength of the power acquired through penance, we would fall in the category of Ravana. (BG, IV, 328)

Self-immolation

1070. People think that self-immolation by burning oneself is non-violence, but in reality it is an extreme form of violence. Just as it would be violence to kill others by burning them, likewise it is violence to immolate oneself in that manner. However, people have come to hold that if extreme steps are undertaken, they are bound to have an impact on the world. But it is a totally mistaken idea. (VC no. 6,29)

The Nonviolent Process of 'From Gentle to Gentler'

1071. In the domain of violence they proceed from gentle weapons to fast and faster ones. But the process of the working of nonviolence must be entirely different. If our gentle Satyagraha does not yield the desired fruit, we must infer that there is something wanting in our gentleness itself and we must, therefore, render it finer, gentler. (H, 30.4.1955, 71)

International Satyagraha

1072. We would not find any precedent in Gandhiji's life as to what should be done when international disputes crop up and peace is disturbed. That will have to be thought out.

(VC no. 34-35, 493)

1073. The citizens of a country which maintains an army, have no right to go into another country and undertake Satyagraha there. Those who intend to do so should first demand the disbandment of the army in their own country. However, there may be a few rare great souls who may do it in any part of the world. They are even doing it today though it is not apparent.

(KKR, 150)

1074. **Question :** How should an international Satyagraha be undertaken ?

Vinoba : Satyagraha denotes a spiritual power. It is neither physical nor psychical. Science has relegated psychology to a secondary place. Hence it is imperative that a search for Satyagraha be made by rising above the mind and soaring into the realm of the supermind. If we aspire to solve international issues by recourse to Satyagraha, then keeping ourselves detached from state power and public opinion, we shall have to ascend to the supramental level. My contact with the persons of various countries during the Bhoodan trek has convinced me that men are fundamentally similar and at the same level of evolution. We must, therefore, possess a power which will emanate from the soul and influence the whole world. When an individual is able to transcend the limits of the mind in the field of his life and enter the supramental level, then only a power capable of influencing the world will be generated.

(BY, 4.7.1958)

XIII
THE AGE

The Dilemma before the World

1075. The whole world is in a terrible dilemma. While the search is for peace, preparations are going on for war. The world is terrified at the latest inventions of science. It is in despair at its experience cf attempts to establish peace through war and to remove economic disparities through struggles. It is waiting for a method of revolution which is in consonance with our aspirations for brotherhood and which moves onwards establishing cooperation among human beings.

(BYB, 30.4.1954)

Man Controlled by Armaments

1076. So far armaments were under the control of man, but it is not so now. He is under their control. (VP, 17.7.1957)

The Condition of Religions, Love and Wisdom

1077. On one of the buildings (in a high school) there was a significant inscription. It said that religion, love and wisdom must ever go together. Today we find that these three are rarely seen to exist in one place. They are found separately. Learning is confined to the university, love to the family and religion to the temple. Thus these three mighty factors have become virtual prisoners (B,12.9.1956, 6)

The Call of the Age

1078. The establishment of equality is the call of the age, which is hungry and thirsty for equality. When the longing is so intense, equality is bound to come. The only question is how it should be brought about so that it is stable, beneficial and satisfying. That would be the way of compassion. (NA, 66)

1079. The call of this age is that nonviolence and science should combine together, and society be ruled by nonviolence and compassion. Meanwhile, though intellectual power would be required, it is compassion which would rule.

(VC no. 32-33, 441)

1080. Spirituality is needed today because man has acquired the immense power of science. It is fast developing and it would do great damage if it takes a wrong direction.

(Prerna-Pravah, 29)

Need of a Social Outlook

1081. Men spend too large a part of their lives in acquiring money. They should pay greater attention to the accumulation of goodwill. Running after money involves constant growth of envy and ill-feelings. No one cares for others ; neighbours behave like complete strangers. What then can we expect but unhappiness and insecurity ? As individuals, we feel true happiness when we are accepted by a family and share its life. To make our social life more satisfactory, the same feeling of belonging and sharing has to be developed.

Social awareness is necessary for a harmonious personal life. We must be sensitive to the social needs of others because the march of history and science has increased our interdependence. What a society does or omits to do affects a wider circle than before.... The awareness about social interdependence is as much basic to personal happiness as it is to social progress and international peace.

(B, 30.5.1956, 4)

Small Hearts and Big Brains

1082. Remember that the world is becoming one and men are coming nearer to one another. Even the high heavens are not as distant as before. When science has made so much progress, when the intellect has such far-reaching power, it will be a disaster for humanity if the hearts remain small. The problems of today arise from this discrepancy; our conflicts, whether between 'capital' and 'labour', between Hindu and Musalman, between India and Pakistan, or in Vietnam, all spring from the conflict between big brains and small hearts. If the brain had remained small like the heart, there would not be so much trouble. (TP, 101-102)

1083. Man's intellectual horizon has today expanded so much that the attainments of a Newton or a Vyas seem small in comparison. We possess much more knowledge than they did. An ordinary college boy nowadays knows more mathematics than Newton, who knew nothing of the differential calculus, although he was the greatest mathematician of his time. ... Little children in primary schools today know more geography than Akbar did.

So our brains have expanded, but our hearts remain small. We call ourselves Harijans, landowners, Sikhs, Brahmins; we label them as belonging to this party or that party. ... So long as people's minds are filled with these petty distinctions and their thoughts centred on such trivial questions, we are simply unfit for the demands of our times.

Should we then restrict ourselves, throw away our science? That cannot be done. Once science has come, it has come to stay. It is not possible for us to forget it and go back. On the contrary, intellectual progress is going to continue and scientific knowledge is going to expand even further. There is no alternative, if we are to survive, except to expand our hearts. (TP, 102-103)

Need for Clear Thinking

1084. The world has become one. ... The winds of thought blow freely over the continents. We are acting and reacting to one another. All this is very welcome. But unless we have acquired clear thinking, we cannot understand or assimilate the significance of current ideas and movements. Unless we are rooted in clear thought and have integrated minds, we shall not be able to judge anything correctly. We shall be washed off our feet by the currents and cross currents of ideas and modes of action. (B, 25.4.1956, 4)

Men of the Steadfast Wisdom Needed

1085. The conditions today are such that problems become extensive and complicated, and the responsibility of taking quick decisions on them has devolved on us..... Hence never before men of the steadfast wisdom were so much needed as today. (BY, 25.4.1958)

The Three Effective Forces Today

1086. I have already said that three forces are working in this scientific age. The first is 'spirituality' which moulds human life. The second is 'science' which besides changing the externals, influences the internal life as well and requires of man to rise above his mind. The third force which can prove effective is that of 'trust'. On an individual assuring us that he would deal with us in a straight manner, we should take him at his words and accept him with full faith, notwithstanding the fact that his past belies his present professions. Only then can we win him over, transform him and find entrance into his heart. (BY, 5.9.1958)

Frightened Man and Violence

1087. There were terrible earthquakes and floods, but it does not seem that man was ever so much afraid as he is today of his own violence. The frightened man has now somewhat begun to think that the excess of extreme violence must be stopped and a limited and ordered violence be re-established. Efforts are going on for it.

But these efforts of the frightened man to put a stop to the excess of violence, do not have the possibility of success. If this fact is realised, there can be only two developments. In one, man would be completely annihilated, and, in the other, he would have opportunity for full growth.

(S, April-June 1955, 588-589)

Conditions in India Today

1088. What is happening today ? Big industrialists invade the cities. Cities in their turn exploit the villages. Villagers exploit Harijans and landless labourers; they exact maximum work from them, but pay them minimum wages. Harijans and labourers exploit their women....What do the women do? They avenge themselves on the animals under their charge. They do not give them adequate feed and exploit them by making them work to exhaustion. Thus there is an unbroken line of exploitation running all along the social scale from top to the bottom. (H, 10.7.1954, 194)

1089. Society has become disintegrated. There is no organic unity in the elements that go to make up the modern (Indian) society. There is no bond of real sympathy between its members, A spirit of mutual cooperation is naturally absent. We have created all sorts of differences and built walls of separation between man and man. A fragmented society like ours can never survive. (B, 24.4.1957, 4)

1090. Dead traditions, feudal casteism, social inequalities, laissez faire economics and struggle for existence have very nearly killed our ethical conscience. There is hardly anything like a social conscience in our social life. Even when we adopt new values like nonviolence, we stick to the word while the spirit eludes us. Very few seem to have actually realised that force and violence are self-defeating instruments. A mother, a teacher, a reformer, each has within him a lurking faith in the ultimate sanction of force. No results, they think, are possible without a judicious use of force or threat. Unless we re-examine our ethics and values, we shall not be able to get out of this vicious circle. Revolution means constant awareness and rethinking. Never before was independent thinking, that is, revaluation of all our values, so urgently necessary.

(B, 20.6.1956, 4-5)

1091. We must clearly understand that today we are completely devoid of morality, and whatever scheme or method we adopt,we have to do so after careful consideration and with foresight. Expedients creating terror will not do. The whole of social organization will have to be replaced by a new economic order based on equality. And that too alone will not do. We shall have to revise our religious notions. We have not only to be kind to all living beings but also to establish truth in practice. At present it is not only in commercial profession that untruth is rampant unashamedly, it is so even in the fields of literature, service of the country and religion. This untruth must be driven out of them. The immense crisis overcasting the nation would not be avoided merely by a threat of punishment or by an appeal for kindness to all living beings, as long as untruth goes on spreading fearlessly in these fields. All thinkers, social workers, persons given to religious practices, educationists, workers and managers should work for it together.

(VV, III, 34)

1092. We have three kinds of troubles, and we must put our whole strength into getting rid of them, for, twenty years after independence, they are still with us.

The first of our trouble is poverty, which seems to be on the increase. There may be several reasons for this, but our negligence is a major factor. We have not done our duty; we have not provided for the country's basic needs, which ought to have taken precedence over any secondary needs.

The second of our troubles is that we have entirely lost our belief in self-reliance and self-sufficiency. How can we talk about India standing on her own feet when even our food, and the milk powder for our children, come from outside? ... . We no longer believe in Swadeshi, we no longer take pride in producing what we need.

So far as education is concerned, we have made every possible mistake, going wrong everywhere. Education today has no spiritual dimension. It is no longer based on the principles which in the past have been India's strength and stay, and which are still her strength today. This is our third trouble; there is no productive work in our current education. It keeps knowledge and work apart.

(TP, 103, 104, 105-106)

1093. At present, there are no villages at all. There are only houses in India. Where there is no consideration for the village, no scheme for it, no love for it, how can a village be there ? They are only houses. (VP, 23.12.1962)

1094. Formerly power resided in London and from there it was transported to Delhi. This was a matter of great generosity. But now it has got stuck in Delhi and has to be carried to every village. (L, 130)

Imitation Will Not Do

1095. Young men must ponder deeply over the various problems that face us. They must note that our country is vast; we cannot imitate any other nation. It is true that China is also a vast country, but the diversity of languages, religions and customs that we have in India can hardly be found anywhere else. Ours is an ancient country. We carry a big load of tradition. We have the caste system which is peculiar to India. We have strong points as well as weaknesses of our own. In Europe, every language group has developed a separate nationhood. That means that our polity is more advanced than those of Europe. They will have to form a federation of Europeon countries before they come up to our level. The capacity to recognize unity in diversity is our special virtue. There is the caste system, there is poverty and suffering. One has to comprehend the whole picture and then find out how one can serve the country. (B, 1.5.1957, 6)

Need to Change India's Economic Structure

1096. Lin Yutang, the well-known Chinese writer, says somewhere that India is a land of God-intoxicated people. This description of India by him is true of our people even today. ...All this corruption, therefore, which we see around us, is due to the evils in the present-day economy. The organisation of our economic life is bad. People are swept away by the tide of these outer evils and led to commit mistakes. Therefore, if we can change the structure of the economic life, you may be sure that our people can well set a unique example in the world. (H, 27.10.1951, 301-302)

Need of Idealism in India

1097. Swaraj ought to have been followed by a broad penetrating vision, lofty idealism and a new inspiration. On the contrary, the idea of enjoying comfort and luxury has overtaken the country. The best educated and fine people go into the government. If they work there sincerely, they would be able to render service to the country. And there is nothing wrong in it. Employment under a free Government is quite justified. But there is an idealism which cannot be satisfied with the present situation and should make us leap forward. That idealism is missing today. If someone makes a sacrifice, he is dissuaded and advised to go in for some job.

This is the situation today. We have to rise above it and take up some great work. .. This is regarded as idealism. It has grown dim. Without idealism, we cannot have a Rabindranath, Aurobindo and Gandhi. Without idealism, we cannot even become good professors, good judges, good generals, good administrators.

I am not at all disappointed at this situation that has arisen since the Swaraj. It has frequently happened in history as nations got tired after they attained some goal. But this state will not last long. (SE, May 1962, 358)

XIV
VARIOUS ISMS

Isms, A Warning

1098. An ism, born as a reaction, is antithesis to some thesis, and hence it comes to acquire the defects of the original.

(VP, 3.8.1957)

Capitalism, Its Defects

1099. Capitalism advocates efficiency. It says that some are less efficient than others and they should therefore get less, while some are more efficient and should therefore get more. It seeks to promote efficiency in society by remunerating each for his labour according to his work and capacity. It has raised the standard of living of a tiny minority to a very high level. But at the same time it has also pulled down that of a vast majority into abysmal poverty. Capitalism has no remedy for this evil. Indeed, it declares frankly that for those who are unfit there is no alternative except that they remain so.

This is the root cause of much of the misery of the present-day world and that is why capitalism has very few supporters today. And though it still continues in various forms, it is doomed to die sooner or later. (H, 7.11.1953, 285)

1100. In a capitalist society one man's misfortune becomes another's opportunity. No one thinks that there is anything wrong or irreligious in exploiting the misfortune of another.

(B, 12.9.1956, 7)

The First Capitalist

1101. A friend told me that Bhoodan is a front against capitalism. This is true. But the first capitalist whom we have to subdue is our own body. Bred and brought up in a capitalist society, it has acquired some habits which have to be discarded. We would have to work with our own hands. (H, 19.2.1955,411)

How to End Capitalism ?

1102. Capitalism cannot be ended either by love or conflict, but by right thought. Conflict leads to ever more conflict which can only weaken both, while love also cannot bring about a change of things. Love brings forth enthusiasm, but only right thought can initiate and effect a revolution.... Conflict is also one of the factors in progress, but it is essentially the propagation of right thought which alone is qualified to bring about a revolution. (H, 1.8.1953, 170)

Communism, A Reaction against Capitalism

1103. Capitalism is of several kinds. Capitalism means earning capital, which requires centralized administration. It cannot be done in a decentralized manner. Thus those who call themselves communists are also capitalists to the core. The communists want centralization in production and equality in distribution. They are under a delusion that decentralized distribu- tion would follow centralized production. They are born of a reaction against capitalists. Theirs is no independent ideology. They have no life-philosophy of their own. They are a product of a reaction against the evils born of capitalism in Europe. Theirs is not a thesis, but an antithesis against capitalism. (H, 19.2.1955, 411)

The Service Done by Marx

1104. Karl Marx has given a very important idea to the world. It is that all the poor of the world are one, that they can stand up together and become free. (VP, 11.7.1957)

1105. If any one since the Buddha raised the voice of the poor and the afflicted out of compassion, it is Marx, the great thinker. (VP, 25.9.1957)

Marx and Gandhi

1106. What can be a more fascinating study to us in the present age than that of a comparison between the ideologies of Gandhi, the great soul, and Marx, the great thinker ? If the last hundred years or so of the social life of humanity were boiled away, the residue will most likely be these two great names. Lenin is ingested in Marx, and the shadow of Tolstoy spreads over Gandhi. The two ideologies stand face to face, each bent upon swallowing up the other. On the surface it might seem that the two contestants occupying the arena are the Communists led by Russia and the Capitalists under the mask of Democracy by U.S. But ideologically the latter has lost all its vitality and though it might appear doughty on the strength of its military force, I do not regard it as really existent as a rival against Communism. On the other hand, though Gandhian ideology stands nowhere in an organised form, yet inasmuch as it is impregnated with the vitality of right thinking, I believe that ultimately it will be Gandhism with which Communism will have its trial of strength.

(KGM, 15)

1107. I said the other day that if Karl Marx had been alive today, he would have rewritten his *Das Capital.* It has already become out-of-date. He could not have imagined the vast changes that have come about because of the impact of science and technology. He was a great thinker. He would not have failed to take note of the vast changes that have been wrought by the rapid advance of technology. There are many good points in the polity recommended by Manu, but it is not suited to our times. Similarly, Gandhiji also should not be followed blindly. We must understand the changed context and also the spirit behind his words. (B, 15.10.1958, 205)

Marxism

1108. Marxism is not an *ism* that can be translated into practice ignoring the nature of surrounding conditions and environment. It is a method of application. It has to undergo changes according to altered circumstances and conditions of each place.

In Russia, the revolution was carried on not exactly on the same line as enunciated by Marx. In China, we saw the adoption of another form different from that of Russia. In the altered circumstances of each place and in response to the demands of the times, Marxism has to change its methods. (SC, 27)

1109. Marxism was conceived as an antithesis to capitalism. Therefore as capitalism decays, it is also decaying. It provided the means for delivering the people from the clutches of the evils of capitalism, and as such proved very efficacious in those days. But now the world has seen that many of Marx's prophesies have gone wrong. (H, 27.12.1952, 374)

Meaning of Socialism

1110. Socialism has an eye on the whole human society. It says that give work to each according to his ability, take full work from him and provide him with full security. (KD, 58)

Socialism, An Interpretation

1111. Socialism means hundred percent private sector plus hundred percent public sector. 100+100 = 100. But this is not intelligible to planners. What does it mean ? It means that private sector itself should be transformed into public sector. All the businessmen would work in the interests of the public and thus both the sectors would grow and flourish.

(SE, April-May 1972, 435)

The Basis of Socialism

1112. Really speaking, socialism comes into existence when every individual is given to observing restraints. Where everyone considers himself as separate from society, socialism cannot come into existence. (BY, 30.12.1955)

Democratic Socialism

1113. Democratic socialism makes the claim that it safeguards the interests not only of the majority but of all. But the experience shows that it has no remedy for many of the ills which democracy leads to. So long as the interests of the minority are sought to be protected through the will of the majority, it is not possible to achieve full socialism.

(H, 7.11.1953, 285)

Socialism and Sarvodaya

1114. I consider Sarvodaya superior to socialism since there are many varieties of socialism, one of them being that of Hitler.

(BY, 19.9.1957)

1115. The word 'Sarvodaya' is of this country while that of 'socialism' has come from the West, and consequently it has brought a variety of meanings with it. Today it has almost come to signify a 'welfare state'. If socialism means that society would maintain an individual and provide him full opportunity to develop his individuality while the individual would tender all his service to society, there is no difference between Sarvodaya and socialism. But there is opposition between them if it involves sacrifice of some for a greater number of men. ... Besides this, an opposition will also be there if socialism accepts violence for its defence. But there is no difference if violence is not accorded primacy.

(VP, 1.8.1957)

No Abhorrence for Communists

1116. Many abhor the very name of 'communists', but it is not so with me. I hold that they too are inspired by compassion.

(VP, 12.1.1963)

Communism Superior to Capitalism

1117. I have been of the view that communism is a noble and broadminded ideology. It is superior to capitalism in every respect. Yet, it suffers from several drawbacks.

(BG, IV, 43)

Defects of Communism

1118. Capitalism prevailed in Europe. Big factories and large cities came into existence. The world's wealth was being accumulated. Then came disputes between factory owners and labourers. The owners did not allow the labourers to better their condition. Reaction against them gave birth to communism. In other words, it is not a complete ideology in itself. A thought born as a reaction is ever changing. Socialism too is not an independent ideology. While one is a reaction against capitalism, the other is so against individualism. Being products of reactions, both of them lack a fully comprehensive perspective. (VP, 28.7.1957)

1119. Communism being obviously an ideology of attachment, I never considered it worthy of a philosophical examination. Although its votaries have erected an apparently grand philosophical edifice around it, essentially it is devoid of any philosophical content. It is so, because it is not an edifice at all but a pretentious jumble. Their vision is all yellow with intellectual jaundice. For example, they believe in an eternal element which they call 'conflict'. There is nothing else in the world but 'conflict'. ... The breast of the mother overflows with milk for her new-born baby. How does the miracle happen ? From their point of view it is the result of a conflict between the breast of the mother and the mouth of the child. ... How can one argue with such obsessed people? One can only wonder at them. They are not concerned with devising a technique to accord with a true philosophy. They are out to manufacture and trim a philosophy to suit their technique. (KGM, 17-18)

1120. They (Communists) frequently discuss whether the mind has emanated from matter or vice versa. None but a lunatic will doubt that mind has emanated from matter. Had mind been the creator of the Universe, who ever would have had any use for God ? But though mind is the product of the matter, the Atma, i.e., Spirit remains a separate entity beyond both mind and matter. But the Atma is nowhere to be found in the communist laboratory and, if anybody shows its traces to them, they will deny its existence without the least hesitation. To such a dialectician Sankaracharya said, "Friend, I have no quarrel with you. For you, who deny the Atma, are yourself the Atma. If you agree, it will be proved by your acceptance, and if you deny, it will be proved by your denial." ......Thus, on account of the rejection of this third factor, the Atma, who gives form and substance both to mind and matter, communism caught in the whirl of social reconstruction, has no independent and important place for virtue. What to us are spiritual qualities are to them merely the product of economic conditions. A soul-less ideology has no place for the freedom of the individual. (KGM, 18-19)

The Mistakes of Communism

1121. The communists want to eradicate theft through theft and violence through violence. It, on the contrary, only increases theft and violence. (Purnea, 64)

1122. Both Gandhism and communism regard the well-being of the poor and the oppressed with the intensely loving regard of the mother. It often happens, however, that the infatuation to see immediate results gets the fond mother involved in entanglements of indiscretions, which make her overlook the far-reaching results of her methods upon the child. This has happened in communism. (KGM, 29-30)

1123. Communism preaches envy of the haves. The envy of the haves cannot be a moral duty of the poor. (SAS, 44)

1124. Though they (the communists) make great sacrifices, go to the people, live a life of poverty similar to that of the people, but there is no provision for it in their philosophy. (SAS, 50)

1125. My objection to communism is that there is no scientific thinking behind it and it has become outdated. (SAS, 85)

1126. The communists create class struggle. They attempt to excite the utmost hatred on various issues. This does not appear to be a desirable method. We want to bury the past and we do not think it necessary to revive what has been buried in history. But both the communists and the communalists are very fond of bringing the past into light. They excite hatred in the people by reminding them of past events. This is a misuse of history. (SAS, 44)

Gandhism and Communism

1127. They say that Valmiki wrote the *Ramayana* long before the birth of Rama, and Rama conformed to every word of it during his early career and, so, had also no occasion to worry himself about using his own judgment in order to take a decision. He had just to consult the book and act accordingly. ...So, too,is the case with the communists. Lenin acted as Marx had prescribed; we, too, have merely to follow him and straightway reach the goal.

It is quite otherwise with the Gandhian ideology. If communism is a solid and imposing structure of granite, Gandhism is an ever-changing amoeba. If we examine Gandhiji's ideas, we will find them always growing.

(KGM, 20-21)

1128. If the Gandhian thought shows up a halo of spirituality around it, communism has at its back the support of a scientific terminology. Having proved its worth by securing Swaraj for us, Gandhism may no longer be dubbed as visionary and impracticable. And communism too, has for the moment proved its virility by rejuvenating the hoary old China. This tempts some workers to seek a reconciliation of the two systems, and has led to the enunciation of the formula like, "Gandhism is communism minus violence". The fact of the matter is that these two ideologies are irreconcilable; the differences between them are fundamental. (KGM, 16-17)

1129. Whatever differences there might be between Gandhism and communism, there are also points of similarity between them and these too are important. A Sanskrit poet traced similarity between even Rama and Ravana through the common syllable *ra.* There is no wonder then that there are common points between these two ideologies, since both of them have originated from a desire for the welfare of the masses. The cause of the have-nots is the basic sentiment running through the both. (KGM, 29)

Sarvodaya and Communism

1130. Communism and Sarvodaya are not adversaries. They are as brothers. And yet with a difference. That is why I have been emphasizing truthfulness in addition to affection and compassion. This brings out the essential difference between the two. Mere love and compassion may go astray. I admit that there is compassion in communism. But the consciousness of truth born of an all-embracing experience is not there. (SE, April 1962, 316-317)

1131. There is a great difference between Sarvodaya ideology and that of communism. According to Sarvodaya, a thing which is good and correct, should be begun at once. Later pressure can be put on government too. If an individual relinquishes his ownership (over land) first', the action would start. The communists want to begin with the government and legislation and to end with themselves. In Sarvodaya, one has to begin with oneself and end with governmental legislation.
(SAS, 49)

1132. The only persons in the world to visualise the abolition of the state system are the communists on one side and the Sarvodaya people on the other. ..These two ideologies hold that without the dissolution of the state, there can be no full flowering of human personality. As long as the administration would be carried on from above, the people would be oppressed by it and man would have no opportunity for free development. (SAS, 73)

1133. We want to abolish the (economic) disparity found in society through nonviolence. The communists too desire equality, but their concept of equality differs from that of ours. It is not in their concept that every village and individual should be self-dependent. They also think that any means can be employed for desirable ends. (SV, 104)

1134. Question : Can there be any compromise or cooperation between communism and Sarvodaya ?

Vinoba : There cannot be any compromise between the two, but there can be a good deal of cooperation. Sarvodaya will not give up its ideas because it is no reaction to any ideology; it is in itself a philosophy of life. ...Can a sea compromise with any river ? (BY, 7.6.1957)

1135. People say that "your programme does not differ from that of the communists." But the communists want the dictatorship of the proletariat and a concentration of all powers in the hands of the government. We, on the contrary, say that education should not be in the hands of government, but in that of the people. The responsibility of national defence too should be on the people. The land problem should be solved by the people and not by legislation. Is it all communism ? The difference between the two is quite obvious.

(BY, 21.3.1958)

Samyayoga and Communism

1136. Samyayoga bases itself on inner unity and armed with right discrimination it seeks to build, on that secure foundation, a justly balanced order. Communism, on the other hand, is blissfully ignorant of the Spirit, which it denies. And because Spirit alone can provide a base to the equality we want to create, communism is without base. It seeks to impose equality from without, an equality which is wholly artificial....Thus, the two orders, though both seek equality, are as apart from each other as heaven and earth.

(H, 19.4.1952, 68)

1137. Communism declares that equality can never be achieved unless the present upper class is totally abolished. Class war and the extermination of those who hold power offer the only way to this cherished goal. This much violence is inevitable and even obligatory on us.

It is obvious that such an outlook can never make for peace, because violence produces counter-violence. Not only that, it also results in the depreciation of human virtues which are ultimately the only real foundation for any progress worth the name.

Samyayoga, on the other hand, holds that there dwells in every man the same Spirit. It therefore makes no distinction between man and man. It goes even further and recognizes no ultimate difference in the spirit of man and other animals.

This is the difference between communism and Samyayoga. Communism does not accept oneness of the Spirit in all beings. Samyayoga does and seeks to reform and rebuild the entire life of society on its foundation, with revolutionary results in every field—ethical, social, economic and political. (H, 7.11.1953, 285)

Communists, No Destructionists

1138. Some are of the view that the communists are destructionists. I have differed from the communists on several points and hence I have criticised them at several places. But it did not appear to me that communism is destructionist in itself. It is, in itself, an ideology given to contemplation. This is a great quality not found in earlier ideologies.

(Report of 1957 Kaladi Sarvodaya Sammelan, 71)

XV
MISCELLANEOUS

Christ

1139. The three important teachings of Christ are :

1. Love your neighbour as you love yourself.
2. Love your enemy and it will bring change of heart in him.
3. Let all my followers love each other and sacrifice everything for others as I did for them.

These three moral duties come first into my mind whenever I think of Jesus Christ. These are the eternal moral duties and will be there as long as humanity lives.

I am as much devoted to the teachings of Christ as to the Vedic Dharma preached by our ancient saints. Christ's teachings are universal as he never preached any difference of religions, sects, etc. (SE, Jan.-Feb. 1976, 221)

1140. Jesus called upon us to love our neighbour. But though this has been extolled as a great virtue by all nations, few have been prepared to accept it in practice as an immediate obligation... We talk of love and nonviolence and One World, but devote the bulk of our resources to the piling up of armaments for mutual destruction. We despair of our neighbour. This is cowardice. Jesus refused to give way to it. He bore the Cross—the burden of our sins—and embraced martyrdom.

Luckily, this teaching of Jesus is not alien to India. We have been the meeting ground of a multitude of races, creeds and cultures, a land of synthesis and fusions.

I therefore unreservedly declare that Jesus Christ is our own, that to us in this country Jesus and his teachings have never sounded strange or unpractical, that we regard Jesus as one of our family. (H, 26.3.1955, 29)

Christian Teaching and Hindu Philosophy

1141. I can wholly accept the New Testament, especially the Sermon on the Mount. There is no difference between Christian teaching and Indian philosophy. Hindu Dharma has given the basis for ethics; the Christian religion and Buddhism have taken the basis for granted and have stressed the ethical side. (SE, Nov. 1954, 140)

An Appeal to Indian Christians and Others

1142. It is for our Christian brethren, now that their foreign trappings are shed, to subscribe to the indigenous background suited to our own genius. And I also suggest that similar processes of wholesome assimilation may also take place among the followers of Islam and other religions, that Christians and Muslims of India who have hitherto held fast to their moorings and their traditions outside India, may no longer remain strangers to the Hindu cultural background, but assimilate Brahma Vidya with profit. It would broaden their outlook and confer a wholesome spirit of quest and tolerance to their religious and ideological approach and add lustre to their culture. Such a consummation, I submit, would render easier what each one of us wants to propagate, and would make a worthy contribution to the growth of our common culture.

(H, 26.3.1955, 29)

Proselytism Disfavoured

1143. The intense desire which the Christians have to spread the name of their Master, acts as an impediment in their work. I think that the most dangerous thing for the ideas of a preceptor is the wish of his disciples to spread his name.

(KKR, 20)

The Meaning of the Islamic Kalma

1144. I particularly like 'There is no other God except God, and Muhammad is the Prophet of God'. In the first part it says, that Allah is one. Every man would accept this. In the next half it says, 'Muhammad is the Prophet of Allah.' This is interpreted in different ways. Some interpret it to mean that Muhammad is the only Prophet of God. But this is, incorrect. For Islam says, "We make no distinction among the various prophets that have come into the world." This is one of the fundamental tenets of Islam. Therefore the plain meaning of the text 'Muhammad is Allah's Prophet' is that no prophet can take the place of God, not even Muhammad. He was only a prophet of Allah.

Thus if we understand this *Kalma* in a broad sense, it should be acceptable to the whole world. No doubt some people might well say that for them Muhammad was enough. To children their father is enough. Though they would respect others' fathers also, yet for their own purposes devotion to their own father serves them sufficiently. The Sikhs believe that there have been ten Gurus for them and henceforth no more Guru is to come. This may be sufficient for them. But it cannot be so said for the whole world. We cannot limit the doings of God. We can limit our own faith.

(H, 16.2.1952, 432)

Islam, Emphasis on Charity

1145. In Islam, charity is one of the important religious injunctions which its followers are asked to carry out, and I think that its views in this respect are, in their sociological content, more advanced than we find in Hinduism. For example, the Koran has denounced the institution of interest most emphatically which would suggest that they (Muslims) are nearer the true economics. (H, 26.12.1953, 344)

Islam and Christianity, Their Characteristic Features

1146. Everyone agrees that a unique spirit of brotherhood and comradeship pervades the teaching of Islam, and that Islam means PEACE. This is why the moon is its symbol. A man who has no passion for peace and has no compassion in him, is not a Muslim. On the other hand, he who has peace and compassion in him, is a Muslim, whether he has such a label or not. I should call him and regard him a true Muslim.

Similarly, love and service are two characteristic features of the Christian way of life. Now I do yearn to live up to these ideals in everyday life. So I am willing to sit at the feet of their prophets and holy men and learn. And I should love to regard myself, or call myself, part Christian and part Muslim, and look upon it as my good luck to be so, and endeavour to be worthy of all that this means. This I can do, I claim, without the least harm to my Hinduism. I rather feel my Hinduism will bloom and blossom forth and add to its lustre and gain in stature for my doing so. Even so, Christianity and Islam, reinforced in the manner I have just explained, can assume a special significance in preaching universal love and brotherhood and service of all God's creatures.

(H, 26.3.1955, 29)

Gautam Buddha, A Hindu Reformer

1147. He (Gautam Buddha) was a great reformer of Hinduism. He was a Hindu and died a Hindu. That is my belief. Our society recognized it by accepting him as an incarnation.

(Diwan, 4)

The Message of Lord Buddha

1148. The ideas of the Buddha are attracting the whole world today. The world needs them. Their attractions are their rationalism, attack on casteism, renunciation, compassion, non-enmity etc. Among these, I assign chief place to compassion and non-enmity, (ibid, 2)

1149. The message which Lord Buddha delivered to the world was fashioned by him not as a result of any speculative thinking but out of his experiences of life. It has stood the test of centuries and shines even brighter today than ever before.

What is that message? It is : Not by hatred is hatred appeased; not by anger is anger pacified; not by falsehood is falsehood eradicated. Hatred will only inflame hatred, and anger aggravates anger. Hatred must therefore be met by love, anger by peace, and falsehood by truth.

Buddha's message is not new........But the ways of the world have remained more or less unchanged. Because, while the people respected him whoever attained this ideal, they did not consider it worth acting upon in practical life.

There was another reason why this message did not spread among the masses. It was this : Hatred is not likely to disappear as long as the factors which excite it are existent.

(H. 3.7.1954, 142,143)

A Difference between Buddha and Mahavira

1150. Lord Buddha was primarily a humanist, while Lord Mahavira was inspired by extreme compassion for all living creatures. This compassion went to the length of holding that the very life of man is based on violence. Hence he holds that even taking of food is a sin. The less is the food consumed, the less is the violence perpetrated. Consequently, he remained without food as far as possible.

The Buddha prohibited violence and it will have to be said that he was successful. Now we do not find violence practised in Yajnas. Such violence was also there during the times of Mahavira but he did not interfere with it. He simply preached unadulterated nonviolence and for that he was always practising austerities. He remained satisfied with that much. This compassion of Mahavira was *nirguna,* abstract. I think that the level of Mahavira was higher and I am inclined towards it. But I have followed the way of the Buddha. That path is of preaching compassion by taking up some work. The compassion of the Buddha is such that it prompts one to do something.

The religion of the Buddha is based on compassion but detachment is its dominating feature. Its field is that of humanity. Jainism too is based on compassion, but it is not concerned with man only. It is concerned with all living creatures. There is neither any uneasiness in it; nor excitement; there is an aloofness. (Diwan, 66)

Hinduism, No Narrowness

1151. Hinduism gives its followers complete freedom. It does not insist on any particular discipline or prayer....Religion has to release us from bondage. The only imperative commandment it can have is to ask us to purify ourselves. Hinduism has emphasized the need for inner purity. Indian civilization and culture has shown a tremendous capacity for assimilation and absorption. If Hinduism becomes narrow, we shall be destroying our precious heritage. (B, 28.5.1958, 45)

Vinoba's Hinduism Not Exclusive

1152. In fact, I do not find any difference in the various religions—Hinduism, Islam, Christianity, Buddhism etc. Having grown up in different countries, their outward forms are different, but in essence they are the same. So my Hinduism is not exclusive. It includes every other religion.... Though my roots are in Hinduism, yet I have studied the Bible, with as much respect as the Gita. Likewise, I have studied the Koran. The *Sermon on the Mount* satisfies me as much as the Gita. But my mother tongue being Marathi, a daughter of Sanskrit, I am naturally happy at native expressions. They are a source of inspiration to me and so also to those with whom I work. So my environment seems to be Hindu but there is no Hinduism in it. (H, 5.3.1955, 3)

Propagation of Religious Ideas, A Historical Analysis

1153. Among the many metaphysicians and thinkers who lived in this world, there were some who had an absolute faith in the capacity of ideas to propagate themselves. One of them was Lord Mahavira. Whomsoever he met, he enquired of his ideological background and would then proceed on that basis to explain his ideas to him. For instance, if someone believed in the Vedas, he would explain to him on the basis of the Vedas themselves. He used to say that no thought has only one aspect. If it was so, it would be no thought at all, but something without its spirit. Hence he would say, "What you think is right, but what is at variance with it, may also be right. Hence keep your mind open," Thus he would explain his ideas with- out any insistence. He also did not take the help of any physical activity for the dissemination of his ideas.

Forty years later than Mahavira, came the incarnation of the Buddha, who was of a different type. He adopted another method for spreading his ideas. He took the help of a physical activity. It was the work of purifying the Yajnas from the perversions which had entered into them. But this activity was not all for him. It was merely a vehicle to take his ideas to the people. Thus the Buddha initiated another method of thought-dissemination based on the view that a physical activity was required for it.

As time passed, many sects and orders came to be founded. Millions of people accepted them, but the process was slow and the strength behind it was that of the ideas themselves. However, a new force later entered the field. Some rulers became interested in spreading ideas. Constantine, Ashoka, Chandragupta and some others are its examples. As a result of it, these various religions underwent changes.

Thus the third method of the propagation of ideas through political power came into vogue. Under it, such material conditions were created as could help in persuading the people to accept ideas and in dissuading them from refusing to do so. In this way, a close link came to be established between religious ideas and political power, so much so that state considered it its duty to propagate them. The consequences of it are quite well-known. Though there are now tens of millions of people professing each religion, the reality has been lost. It is either finding no expression or the ideas have got perverted.

Later on, it came to be considered essential to break the power of opposition to what were regarded as sacred ideas whose acceptance would result in the good of mankind. This led to the seeking of military help for their propagation or on its plea. In the beginning, it was all done in the name of security. Prophet Muhammad showed great tolerance and forbearance in the beginning. He explained to his followers that their ideas were a gift from God and if they were made to suffer for them, they should bear it. But it so happened that their power of endurance began to give way and they started fleeing away.

Then he had to tell them that it was not proper to behave like cowards. It would be better to take up the sword and face the opponents, but it should only be used to the extent needed. Thus he commanded them to resist when they tried to flee out of cowardice on the pretext of forgiveness, forbearance and nonviolence. That is how violence came to be allowed, not for the propagation of ideas but for their defence. The example of Prophet Muhammad is not a solitary one. We find the same thing in the Mahabharata. The temptation of the propagation of ideas, led us to adopt an aggressive attitude and it resulted in depriving them of their real spirit.

(Hindi Report of 1958 Sarvodaya Sammelan, 108-111)

Animal Sacrifice

1154. If God becomes happy at the sacrifice of a goat, why should not man be sacrificed to add to his supposed happiness ? It is a fantastic and baseless practice.

(H, 13.11.1954, 295-296)

Vegetarianism

1155. I believe that India's special contribution to the history of nonviolence is the giving up of animal food. Not that all Indians are vegetarians, but the idea commands the respect of all. I have seen many a cruel person among habitual vegetarians and many a kind one among meat eaters. In spite of this, I believe that vegetarianism will go a long way to help the evolution of nonviolence, and humanity will be imperfect without it. (H, 8.1.1950, 389)

1156. With me it is also an article of faith that the modern man has got to attain, sooner rather than later, an adult status, when he shall kill no creature of God for food or sport, when he will refuse to look upon any living being as his food. ... For, mankind must reach the conclusion soon enough that vegetarian food is the best food for man so as to enable him to outgrow the beast in him. I am also aware that enough vegetarian food is not available in the world today. Nevertheless, I submit that the reform is essential for the evolution and perfection of man and for the unity of religious and spiritual endeavour of all mankind. (H, 26.3.1955, 30)

1157. India has her own mission—to rid the people all over the world of meat diet. ... If man depends upon meat, he requires four acres of land; if he relies upon milk, he needs two; but if he confines himself to cereals only, one acre is enough. Now population is rising day by day and the extent of land per capita is going down. Hence more land would be required if we use animals for food and they in return use cereals for theirs. This question is soon bound to crop up before the whole world. (SE, Oct. 1973, 146-47)

1158. I suggested two things to a Christian friend : collective silent prayer and voluntary vegetarianism. I told him that vegetarianism is India's gift to the world. Saint Paul says, "If meat hurteth my brother, I will not take meat all my life."

(ibid, 47)

1159. If we want to do away with non-vegetarianism, we have to grow more fruits and vegetables and increase the supply of milk. (SE. Aug. 1956, 37)

Cow Protection

1160. Protection of the cow and the bullock is a characteristic of the Indian social philosophy. We are, in this respect, a step ahead of the Western socialism. Western socialism asks for a full and equal protection being given to all men, but there it stops. We in India have gone a step further. We have included the cow as a member in the family. True, we have not followed this principle in practice fully. We merely pay respect to the cow but do not look after it so well as they do in the Western countries. Nevertheless we have deep regard for it and consider it worthy of our care and protection in the same way as the human members of the family. We do not drive out the latter when they grow old. In the same way, though we make full use of the cow and the bullock—take milk, get our fields ploughed, use the dung for manure, and use even their hides after they are dead—we do not kill them.... But now we must link up this regard with a scientific attitude. Superstitious respect will not do. We must open good dairy farms, Gosadans, and the wealthy amongst us should come forward to provide for the upkeep of decrepit cattle.

(H, 29.8.1953, 202-203)

Ban on Cow-slaughter

1161. Some people are under serious misapprehension in regard to the secular character of our State. They think that there is some kind of incompatibility between cow protection and a secular State.... There is no incompatibility between the secular character of our State and the protection of the cow. No religion in India says that it is meritorious to kill a cow, and therefore there is no conflict among our different religions about the desirability of the protection of the cow. ... Therefore I say that there is nothing to prevent the secular State from striving to protect the cow, and our State must do it,

(ibid, 202)

1162. When people inquire of me, "Have you no pity on other animals?", my reply is, "First let me show my compassion to the cow. If I could save the cow, I would proceed to show pity for saving other animals." (KW, Vol, 1, 98)

1163. I am simply amazed that cow-killing goes on in Calcutta day in and day out. Yet there is no attempt to stop it. You might say that there is politics behind the movement for banning cow-slaughter. But this does not absolve you of the responsibility of stopping a great disaster which is daily sapping the very vitality of the nation. Let apart the political motive behind the movement, why not go and see the horrible crime committed daily in the killing of our finest cows ? I believe that in a country like ours every cow and bullock must be given full protection. But what is happening in Calcutta is so horrible that no self-respecting man or government would be able to bear the sight. (H, 12.3.1955, 14)

Prohibition, Its Benefits

1164. Wherever prohibition has been introduced, the condition of the workers has improved. Ask the womenfolk or the workers of Ahmedabad and Madras. How grateful they are to prohibition. Their lives are happier.

(H, 19.1.1952, 394-395)

The Problem of Liquor, Its Two Aspects

1165. The problem of liquor has two aspects, one relating to the village and the other, to the city. As far as the village is concerned, there should be a Gram Sabha or Village Assembly in every village. ... It would explain the matter to the villagers and if it has influence over the village, all the villagers would collectively decide against the consumption of liquor in the village. If, in spite of it, the government opens a liquor shop there, the people would have the right of picketing it. If we want to work on the basis of people's power, we shall have to go to the villages we have not been able to reach so far.

In the city, the approach will be different. Some persons will have to be issued permits in a planned manner. Where liquor is to be supplied, it would be done by the government, which would also be manufacturing it. In other words, the manufacture of liquor would be nationalised. The percentage of alcohol in the liquor would also not exceed a prescribed limit. Such a liquor would be provided to those who have grown habituated to it. However, the right of picketing the shop and dissuading the people would also be there.

(Maitri, Jan. 1973, 1147)

The Devanagari, As a Common Script

1166. There is no objection to Hindi as the national language being written in the Devanagari script, but we have yet to decide that the various other languages of India be *also* written in it. Such a decision would not mean rejection of the present scripts used for them. It will only mean that both the original script and the Devanagari script will be used.

Some people propose to give this place (of a national script) to the Roman script instead of to the Devanagari. I have thought over the suggestion and have tried to take an objective view. There is no doubt that the Roman script has many virtues, but it is equally true that it has many defects as well. These defects are so conspicuous that George Bernard Shaw wanted the invention of a new script for the English language, and even set apart a portion of his estate for it.

This does not mean that the Devanagari script is perfect or that there is no room for improvement in it. I also count myself among those who think that there is need for improvement in that script.... But I do not hold that the script should not be used for other Indian languages in its present form. On the contrary, I sense a danger in the proposition that the Devanagari script should first be improved and then adopted as the common script for all the Indian languages. My opinion is that even in its present form it can and should be adopted as the common script for all of them.

During the course of my present Padayatra, I had an occasion to learn the Japanese language, I found that the construction of the Japanese language is similar to that of the Indian languages. The syntax and the use of the preposition are also similar. The sentence begins with the subject, followed by the object with the verb at the end. The Japanese are in search of a new script because theirs is a picture script and hence being composed of innumerable signs, it is unfit for wide use. Under these circumstances, if we adopt the Devanagari script for the whole of our country, there is a possibility of its being adopted for the Japanese language as well. The same applies to the Chinese language.

(SE, May 1960, 459, 461)

The Devanagari Script and South India

1167. It is wrong to think that the Devanagari script will not be liked by the people of the South. It may be so due to a misunderstanding born of confusing this script with the Hindi language. Some designate the Devanagari as the Hindi script. In fact, it has no relationship with Hindi. This script is also used for Marathi, Sanskrit, Ardhamagadhi and Pali. Sanskrit, Ardhamagadhi and Pali are ancient languages.... and Marathi is among the modern languages. Other languages of the North too are written in that script with slight modifications. It is this which leads to the misconception of identifying it as the Hindi script when Hindi has no relationship with it.

(Nagari, 56-57)

Devanagari, As an Additional Script

1168. I do not say that only the Devanagari script should be used for other languages. What I say is that it should *also* be used.

(ibid, 59)

Why the Additional Devanagari Script ?

1169. My first objective is that all the four languages of the South should come closer. There are such fine writers in Kannada as Bendre, Puttappa, Karant etc., but their literature is not read by the Tamilians, though Tamil and Kannada are very near. ... Thus, what I want first is that the languages of the South should get closer.

The second objective is that the whole of North India should become one.

The third objective is the integration of the South and the North.

The fourth objective is unity between India and other countries of Asia.

The fifth objective is the unity between India and the world. This programme will, however, commence when the question of the unity of the world will arise. For that, I can accept both the Devanagari and the Roman scripts.

(ibid, 59-60)

Upavasadana, Donation of Money Saved by Fasting

1170. I have a suggestion. The Sarva Seva Sangh may be needing some ten lakh rupees for its yearly activities in India. This has led to an idea that if our fellow-workers, helpers and others in India having faith in Sarvodaya keep fast for a day every month and donate the amounts so saved in a year to the Sarva Seva Sangh, it would be a big thing. My daily expense on food comes to three rupees. It might be two rupees in the case of a worker, thus coming to some twenty-four rupees for the whole year, which, for calculations, be taken as twenty-five rupees. In other words, forty thousand persons would be needed to observe fasts to contribute ten lakh rupees to the Sangh. I think that the number of the lovers of fast in India must be in lakhs.

Such a donation would have three merits. A person keeping fast, would gain spiritually. For, on that day he would be engaged in contemplation and be nearer to God. Merely abstaining from meals does not amount in an *upavasa* (fast). It must lead to spiritual benefit as well. The second benefit would be physical. According to naturopaths a few fasts must be kept every month. Thus a monthly fast would keep the workers in good health. The third advantage would be that this donation would be an untainted donation. When the Sarva Seva Sangh would receive such donations, it would also utilize it well. There would be less possibility of its misutilization.

(M, Oct. 1973, pp. 93-94)

Mystic Powers, Not Enough

1171. I have no faith in mysticism. The visions of the mystics and of the meditating devotees are but projections of their yearnings. In truth, they are not seen; they are felt in the heart as Divine assurances, or as wishes of the devotees fulfilled by God. He who is satisfied with such visions and gives up the deeper search will only forfeit the bliss of real seeing, of realization. Of course, the mystic sees far into the deep. Within him lies the great power to get the direct vision of the Unmanifest. But we cannot rest with the acquisition of this power. (B, 9.7.1958, 92)

Supernatural Powers

1172. The practice of Yoga, *yoga-sadhana,* leads to the attainment of supernatural powers, but that is not liberation. They work rather as obstacles in its way. (Diwan, 101)

Kingdom of God

1173. I do not know if there was any period in ancient times when a kingdom of God existed. It might have or might not have existed, but I do feel that it is possible to bring about such a kingdom. It has to be created in the mind and heart of man as well as in the world outside. (B, 3.4.1957, 4)

Place of Forgetfulness in Life

1174. I want people to forget their past, not the whole past but only that past which has become defiled by guilt, passions, sins and bad habits. And not only our own sins and bad habits but those of others also. It seems an unattainable state of mind because to remember is a natural attribute of the mind. But to make it forget the sordid chapters of one's past is the essential training we need to give to our mind. At the same time, the mind should remember the good deeds it inspired us to do, not in detail but in essence. It is like extracting butter out of buttermilk and preserving it.

(SE, Aug. 1973, 51)

Love, Friendship and Tenderness

1175. When persons gather because of mutual attraction, there is love; when the attraction is of ideas, it is friendship; and when the attraction is that of a teacher, it is a feeling of tenderness.

(AD, 70)

Impact of Great Men

1176. The impact that great men have on society can never be measured in mathematical terms. They continue to influence generations for thousands of years afterwards.

(B, 1.5.1957, 8)

How to Control One's Mind ?

1177. Outside regulation has no effect. What is needed is inner regulation. One should not act according to the desires of the mind. It is necessary to listen to the commands of the intellect. On resolving to do so, one is able to control one's mind.

(Diwan, 52)

Should Evil Propensities Be Suppressed ?

1178. The idea that evil propensities should not be suppressed or restrained is wrong. If we are not to suppress them, should we allow them to oppress us ? Should we be a prey to them ?

Should we permit them to control us ? To leave them unbridled is to lack courage and spirit of adventure. (Diwan, 102)

Escapism, A Defence

1179. Those who retire from the activities of the world and mundane efforts are scoffed at as escapists. I am an escapist. The house is on fire and they ask one not to run away. Should he be burnt to death in it ? (Diwan, 119)

Purity of Intellect Needed

1180. The intellect of some is acute and of some dull. But this acuteness or dullness is not important. If the intellect is pure, even if dull, it will decide correctly and provide right guidance. It is bound to arrive at wrong decisions if it has the *rajas* and *tamas* elements, even if it be acute. Hence what is of importance is its unpollutedness.

(HS, 10.7.1949, 154)

Satisfaction with Little and Satisfaction with Self

1181. Some Vedantists preach that man should be satisfied with little, but it is absolutely wrong. Man should not be satisfied with little but should have satisfaction with self. Self-satisfaction is one thing and satisfaction with little is another. The latter indicates weakness, while the former points to the highest endeavour. (HS, 18.9.1949, 251)

Literature Must Be Universal

1182. Literature is for all and must be universal. All should be attracted by it, should be able to enjoy it and should like to preserve it. That which people like as having with them (*sahit*) is *sahitya,* literature.

Good literature should maintain its attraction at all times and in all periods of life. (B, 28.5.1958, 46)

1183. A good work of literature is that which is capable of multifarious interpretations.... When one reads Valmiki's Ramayan, one does not come across many sermons. Like the flowing Ganga, it makes a fluent reading, and different people interpret it in different ways. Nay, the same man interprets it differently at different times. (H, 2.7.1955, 142)

Qualities of a Great Writer

1184. I submit that a great writer must have deep humility. There is no place for humbug in literature. The sense of 'I-ness'is one of the great impediments to any artistic creation. A literary artist must be able to forget himself and become a silent witness.

A thermometer has the quality of an ideal artist. It can measure temperature objectively. It remains unaffected and records faithfully one's body temperature. A literary artist must have the quality of detachment. He must be free from predilections and prejudices. Like an umpire in a game, the artist must be able to watch the play of life around him with deep interest and attention but without any bias.

(B, 28. 5. 1958, 46)

1185. Men and women who have given themselves to the pursuit of literature are never sectarian; they do not belong to any religion or sect. Why ? The very fundamental characteristic of the men of letters is that they are above narrow sects or sectarian loyalties. Those who are bound by sectarian loyalties can never hope to create permanent literature. They can only produce literature which merely serves the need of the moment. (H, 2.4.1955, 37)

Who Is a Poet ?

1186. The word used in our ancient language for men of letters is *kavi,* poet. The poet is he who can perceive change or revolution. Merely writing out the letters of the alphabet in a particular order does not make a poet. The poet is he who has the capacity to perceive the on-coming change, he who can see the future, the beyond. (ibid)

Literature and Nonviolence

1187. When in my heart I analyse the word 'literature' *(sahitya),* I reach the conclusion that it connotes nonviolence. You will wonder at this analysis and call it sheer idiosyncrasy to bring in nonviolence everywhere. But men of letters have themselves observed that the best literature is only suggestive. (H, 2.7.1955, 142)

Litterateurs and the Means of Living

1188. I am of the view that artists, including literary artists, must take up such small industries as will give them enough for their livelihood but will not fatigue their minds. Kabir would not have been Kabir had he not been a weaver. The poets who lived as the poor masses lived and worked, achieved unity with the people, and their compositions in song or poetry or fable endured without the help of the printing press. The more the poets identify themselves with the creation, the more would their poetry gain in depth and meaning.

(H, 6.6.1953, 40)

The Ramayana

1189. The theory that the Ramayana is the story of the conquest of the South by the North is fantastic. It was first conceived and put forth by some Western historians. Intentionally or unintentionally they have put forth some imaginary and untenable explanations about social development in India. They have never understood correctly that this subcontinent has been from times immemorial an 'ocean of humanity'. It has welcomed and made attempts to assimilate various racial groups who have come in wave after wave here. They have, therefore, emphasised differences and racial conflicts which lack a proper perspective. The picture they present is often out of focus.

No book of history has depicted a person with more than one head anywhere in the world. Therefore a drama which depicts one of its main character as having ten heads can surely have no historical authenticity. ... So I had never a doubt in my mind since my childhood that the Ramayan was not a book of history. It was an allegory. It depicted war between the gods and the demons.

This war is being waged in every human heart.... Ravana represents the active, *rajas,* principle in man, Kumbhakarna represents the indolent, *tamas,* principle and Bhibhisan, the good, *sattvik,* principle. The ten-headed Ravan rules over the human heart. Man can get peace and happiness only when this hydra-headed demon is annihilated.

1 have not come across any other book which has helped man to purify his mind to such a degree as the Ramayan. I would go to the length of saying that as far as Hinduism is concerned even the Gita takes the second place. The Bhagwad-gita may be compared to butter, whereas the Ramayan is pure milk. Even a child can assimilate it easily.

(SE, Oct, 1956, 109-112)

The Clash of Generations

1190. Every generation is inspired by a new idealism. Often the vanguards of the old idealism are not able to appreciate the new one. Hence they complain of the want of discipline in the new generation. The fact is that the old discipline does not suit the youth. New generation, new idealism ; they can only pursue the new ideal. Should they be stopped from reaching it, they are diverted along the wrong path. And this term as 'indiscipline'.

The old leaders are like a bow. The experience of an old aged coupled with ten enthusiams of the youth can work wonders. Otherwise, a gulf grows in between and ten young are blamed as indisciplined..

There is no indiscipline in them; only a new idea, a new music has caught them. If you strike a new symphony and play their right chord, they would simply dance at your behests But they do not obey you because you have nothing to offer them worthwhile. (H, 19.2.1955, 409, 410)

Attitude towards Films

1191. You know that I have repeatedly stated that I am not opposed to the film industry. On the contrary it can prove to be a good medium of education as well as entertainment, provided it is regulated and planned properly. As Ruskin has observed, every industry ought to keep before it the public good as one of its objectives. Within this broad objective there can be a place for fair profits also, but it would be intolerable in this age of science if the film industry is guided solely by the profit motive and does not care for the public good even when the harm that is being done to the public is obvious.

I would go a step further and say that if the film producers continue to have this attitude, it would be regarded as dangerous to allow an industry which exercises such powerful influence on the public mind to remain in the private sector.

I do not have any conservative or outmoded notions about what is decent or indecent in films. I insist on scientific thinking in these matters.... It was painful for me to launch a Satyagraha against indecent posters, but I was forced to do that. Posters are but the external symptoms of an internal malady.

Along with the curb on posters, censuring of indecent films and indecent songs is also necessary. I am therefore happy that the Government is now attending to it. I would appeal to the film producers to adopt a cooperative attitude and give a lead in building a healthy and dynamic younger generation in the country. (SE, Sept. 1961, 70-71)

Labour-Capital Relations

1192. Those who are engaged in labour welfare work generally talk of wage increase and payment of bonus. It is all right so far as it goes. But it will be better if a new relationship is established between mill-owners and workers. Mill-owners should come to regard their employees as co-partners in their undertakings. An employer and his employees should work together in a cooperative venture as partners. He should come to regard his wealth as a sacred trust for the well-being of society. Whatever profits are earned in a year, a portion of it should be earmarked for the expansion and development of the undertaking, another portion should be distributed among the workers and a third and smaller portion should go to the employer, not by way of return for his investment but by way of the remuneration for service rendered by him, and the ability and skill he has displayed in managing the affairs of the undertaking.

Whatever wealth he has belongs to the nation and he is a servant of the people. His share should be decided by mutual agreement. If industrial relations are organized on these lines, all labour-capital conflicts will disappear, and not merely workers but the country as a whole will prosper.

Labour, on its part, should also become more enlightened, Nowadays talks of strikes and presentation of a charter of demands are considered as hallmarks of enlightenment among the working classes. But the kind of enlightenment I want is education on the right lines. By that I do not mean attainment of mere academic learning but technical and vocational skill as well. Only when people become experts they will be respected and their advice taken by their employers. (H, 19.1.1952, 394)

Mercantile Community and Social Welfare

1193. The mercantile community should assume the responsibility of running the essential services of society, such as health and education, as an article of faith. That would enable them not only to regain their lost prestige but would also help them to be benevolent intermediaries between the state and society. (SE, June 1959, 476)

Advice to Businessmen

1194. The work you are now doing is described as private enterprise. But it is generally held that trading should no longer be left in private hands. However, if the use of your intelligence and enterprise is made in the service of society, all businessmen will become a part of public enterprise.

The conditions today however are such that neither the government nor the people have any confidence in businessmen. They too are apprehensive about the intentions of the society. People generally feel that businessmen are out to exploit and cheat them. I do not think so. I think that it is the peculiar economic structure we now have which has made men overconscious about self-interest. I do not think any particular class is specially blameworthy in this respect.

Nevertheless, the only way out is that businessmen prove to society that they are working for its good and that of others.

Traders should now stop doing business individually. They would do better if they worked together in groups of five or ten persons. This would enable them to give better service; dishonesty, which a small trader might indulge in ordinary course, may be curbed when a large group is formed. ... This in turn will raise the opinion of the people about businessmen. Such traders' cooperatives will also create a favourable impression on the government. (B, 14.11.1956, 6-7)

Controls and Merchants

1195. Two years ago, I had said at Indore that the government, on the advice of Gandhiji, had removed the controls and had warned the merchants to be honest. But the merchants failed and the rates went up very high. I had to say then to the merchants that they had betrayed Gandhiji and had proved treacherous to the people. I said that it left no alternative to nationalisation and the merchants have forfeited their rights. Some socialist friends gave wide publicity to my words. Even today, I do not think any need to revise my opinion.

(H, 7.7.1951, 168)

East and West

1196. I do not distinguish between Eastern and Western societies, saying that the Western is selfish and the Eastern is religious. That is not true. Human tendencies are the same everywhere. The only difference is that science has developed in the West in the last three centuries. Previously science had developed in the East also, but in the last three centuries the West has far outstripped the East. The science has come to dominate all Western thought. (SE, Nov, 1954, 140)

What Can India Learn from the West ?

1197. We have to learn a lot from the West in the field of science. But so far as the science of social organisation is concerned, we must rely more upon our old experience. There is not much to learn from the West in this respect. (H, 3.4.1954, 35)

Science and the Teachings of Saints

1198. The rapid development of science has created conditions in the world which give relevance and urgency to the teachings of saints. Men all over the world are hungry for words which will give meaning and significance to life. Science can be a boon to humanity if it is wedded to spiritual wisdom. The teachings of saints had a meaning for spiritual aspirants in old days. Science has now given a new relevance to their teachings. (B, 4.6.1958, 52)

Science and Metaphysics

1199. Science is the systematic study of the laws governing the process of the physical world. It investigates the nature of water, air and other forms of matter, and the law by which they operate.

Metaphysics is different. A metaphysician reflects on the basic nature of creation. He also asks how the physical concept of the world came into being and what is its relation to the concept of 'Spirit'? He considers the nature of God and the individual soul. A metaphysician in short considers the question 'why', while science answers the question 'how'. (TP, 41)

No Conflict between Science and Religion in India

1200. No instance like the prosecution of Galileo has been reported in our history. On the contrary, all theologians assert that whatever be written in the Vedas, nothing should be accepted that is contrary to science. Even if hundred scriptures affirm that fire is cold, they cannot be taken as correct. The Vedas or the Shruties could not be in contradiction with direct knowledge. There never has been any struggle between science and religion in India, nor is it likely in future, for here the marriage of spiritual life and knowledge has been happy and fruitful. (B, 27.2.1957, 1)

The Scientific Attitude and Life

1201. The scientific attitude is a respect for facts; it is characterised by an objective, experimental attitude towards life. If we have a scientific outlook, we shall regard every aspect of life as a field for research.

A scientific life is a simple life. People often think that science makes life more complicated, but this is a mistake. Science will help us, for example, to understand the value of fresh air. We are in the habit of covering ourselves with clothing all the twenty-four hours; some parts of the body are never exposed to the sunlight, and the body loses its vitality. Science teaches us to wear fewer clothes and so to simplify life. In a scientific society men will build houses of one storey rather than ten, and see that each house has open space around it so that light and air can enter. Science will improve health so much that medicines will scarcely be needed, though the very best remedies will be available if need should arise. There will be doctors, but their services will not be much in demand. Good spectacles will be available, but men of scientific outlook will take care of their eyesight. In the same way aeroplanes will continue to fly, but they will be needed only occasionally; men will prefer to walk, and to enjoy themselves by rambling in the forests. And in a scientific world there will be little need of artificial lighting, for people will prefer to spend the night sleeping under the stars. Science will not be used to deprive man of healthful bodily labour, but to lighten his burdens and to increase his vitality and vigour.

Science has expanded, no doubt, but the scientific attitude is still lacking to a large extent; life in general has not become scientific. (TP, 46-47)

The Warning of Science

1202. There may be some dim mental life in even the lowest order of animals, but it is their instincts which primarily control them, whereas in man, it is the mind which takes control. He is swayed by his mental states, his emotions, desires, hopes and fears. He is played upon by courage and by terror, by honour and dishonour, by love and hatred, by attachment and contempt, according to the bent of his mind.

Science, however, is now warning man that this mental equipment is no longer sufficient, and that he must now build his life on a scientific foundation. His old psychological equipment is useless. For man now holds in his hands the power of the atom—the very building block of creation, and at the same time the energy which can destroy the creation itself. For life or for death, the atom is in man's hands.

Science operates on a higher plane than that of the mind. The fact that science is higher than self-conscious mind has been known from ancient times.... In those early times the scientific plane of living was known, but it was not then essential for all men. Some men attained to it in the course of striving for self-development, but it was thought of as an individual achievement only.

That is why Sri Aurobindo spoke of the supramental state. He thinks of the mind as rising above itself to taste the immortal bliss of the vision and touch of God, and then returning to the earthly plane as what he calls an *avatar.*

This is a magnificent vision, but we may not all aspire to become *avatars.* Even if we are not capable of such great things, we must still raise ourselves above the mental level. (TP, 41-43)

All Societal Forces Must Cooperate

1203. For individual and societal health five forces should be strong and there must be good cooperation between them. Only then can the individual and society be healthy. I indicate them by fingers lest they be forgotten.

The first force is that of the thumb which is strong. 1 call it people's power.

The second is that which provides inspiration to mind and heart. It is represented by the small finger and it is the force of such servants of society who pattern their lives on the basis of truth and other ethical principles and who ever serve the people according to those principles.

The third is the index finger. It is used to point out the way. It represents the power of the intellectuals who provide objective guidance to all.

The fourth force is that of the moneyed people who include big and small industrialists and businessmen. They set the example before the people—of the path that should be trodden by them. (It is the middle finger.)

The fifth is the ring finger. Its function is to cooperate with other fingers, which have independent functions of their own. Here it represents the force of the government, which should only supplement the work done by other forces. However, the condition these days is such that whether it is India, Russia, China or America, this force has become all in all.

(Culled from a Paunar speech of 8.9.1973)

Be Appreciative of Foreign Countries

1204. When visiting other lands, we should have an appreciating attitude. While doing so, it is not necessary to appreciate one's own country as well. We may well be critical of it. But this difference of attitude will only last till distinctions exist between various countries. As they disappear, and disappear they must some day, there would be nothing but appreciation everywhere. God looks into the motive; we should grasp the essence. It is the essence which is *satya,* real. Hence we should be *satya-graahi,* i.e.,one who grasps the *satya,* reality. In such an outlook, both appreciation and criticism meet together. (Balkoba, 15)

Jawaharlal Nehru as Heir to Gandhi

1205. **Question :** Gandhi committed a big mistake in declaring Jawaharlalji as his heir. We think that it is you who are his real heir. For, we hold that Gandhi's personality was not political but spiritual, and you too subscribe to this view. What is your opinion about it ?

Vinoba : Gandhiji had the international world in his mind. That work of his still remains to be done. He expected Jawaharlal to take it up. It was with this view that he made it known that he was his heir. That is how I think. Jawaharlalji is carrying out that work in his own way. It is well-known that his attitude towards Khadi and village industries is different. Gandhiji was aware of it. Though he looks differently in economic matters, I feel that since my meeting with him at Chandil he accepts that village industries are not unscientific. It is not correct to say that Bapu should not have named him as his successor. Bapu acted in his own way. I was already his, while he expressed his trust in Jawaharlalji (by nominating him) as his heir. There is not the least doubt that he would justify it. If Jawaharlalji's way of looking at things has been different, mine too has been different. This too must be taken into consideration. (Divan, 69)

Essentials for a Shanti Sainik

1206. (i) Faith in Truth and Nonviolence.

(ii) A fearless, non-malicious and non-party attitude.*

(iii) Making no distinctions on the basis of country, creed, race, caste, language, etc.

(iv) Standing fully aloof from power and party politics.

(v) No support to war.

(vi) Preparedness to undertake even risk to life, in calming disorders.

(vii) Observance of the Shanti Sena discipline.

(Gogras, no. 41, 134)

Shanti Sainik and Exercise of Franchise

1207. Some colleagues have been of the view that the right of franchise is a sacred right. It is a step to wean citizens away from the path of violence and to induce them to adopt non-violence. Hence it would be an unprincipled action to prohibit Shanti Sainiks from exercising their fundamental right of franchise. It does not mean that they must vote; but to prohibit them from doing so would be improper. Rules can, however, be laid down regarding the types of candidates for whom they may vote, and for whom they must not.

Vinoba : A Shanti Sainik should not vote for any party. However, if a party declares his support to (full) disarmament,

* According to the Bharatiya Shanti Sena Pledge Form, approved by Vinoba, non-party attitude implies not to vote in elections.

it may be voted for. But it is extremely doubtful if there would be any such party. (ibid, 135)*

Formation of Acharyakul

1208. The teachers, *acharyas,* and professors of Bihar are undertaking a great step in founding this Acharya-kul....There are reasons which led me to choose the name Acharya-kul. *Kul* is a beautiful word, and it is one of those words which have links with both Arabic and Sanskrit. It includes *all (Kul)* teachers; there is no question of high or low, of great or small. All teachers are to be equally honoured; all will work together. These are the conditions of success. (TP, 99)

Acharyakul, Not Confined to Teachers Only

1209. Such persons may also join Acharyakul, who are objective and balanced in their thinking, scholarly, men of character and free from all party affiliations. (AK, 86)

1210. **Question :** Will it be right to admit only educated women to Acharyakul ?

Vinoba: Literacy is not essential. What is needed is intelligence. It is not necessary that only the educated should join it. The illiterate can also do it. But they should not belong to any party. It is of no good to be in any party, whatever it be. It will not add to strength.

(M, May 1980, Appendix, 3)

Functions of Acharyakul

1211. The word *kul* means a family, and all of us teachers are members of one family. Every aspect of the work we mean to do—to commit ourselves to knowledge, to strive for mental purity, to watch over the development of our students with affectionate care, to study the problems of society and to make a disinterested endeavour to reach agreed conclusions for the guidance of the public—all these are part of the task of establishing the unity of the family. (TP, 99)

---

* The above statement of Vinoba should not be taken to mean that a Shanti Sainik may vote for an independent candidate. He made it clear later.

1212. There is nothing new in what I am going to say. I put six programmes before you :

(i) Make the Acharyakul organisation as it ought to be. Acharyakul stands for fearlessness, non-maliciousness and non-partisanship. Form a strong organisation of this type in every village. If it has a school, there must be teachers, and then there should be an Acharyakul.

(ii) Organize Shanti Sena. All, men and women, present here should be fully prepared to join it. If an adversary comes to kill, they should not run away but bare their chests before him and suffer everything cheerfully.

(iii) Get Sarvodaya Patra maintained in every home.

(iv) The work of getting cow slaughter banned should be carried on throughout the country.

(v) Padayatras should be organized. As Malaviyaji (Madan Mohan Malaviya) once said, "Meetings should be held in every village; inspiring stories should be narrated in every village; schools should also be places of physical exercise; and there should be *gosadans* (cow homes) in every village."

(vi) Select a village and take up integrated work there. It will have an impact on other districts and on the whole country.

In addition to these, also propagate *Devanagari* as a world script. (Sansthakul, March 1980, 1-2)

1213. It is the work of the police to establish law and order through repression; it is the function of the Acharyas to establish peace through pacification and reconciliation.

(AK, 90)

Acharyakul and Politics

1214. We should stand aloof from politics. This is a *svadharma* of the Acharyas. Acharyakul would take to a study of politics, but it would be the world politics, studied by rising above power and party politics. Thus, if freeing themselves from politics and associating themselves with Lokniti, the Acharyas resolve to stand aloof from power, party and parochial politics, their status in society would improve. The people would come to look upon them differently. When they stand before the country as teachers providing guidance, they would find that people have faith in and respect for them.

(From an Acharyakul pamphlet issued from Vinoba's Ashram)

1215. Question : If there are persons not prepared to give up their membership of political parties but otherwise fulfilling all conditions laid down for Acharyakul membership, can they be admitted as 'Acharyakul friends' ?

Vinoba : No, they should not be admitted.

Question : It has been decided that the *Acharyakul,* the monthly organ, should carry teacher-centred material. What are your views concerning articles and other items in it ?

Vinoba : Articles may be published, but they should not deal with politics.

Question : It is obvious that they should not be concerning party politics. But can they not be such as to give the people an understanding of politics so as to educate them about it ?

Vinoba : Yes, they can be such so as to educate them about politics, but this politics should not be the politics of this country but of the world. (M, March 1980, 169)

Acharyakul and Exercise of Franchise

1216. Question : Can the members of Acharyakul vote (in the elections) ?

Vinoba : They must not vote. (ibid, 171)

Superiority of Acharyas' Discipline over Government

1217. While those who are in power govern, the Acharyas exercise discipline. We should clearly understand the difference between the exercise cf discipline and the act of governing. If the world will be guided by governments, there will never be peace in it. ... There will be peace if it is under the discipline of the Acharyas. They are, in the language of Guru Nanak, fearless and without malice. I have added to these 'non-partisanship' as well. The minds of the Acharyas are never perturbed and agitated. They never use (coercive) pressure in the shape of fasts or in any other way. They think over each and every problem calmly and put before the public those things on which they all agree. If people accept their guidance, it will be good for them and peace will reign in the world. This is what is signified by the 'discipline of the Acharyas'. (M, Jan. 1976, 8)

Cow-protection, Man's Limitations

1218. It is only God who can protect the cow. Hence Baba does not talk of protecting it. He talks only of serving it as much as he can, and, if need arises, of sacrificing himself for it.
(M, Dec. 1978, 1057)

Glossary of Indian Terms

abhaya : fearlessness
abhyasa : practice
acharya : teacher; example of good conduct
adhyatma : spirituality
Advaita : Non-dualism; Monism
ahimsa : nonviolence
anasakti : non-attachment
aninda : not to speak ill
aparigraha : non-possession; non-accumulation; non-acquisitiveness
apravritti: not taking an active part in world affairs; inactivity
ashram : 1. abode of spiritual teacher; centre of Gandhian activities
2. a stage or period of life out of the four stages or periods of life into which the life of a Hindu has been divided.
ashram-dharma : the *dharma* of the various stages of life.
ashram-vyavastha : the division into the four stages of life, viz., *brahmacharyashram, grihasthashram, vanaprasthashram* and *sannyasashram*
asprishyata : untouchability
asteya : non-stealing
aswad: literally non-addictions to deliciousness; control of the palate
atma : the soul; the individual soul; self; spirit
atma-jnana : self-knowledge
avatar : descent or incarnation of God
bhakta : devotee to God
bhakti : devotion to God
Bhishma : a character in the *Mahabharata*
Bhoodan : land-gift; a movement for it initiated by Vinoba

Brahma : the Ultimate Reality; The Supreme Being

brahmachari : one observing *brahmacharya*

brahmacharya : a discipline which implies a way of life moving towards the realization of the Ultimate Reality; generally translated as 'self-continence'

brahmacharyashram : the first of the four stages of life; the student stage of life

Brahmin ; the name of a caste; a priest; one who knows *Brahma*

buddhi : intelligence; intellect; reason

dahej : dowry; gift

dan : gift; act of giving

dhyana : meditation

dhyana-yoga : the yoga of meditation

dharma : a word that may stand for law, virtue, intrinsic quality, duty and religion, either jointly or severally

Drona : a character in the *Mahabharata*

Dvaita : Dualism

gram : village

gramdan : village-gift; a development of **bhoodan** in which villagers give up private property in land to vest its ownership in the village and agree to administer the village as a family unit.

gramkosh : village chest

gram-panchayat : village council

gram sabha : village assembly

gram swaraj : village self-government

grihasthashram : the second stage of life; the householder stage

guna : quality; any one of the three properties belonging to all created things, viz., *sattvaguna, rajoguna* and *tamoguna*

guru : a spiritual guide, a teacher

Jai Jagat : Victory to the World

jana-shakti: people's power

japa : repeating prayer in an undertone; repetition of the name of God or of any thought

jnana : true knowledge; knowledge

jnani: one having true knowledge; seer

kama : craving

karma : action entailing consequences

karma-yoga : the yoga of action

karmayogi : a man of perfect action

kriti : act

krodha : anger; Vinoba uses it in the sense of agitation

kshattriya : defender of the good; a warrior; name of a caste

lahej : demand

lok-lajja : people's disapprobation

lokniti: politics of the people; polity based on the moral power of the people with no exploitation and coercion

lokshakti : power of the people

mahila : woman; literally 'great'

moksha : liberation; salvation

mukti: synonymous with *moksha;* freedom

Nai Talim : literally 'New Education'; a name for Gandhiji's system of education

nirguna : without attributes; the impersonal; formless

nirvana : reunion with the Supreme

nishtha : belief; fixedness

nivritti: renunciation of the world in spirit; withdrawing from a thing; cessation of worldly actions

pativrata : a woman who shares in her husband's vows; a woman dedicated to the good of her husband

pativratya : the abstract noun of *pativrata*

prajna : wisdom, intelligence, intellect, understanding

prana : vitality; breath

pran-shakti : the vital force

pravritti: active life; taking an active part in worldly affairs

rajas, rajoguna : the second of the three properties which is supposed to be the cause of great activity

rajaniti : the politics of the state

rakshasa : a demon; one partaking of a demon's nature
Ravana : the demon king in the *Ramayana*
rishi : sage; seer
sadhaka : spiritual seeker ; seeker ; aspirant
sadhana : effort or endeavour for spiritual growth in a disciplined way
sagun : with attributes ; the personal; with form
samadhi : experience of oneness; a state of inner equilibrium and tranquillity of mind
samaj-dharma : the *dharma* towards society
samanvaya : synthesis
sampattidan : wealth-gift
samya-yoga : the yoga of equality or sameness or evenness
sannyas : renunciation; complete renunciation of the world and its possessions and attachments
sannyasashram : the fourth stage of life when one renounces worldly possessions and attachments
sannyasi: one who has taken to *sannyasa*
sanskaras : effects of the previous birth ; tendencies developed by repeated actions
sarva-dharma-samabhava : feeling of equality for all religions
sarvodaya ; uplift or welfare of all
sarvodaya-patra : a vessel for daily donation of a handful of grain for the cause of *sarvodaya* by the youngest member of the family
sattva; sattvaguna : the first of the three properties supposed to exist in all creatures, representing purity and goodness
shanti ; peace; tranquillity; calmness
Shanti Sena : Peace Army
shastras : Hindu scriptures
shraddha : faith
shudra : the last or the fourth *varna* of the Hindu social order
siddha : the perfected one
siddhi : superhuman power or faculty
sparsha-bhavana : feeling of touchability

sthitprajna : man of steadfast wisdom

sutanjali: yarn-offering

svadharma : one's law of being ; one's own *dharma*

svakalin-dharma : the *dharma* of one's own times

swadeshi : of one's own country

swaraj : self-government

tamas, tamoguna : the third property representing inertness, darkness, ignorance, and *status quo-ism*

tapat tapas, tapascharya : penance; austerities

vairagya : non-attachment; a distaste for the world and life

vaishya : the third *varna* of traders or businessmen; a caste in India; formerly included cultivators and cattle-breeders also.

vanaprastha : the third stage of life which is that of a hermit

vanaprasthi : one who has taken to *vanaprasha*

varna : usually understood to mean 'caste' but differentiated from it as a system taking advantage of the hereditary tendencies without any rigidity; colour

varnashram : a combined word which stands both for the *varna* system and the *ashram* system

varna-vyavastha : the *varna* system

Vedanta : a philosophy based on the *Upanishads*

vichar-shakti : thought-force; the power of thought

Vidur : a character in the *Mahabharata*

vikarma : special action; action for purifying oneself

Vishisthadvaita : qualified Monism

vishwastavritti : literally an 'attitude of confidence;' Vinoba's word for 'trusteeship'

vritti: attitude; mode of action

yajna : religious sacrifice

yug-dharma : the *dharma* of the age

(This glossary has mostly been compiled with the help of the various English publications of Vinoba by the Sarva Seva Sangh Prakashan and V. S. Apte's *The Practical Sanskrit-English Dictionary*. Vinoba, however, sometimes used words in his own sense).

INDEX

References are to the numbers of the passages in the book.

SELECT PUBLICATIONS OF THE NATIONAL GANDHI MUSEUM

No.	Title	Author	Price
1.	Birth of Free India's National Anthem: A Gift from Netaji Subhas Bose	Y.P. Anand (Comp.)	25.00
2.	The Essential Relationship between Netaji Subhas Bose and Mahatma Gandhi: The Supreme Martyrs in India's Freedom Struggle	Y.P. Anand (Comp.)	25.00
3.	What Mahatma Gandhi Said about the Atom Bomb	Y.P. Anand (Comp.)	5.00
4.	Into the Sun: An Autobiography	Ramadevi Choudhuri	100.00
5.	Piletermaritzburg Railway Station: The Start of the Journey from Mohandas Karamchand Gandhi to Mahatma Gandhi	National Gandhi Museum	20.00
6.	The Little Princess and the Birds	National Gandhi Museum	20.00
7.	Exploring Gandhi (Reprint)	Manmohan Choudhuri	90.00
8.	Mahatama Gandhi the Journalist (Reprint)	S.N. Bhattacharyya	225.00
9.	Gandhi's Social Philosophy: Perspective and Relevance (Reprint)	B.N. Ganguli	450.00
10.	In Defence of Freedom: Exciting Times and Quiet Meditations	Amlan Datta	125.00
11.	Gita and Gandhiji	Ramesh S. Betai	450.00
12.	Gandhiji's Lost Jewel: Harilal Gandhi	Nilam Parikh, Kalpana Palkhiwala, Tr.	135.00
13.	Gandhian Sarvodaya: Realizing a Realistic Utopia	Thomas Vettical	150.00
14.	Selected Conversations of Vinoba Bhave, Nov. 1969 to Dec. 1971	Kusum Desphande, Ed. Vishwanath Tandon, Tr	95.00
15.	गांधीजी किस प्रकार इस निष्कर्ष पर पहुंचे कि अन्तर्जातीय विवाह से जाति प्रथा का उन्मूलन करना होगा	मार्क लिन्डले, सं.	20.00
16.	पीटर मेरित्सबर्ग रेलवे स्टेशन: एक यात्रा जिसने मोहनदास करमचन्द गांधी को महात्मा गांधी बना दिया	राष्ट्रीय गांधी संग्रहालय	20.00
17.	महात्मा गांधी ने अणु बम के बारे में क्या कहा?	वाई.पी. आनन्द, सं.	5.00
18.	नन्ही राजकुमारी और हज़ार पक्षी	राष्ट्रीय गांधी संग्रहालय	20.00
19.	कामरेड रामकिशन: व्यक्तित्व और विचार	वी.पी. गुप्त एवं मोहिनी गुप्ता, सं.	250.00
20.	राजकोट सत्याग्रह का ऐतिहासिक महत्व	बालुभाई वैद्य, अनु. हसमुख व्यास	65.00
21.	गांधी जी का खोया हुआ धन: हरिलाल गांधी	नीलम परीख, अनु. योगेन्द्र परीख	135.00
22.	महात्मा गांधी का ट्रस्टीशिप सिद्धान्त	तत्त्वमसि	130.00

Gandhi Literature Centre
NATIONAL GANDHI MUSEUM
Rajghat, New Delhi-110002,
Tel.:23311793, 23310168, 23328310 Fax: 91-011-23311793